The Practice of Process Meditation

The *Intensive Journal* Way to Spiritual Experience

Books by Ira Progoff

The Practice of Process Meditation:
The *Intensive Journal* Way to Spiritual Experience, 1980

At a Journal Workshop: The Basic Text and Guide
for Using the *Intensive Journal* Process, 1975

The Symbolic and the Real, 1963

Depth Psychology and Modern Man, 1959

The Death and Rebirth of Psychology, 1956

The Cloud of Unknowing, 1957

The Image of an Oracle, 1964

Jung's Psychology and Its Social Meaning, 1953

Jung, Synchronicity and Human Destiny, 1973

The Star/Cross, 1971

The White Robed Monk, 1972, 1979

The Well and the Cathedral, 1971, 1977

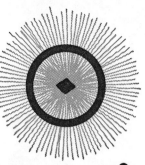

The Practice of Process Meditation

The *Intensive Journal* Way to Spiritual Experience

by
Ira Progoff

DIALOGUE HOUSE LIBRARY | NEW YORK, N.Y.

Published by
Dialogue House Library
80 East Eleventh Street
New York, New York 10003

Library of Congress Catalog Card Number: 80-68847

ISBN 0-87941-008-6

Printed in the United States of America

THIRD PRINTING 1981

Contents

PART III:
CONNECTIONS:
THE MAKING OF OUR SPIRITUAL HISTORY

PART IV:
MANTRA/CRYSTALS

PART V:
PROCESS-PLUS-ONE

The Practice of Process Meditation

The *Intensive Journal* Way to Spiritual Experience

PART I

The *Intensive Journal* Way to Spiritual Experience

Chapter 1

The Personal Renewal
of Bibles

INTRODUCTORY

When I returned to civilian life after my army service in World War II, I often lost myself in unhappy contemplation of the destructive events of recent history. In one decade from 1935 to 1945, civilization had come precariously close to destroying itself. I found myself especially reflecting on the massive burning of books that had taken place during the Hitler era. Again and again I asked myself what would have happened to civilization if the ritual Nazi burnings of the books had been continued until all the recorded wisdom of mankind had been destroyed.

I answered that question in two parts. The sciences, I concluded, would be retained in the technology of the engineers. Science would be preserved, although in a stunted form, if only because science is necessary for making weapons of war and for producing commodities to sell. But what of the sacred scriptures, I asked. Suppose all the Bibles of the world were burned, the Old and the New Testaments, the Tao Teh Ching, the Upanishads, the Koran, and all the others. If that happened, what would befall mankind?

I used to lie awake wondering what the human race would do if all its sacred scriptures were destroyed. Finally one night the answer was given to me. It came as a simple practical statement spoken in everyday tones. We would, the voice said, simply draw new spiritual scriptures from the same great source out of which the old ones came.

In that moment I became aware of how vast and self-replenishing are the resources of the human spirit. The fires of Hitler could burn the sacred books, but they could not destroy the abiding depths out of which those scriptures had emerged. I heard also the words of the Polish rabbi chanting as he was being buried alive: "Green grass lives longer than Nebuchadnezzar." God's smallest creations will outlast the power of tyrants. And this is because, as Walt Whitman knew, the simple leaves of grass come from the same infinite, re-creative source as the depths of the human spirit, from which the wisdom and the strength of civilization also come.

That understanding opened a new range of hope for me. Mankind would not be destroyed. No matter what foolish, destructive acts man would perpetrate on the physical level, new fountains of life would continue to rise from reservoirs deep within. Recognizing that there are indeed infinite dimensions to our universe, the immortality of life began to be a fact for me.

Soon another realization arose in me. If mankind has the power to draw additional spiritual scriptures out of the depth of itself, why do we have to wait for a Hitlerian tyrant to burn our Bibles before we let ourselves create further expressions of the spirit? If it is indeed true that each human soul contains a Bible within itself, may it not be that each person contains the possibility of new spiritual events and awarenesses taking place in his and her own experience? Perhaps there are new Bibles, many new Bibles, to be created as the sign of spiritual unfoldment among many persons in the modern era. It may indeed be that the creation of multiple spiritual scriptures, and especially the extension of old scriptures, is an event that needs to happen in our time as part of the further qualitative evolution of mankind.

This thought led me to additional explorations concerning the Bibles of the world. I soon realized that each of the Bibles of mankind is a spiritual source book for the civilization it serves. As the "Scripture" for its society, a Bible is not a book that comes into existence by means of a single individual. It is a product of many experiences and numerous lives. It reflects the experiences of many persons as they reach toward a contact with divinity in the midst of the harsh social and economic facts of history. Each Bible expresses the social and spiritual struggles that formed the life of its civilization through the centuries. The Bibles of the major civilizations provide a tradition and a wisdom from which those who are attuned to them can draw sustenance for their lives.

The Bibles of each of the major civilizations are connections to the past. They do not restrict us to the past, but they link us to it. They give us a sense of continuity so that each generation can be reminded that the present moment has been preceded by many that have gone before. No matter how intense our own experience may be, we are not the first who feel it. We are not the first to be groping and leaping our way toward the truth. We need therefore to be aware of what has taken place in earlier times so that we can live our present experiences in an organic relationship with the past.

In addition, the major Bibles of the world contain the profound recognitions of wisdom in life that have been achieved or have unexplainedly "happened" in the lives of the great historical persons. The texts express, sometimes in obscure esoteric and symbolic forms, perceptions of the mysteries of human existence as well as profound philosophic guidance for the conduct of life.

Bibles are teachers of the various meanings and possibilities in human life. Consequently, when individuals come to crossroads of decision or to points in their lives where they are tested by adversity, they can find not only a deep source of guidance but the energy of re-inspiration in the pages of the great scriptures. The Bibles take the form of books, but they are more than books. They are teachers of persons because they are carriers of ageless wisdom in forms that can speak to the condition of individuals at the particular time and place of their existence. Thus they have the capacity to renew the lives of individuals. And that is one reason why the Bibles of all civilizations are venerated as *holy* scriptures.

Because they each contain the profound teachings that carry the wisdom of their civilization, the Bibles of the world are indeed worthy of being regarded as *holy*, of being revered and lovingly preserved by those who are devoted to them. In all their forms, as oral traditions and as written texts, they are the composite record of the major moments in history when chosen individuals, in caves and on mountain tops, in desert retreats or casually going about their chores, were touched by a power greater than their own personalities and given directions that were meaningful to a large part of their society as well as to themselves.

The source of these guidances has been attributed to many gods, called by many names, depending on their time and place. But with all their variations it is clear that each involved a contact with a depth of being that expresses the underlying unity and wisdom of the universe in some special aspect and degree. Each of the Bibles carries its share of this contact with the great Unity of Life. The origins of the Bibles reach far into the primordial past, but even in the modern day, wherever individuals are attuned to the holy scriptures of their particular tradition, they have access to a resource of wisdom that strengthens their present life.

One problem, however, is that for many people in the modern age the great Bibles of history no longer speak with their original power. The style of language is that of ancient books, and it now sounds strange to the modern ear. Not only the language, but the concepts of thought and the symbols that carry the ancient perceptions of reality seem strange and distant. In the historical texts these are so different from the terms of modern science and technology that many persons feel them to be alien and irrelevant to their lives. To many they seem as foreign as if they came from another universe.

In a certain sense this perception is true. The teachings of the ancient Bibles do indeed come from another universe, another cultural world inhabited in a distant historical time. The disparity in styles of language and thought as well as the vast differences in the conditions of daily life create a chasm of communication. And this has made it increasingly difficult for the Bibles of bygone days to serve in the modern world as effective sources of personal guidance and life wisdom. It is a great loss, for it means that a profound spiritual resource has been obscured and rendered inaccessible for many persons.

A second difficulty is more general and subtle, and it has an important effect on the religious life of our time. There are many modern persons who accept the validity of the ancient religious teachings even to the point of revering them, and yet do not have an effective way of relating them to the urgent and immediate needs of daily life. These persons honor the old traditions, refer to them as authorities, and quote them as models for current behavior. The pressures of the environment, however, give them no option but to follow other values, modern secular values, in the actual conduct of their lives. It is like the pious regard bestowed upon ancestors or venerable great-grandparents who are revered but are no longer felt to be relevant to life. The old traditions are appreciated, but the principles that made them effective are no longer experienced as being present. They are not felt to be living realities any more, but are emptied of their power. They are given respect and love, but they are not in fact an active presence in life.

There is a delicate and painful irony in the fact that the Bibles of the world have lost so much of their reality and effectiveness as a force in human experience. They have not been destroyed physically as Hitler's fires might have done, but they have been atrophying spiritually from within. Steadily the center of gravity in the conduct of life has been drawn away from their interior principles in favor of the secular concerns and external pressures of the modern economic society. Mankind's Bibles have not been burned, but their inner flame is dwindling away.

Reflecting on this situation has reminded me of the phrase that I heard spoken when I was worrying about the fires of Hitler. The perspective that it gave me seems to be equally applicable. The source of spiritual knowledge is as available to mankind now to renew its old Bibles as it would have been if we had needed to create new Bibles altogether.

The great source is there to be contacted where "deep calleth unto deep," but each civilization and period in history has to find its own way of reaching it. Wishing for that contact, or being in favor of having it, does not make it a fact of reality; but desiring it strongly is a good first step. That establishes the personal commitment, and then the earnest work can begin. It is essential that we take it personally.

Bibles express the spiritual and cultural life of entire civilizations and periods of history, but the inner experience by which their meaning can be known is individual. For that reason, the work of re-establishing contact with the Bibles of the past and extending their meaning in the present is a work with large social implications, but it is a work that can be done only person by person. Spiritual contact, the awareness of the profounder meanings of life and the experience of its symbols, is an individual endeavor that can be carried through only in the silence of one's privacy. It is a work that each person has to do alone, but it is helpful to know that many of us are working alone together. It is helpful also to understand that we do not all have to hold the same beliefs in order for us each to contribute an atom of spirit to the human atmosphere. It seems important that as many persons as possible do their private inner work as deeply as they can. For that we require a methodology that can be used in the modern age by individuals whatever their faith or lack of faith, and whatever their level of intellectual development and personal interest. That is what we seek to provide in this book.

PROCESS MEDITATION IN THE Intensive Journal PROGRAM

When I appreciated the dimensions of the spiritual need confronting this period of history, it seemed to me to present a task that many of us had to undertake personally. I therefore set myself on a path of exploration to see if I could discover or develop, primarily for myself as a modern person, a viable means of access to the sources out of which the Bibles of the world have been drawn. More than three decades have passed since then, with much trial and error, testing and expanding. Eventually, out of my personal searching and my professional researching, first in the historical study of society and then in depth psychology, a set of underlying principles took shape. From these there evolved the *Intensive Journal* system of thought and practice of which the practice of Process Meditation described in this book is a further development focused first toward spiritual experience and, as I later discovered, toward creativity as well.

The *Intensive Journal* concept was first formulated in 1966. Since that time it has been the subject of considerable research that has led to substantial extensions and applications. The pace of this development was accelerated in 1975 by the publication of *At a Journal Workshop*, the book that serves as the basic text and reference manual for the *Intensive Journal* system.* As the method came to be more widely known and used, the National *Intensive Journal* Program was formed to make *Intensive Journal* workshops available throughout the United States, and more recently in other countries. By means of the national program it has become possible to offer to the general public a sequence of *Intensive Journal* workshops with a standard, carefully organized curriculum of exercises taught by *Intensive Journal* consultants specifically trained for each module of the work. A *Process Meditation* workshop is one of the modules in the national program. By standardizing the curriculum of the workshops, it has become possible for individuals to focus on the

* Ira Progoff, *At a Journal Workshop*, Dialogue House Library, New York, 1975, paperback edition, 1977.

particular areas of experience that seem most appropriate, or urgent, at a given time in their lives. And they can do that special focusing within the context of their life as a whole, thanks to the *Intensive Journal* system.

The basic instrument for the national program is the *Intensive Journal* workbook. It has been described by persons other than myself as "deceptively simple." I agree. If you examine it apart from the program in which it is used, the *Intensive Journal* workbook may seem to be nothing more than a notebook with twenty-five colored dividers. In practice, however, it turns out to be a highly specific structure of inter-related moving parts based on the various *hypotheses of process* of which we shall speak later, each of the Journal sections being a channel for a particular inner process of personal life. Each section is used with specific active procedures that serve to evoke the contents of a person's life without analysis or diagnosis, but in such a way as to stimulate additional inner perceptions and movements of many kinds. The sections tend to cross-fertilize and activate one another, releasing new energies and bringing about new combinations of ideas and feelings. Even in short periods of use, the process carried by the *Intensive Journal* structure is able to build a cumulative energy that often has a transforming and redirective effect upon a person's life.*

A special value of the *Intensive Journal* approach is that it enables individuals to break through situations of stalemate where their lives had seemed to have reached a dead end. It achieves this in part because its non-analytic approach generates a movement of inner energies. The progressive, interrelated continuity of exercises within the *Intensive Journal* program has the effect of evoking new ideas and opening new contexts of understanding. The inner activity that it stimulates leads to new courses of action, and the newly built momentum of energy provides the strength to set them into motion. These are the specific steps by which the *Intensive Journal* program functions non-analytically to set people into motion on the track of their lives.

The sequence of inner events by which this takes place can be very energizing, and therefore it may sometimes build strong enthusiasms. But the *Intensive Journal* program provides protection against making and carrying out errors of judgment that may arise while we are seeking

* A complete *Intensive Journal* workbook is printed in this book as an Appendix, beginning page 317.

to re-establish our lives. The wholeness of its structure establishes a perspective for the movement of one's life, so that the past, present and future are included in a single, comprehensive framework. The fullness of this context is a protection against acting on momentary enthusiasms, a danger that is often very great when people feel their lives to be in crisis.

Too often, when we are trying to help ourselves in times of desperation, our actions only prove the truth of the old adage, "Out of the frying pan into the fire." The *Intensive Journal* structure is a protection against this because it sets the sequence of its exercises in such a way that the contents of a life can be experienced in perspective. Over-reactions to adversity or over-enthusiasms of hope can then equally be set in context and brought into balance in the course of the Journal exercises in the continuity of the process.

Context and continuity are two basic aspects of the work that the *Intensive Journal* structure makes possible, enabling us to draw our lives into focus at a given moment in the midst of the pressures of a crisis so that we can resolve the immediate issues. Then, at a later time, we use additional Journal sections and exercises in order to reconsider the situations of our lives from additional vantage points as we move through new circumstances and events. In this way the *Intensive Journal* program serves as a vehicle that carries people through the difficult and confusing transitions of their life. In addition to providing perspective, it acts as a self-adjusting compass, seeking the "true north," the special meaning and direction of each individual life.

As it brings an inner self-guidance for life's problems, the *Intensive Journal* approach has also produced an interesting, if unexpected *extra*. In the course of its work it deepens the level of experience, and this draws an individual into contact with the profound sources of inner wisdom. Many persons have found that as they involved themselves in the *Intensive Journal* process to resolve the immediate problems of personal life, they have inadvertently opened awarenesses that are transpersonal in scope. Without intending it, they find that they are drawn beyond themselves in wisdom to levels of experience that have the qualities of poetry and spirit.

The reason that this takes place is fundamental to understanding why and how the *Intensive Journal* process has been able to be helpful to so many persons. And it is the key to Process Meditation. The source of it lies in the *Intensive Journal* structure, for it is the structure that gives the method its capacity to generate new energy. Through the relation of the Journal sections to each other, an inner dynamic is built, and this dynamic moves in two directions. One is outward toward the activities of the world. The other is inward. Both are integral to the process as a whole, but it is by the progressive and cumulative deepening of the inward movement that the new energy is built. This is true whether you are at a Journal workshop with many other persons or are working alone in your own privacy. The process of the method draws you systematically inward until it establishes an atmosphere of quietness and depth in which the refocusing and then the reintegration of the life can take place.

It is apparent that this inward movement has an inherently meditative quality. During the early years of this work it was common for people to comment, often in surprise, that the feelings stirred in them at *Intensive Journal* workshops reminded them of profound prayer or of deep meditation. And yet they also observed that the process was dealing factually with the nitty-gritty of their lives and that it was not prescribing for them any particular religious philosophy.

An indicative example of this experience at an *Intensive Journal* workshop was expressed some years ago in a syndicated newspaper column written by Father Dennis Geaney. After attending a workshop, Father Geaney was describing what had taken place and was ruminating on its significance. He concluded his column by writing:

> Come to think of it God was not mentioned during the weekend, but I could sense that the people around me were going down into the depths of the well and experiencing Him in the image of the living stream or however they get access to the living God.*

The *Intensive Journal* work is indeed a species of prayer and meditation, but not in isolation from life and not in contrast to active life involvement. Rather, it is meditation in the midst of the actuality of our life experiences. It draws upon the actualities of life for new awarenesses, and it feeds these back into the movement of each life as a whole. The fact is that the fundamental *process* in Process Meditation is each life

* The Pittsburgh Catholic.

itself. We shall recognize the many practical as well as spiritual consequences of this statement as we proceed through the varied exercises of our Process Meditation work.

At the surface of our life we are conscious of the many pressing problems that beset us, the conflicts, the anxieties, the angers, the decisions that we feel we must urgently make. But one reason that the *Intensive Journal* method has been effective for many people is that it practices an *indirect* approach to solving our life-problems. Rather than move head-on to encounter problems in the external form in which they appear in our lives, we step back and inward to meet them at a deeper level. And this way of approach is made possible by the principles that are at the base of Process Meditation.

Over the years my personal experiences as well as my observations had led me to question whether we solve our life problems best by reacting directly to the pressures they place upon us. Eventually I discovered that the *Intensive Journal* structure makes possible an alternate strategy, an indirect strategy. The first step is to acknowledge the problems of our life as we find them, to observe them and describe them as objectively as we can. That gives us a reference point in outer reality, but we do not establish our position there. We draw back. We move away from the surface of things. We move inward in order to return with a greater resource to use in re-approaching the situation.

It is basic to this inward phase of the work that we begin by setting the movement of our life as a whole in a full perspective. Once we have established our life context we have parameters within which we can move deeper and deeper to explore the contents and resources of our life. The purpose and style of that exploration is neither to diagnose nor to judge, but to enable our life to disclose to us what its goals and its meanings are. In doing this, we each find different meanings, different directions for our lives. But we discover that, regardless of the diverse conclusions we may reach, we are all impressed by the quality of experience that comes to us as individuals when our attention is focused inwardly in this way, especially when our inwardness has established an atmosphere of depth and stillness of being. The atmosphere of inward attention seems to possess a profound validity that dwarfs any particular opinions, or any particular anxieties we may hold about the details of our existence.

The set of procedures to which I have been alluding is the means by which we build the inward dynamic of the *Intensive Journal* work. It is called *progressive deepening*. Originally this was a psychological procedure, and it still is. But the years of using it to draw personal lives into focus have demonstrated a truth of more--than-psychological significance. It is that there are resources for a profound knowledge of life that become accessible to us when our attention is focused inwardly at the depth of our being in the context of the wholeness of our life.

Process Meditation is the method that has been developed for working actively and systematically at this inner level, reaching toward an experience both of personal meaning and of a meaning in life that is more than personal. It is in one sense an outgrowth of the *Intensive Journal* concept and in another sense a fulfillment of it. The practice of Process Meditation makes it possible to work tangibly with the dimension of spiritual meaning in the specifics of our individual life history. To this degree it also fulfils the fundamental vision that was stated many years ago as the goal of Holistic Depth Psychology: to provide an integrative method by which the psychological and the spiritual can be experienced as two sides of a single coin.* It may be that all psychological work has been implicitly seeking this ever since William James and C. G. Jung recognized that there is no lasting personal healing without an experience of meaning at the depth of one's being.

The methodology that is described in the present volume has passed through a number of stages of testing and revision in the course of its development. Process Meditation first became part of the *Intensive Journal* program in 1970; the program had been created in 1966. In 1970 the principles underlying Process Meditation were sharply enough defined to enable me to use at least some of its techniques in *Intensive Journal* workshops. Some of the procedures and certain aspects of the concept behind the method were still in an exploratory stage, however, and I did not feel ready to include them in *At a Journal Workshop* when I published it in 1975 as the basic textbook for the *Intensive Journal* method. The Process Meditation methodology was thus not described in that book.

Since that time, however, I have been able to take substantial strides in developing the underlying conception of Process Meditation and in working out the details of its procedures. For one thing, the increased

* See Ira Progoff, *Depth Psychology and Modern Man,* 1959. McGraw-Hill paperback, New York, 1973, p. 268.

public participation in the *Intensive Journal* program as a whole has provided me with extended opportunities for gathering empirical data regarding the various Process Meditation procedures. It has enabled me to explore and test new principles and techniques.

As an outcome of this extended exploration, a full Process Meditation component containing five separate sections for active inner work has been added to the *Intensive Journal* workbook since *At a Journal Workshop* was published. By now they are well established as a functional part of the total structure of the *Intensive Journal* method. It is the principles and procedures for using these Process Meditation sections that we shall be discussing and practicing in this book.

The purpose and style of this book parallels that of *At a Journal Workshop*. In that volume our goal was to make available in written form a description of the *Intensive Journal* structure and the exercises that accompany each of its sections. For many persons the text of that book has served as their total guide to working with the *Intensive Journal* method. For others the text has served as a starting point and has been supplemented either by college courses or by participating in the workshops of the National *Intensive Journal* Program as they are available locally. And for the large number of people whose first experience of the *Intensive Journal* method has been by taking part in a workshop, *At a Journal Workshop* has served as a reference book to support them as they continue their Journal work privately.

The present volume has the same multiple purposes, here applied to the five Process Meditation sections that have been added to the *Intensive Journal* workbook. In this volume we shall discuss the principles that underlie Process Meditation as an approach to and method for spiritual experience and also its role in the *Intensive Journal* concept of whole-life development. We shall then describe each of the sections and the various procedures for using them. Since this is a method for carrying out a program of inner work, portions of our text are designed to lead us into the actual exercises. When these sections appear, it will do no good for you to remain a merely passive reader. It will be necessary for you at least to begin your inner work by participating in the exercises as we proceed. Working in the exercises may slow down your reading time, but you will find that as you carry out the exercises you are filling in the structure of Process Meditation with your own experiences. The concepts and principles that are involved in Process Meditation will thus become more meaningful to you as you proceed because they will be made specific by the contents of your own life and especially by your own ongoing inner experience. Step by step, as we work with each of the Process Meditation sections, we shall be setting the process of our inner life into motion, deepening it, evoking new experiences and generating an interior energy as we proceed.

To help in carrying out the exercises, I shall describe the sequence of the steps to be followed much as we do at a workshop, setting the atmosphere and leading into the experience. We shall also discuss here the additional steps and the variations that may be drawn upon in continuing our Process Meditation after a workshop. My desire in this volume is to provide a sufficient store of information with respect both to the theoretical and the practical aspects of Process Meditation so that you can use it as an ongoing spiritual discipline largely under your own direction once you have learned it. It may thus serve as a background book to be referred to as you proceed in your work, and also as a direct guide to working in the exercises that build your own experience.

Do not content yourself with reading the descriptions and merely thinking about what you would write *if* you did the exercises. Thinking about what you would write is not the same as actually writing it. The act of writing in the atmosphere that is created by Process Meditation and that builds cumulatively as we follow the format of its exercises seems to evoke depths in us that mere thinking does not reach. You will find that the act of carrying out the steps of the work and actually recording them in written form has the effect of stimulating a movement within you that draws forth awarenesses you would not have thought of in advance.

To get the benefit of this method it is necessary actually to use it and to do so in writing. Thinking about it and figuring it out is not enough, because that gives us the illusion that we understand it conceptually when we cannot in fact understand innerly how the dynamic of its principles operates without working with it over a period of time. We should not place ourselves in the position of talking *about* a process that we do not actually know as facts of our inner experience, for that leads to intellectual chatter rather than to spiritual reality. The Process Meditation procedures give each person a means of taking whatever meaningful experiences they have already had in their lives—whether large and dramatic or small and inconspicuous experiences—and using them as starting points for new, and often unpredictable, inner events. We shall see step by step how this works.

I wish to address a special word at this point to those who are coming to Process Meditation without having worked in the *Intensive Journal* program before. I have tried to write the descriptions, and the instructions for the exercises of Process Meditation, in such a way that you will be able to begin here with this book, and then do the rest of the work later on. The important thing to bear in mind is that Process Meditation is part of an integrated program and that it achieves its major results within the encompassing context of the *Intensive Journal* work as a whole.

In computing their calendars, some societies think of the day as beginning at sunrise; in other cultures the unit of a twenty-four-hour day is measured from sunset to sunset. These alternate conceptions may be one way to think of the question of whether you should begin your work with the basic *Intensive Journal* material described in *At a Journal Workshop* or whether you should begin with Process Meditation. The important thing to remember is that whether you begin at sunrise or at sunset, it is not a complete day until the entire twenty-four hours have been lived through. Thus, those who have begun their *Intensive Journal* day with the basic experiences described in *At a Journal Workshop* will not complete the day until they have worked with Process Meditation. And those who are beginning their *Intensive Journal* experience now with Process Meditation will need also to move through the Life Context phase of the work in order to complete the full unit of experience.

Once you have learned how to use it, the *Intensive Journal* method becomes like a musical instrument you can play; and its melodies are the themes and the intimations of meaning in your life. Going to great heights and to great depths, the life music that persons find themselves playing upon their *Intensive Journal* instrument is often startling to them. They did not expect to find in themselves sounds of such strength or such sweetness, such sensitivity in the midst of pain, such capacities for harmony or such inner vision.

Quite often as I sit at workshops, listening to persons read the experiences that have been evoked in them during their Process Meditation exercises, I find myself reflecting that the words that were spoken to me (or within me) years ago are being fulfilled now in ways I could not have imagined at the time. Individuals, working in their own lives and in the depths of their own being, do in fact activate spiritual knowledge they did not know they possessed. They did not know how wise they were, nor the power and range of their visionary capacities. Nonetheless it comes from within them undirected, evoked in the spontaneity of their experience by the Process Meditation procedures. Bibles are indeed being renewed and extended in the depth of individual experience. It must be that, as we work in our personal depths, we make contact each in our own way and in varying degrees with the same inexhaustible sources out of which the old Bibles came. Whenever an individual touches those sources, regardless of the language or the doctrine or the symbols in which the experience comes, new sparks of divinity enter the world. And these sparks ignite fires that give warmth and light but do not consume.

For many people Process Meditation has evolved into a spiritual discipline that fulfils the creative role of awakening and extending the Bibles that have been sleeping in their souls. In the discussions and experiences that follow, it will be good if we can bear in mind this large frame of reference as the background and purpose of what we do. In the practice of Process Meditation we are reaching back through our heritage as civilized persons to the inner source of that heritage in order to touch the power by which it originally came to be. And we seek to give that old reality a new life through our individual experiences.

Chapter 2

The Depth Beyond the Doctrines: Meditation As Spiritual Methods

As its name suggests, Process Meditation achieves its results by combining two primary factors: meditation and process. It draws them together in a distinctive way that is made possible by the structure and the principles of the *Intensive Journal* system.

In the course of our using the Process Meditation procedures, and especially after we have moved through a full cycle of experience with them, these terms will likely appear to us in a new light. We shall be enlarging their range of content as well as their role in our inner lives. But that will come about as one of the by-products of our work with Process Meditation, and therefore we can discuss it more fruitfully if we wait until after we have had our first experiences with it. In the meanwhile we have to begin our work in the midst of the current conceptions and understandings. It will be useful, therefore, for us to start by examining some of the basic aspects of meditation and process as they relate to the purposes that Process Meditation seeks to serve. This will give us historical background as well as a perspective of the goals of our work. It will also prepare us for the range of exercises and ongoing procedures which we shall be learning to use.

Coming into the last third of the twentieth century the use of the term, Meditation, has achieved a prominence in Western civilization that it has not had for several centuries. The practice of meditation had receded to so low a point in the Judeo–Christian religions that by mid-twentieth century many persons had come to assume that meditation is not a part of the Western heritage. It became increasingly common to speak of Western religion as "extroverted," meaning that its attention is directed toward outer activities, while the Oriental religions are primarily "introverted." The implication of this distinction is that the Eastern religions are well attuned to inner realities but that Western practice is not on familiar terms with the spiritual side of religion. This view has become quite a common attitude, especially because the dominant religions of Western civilization have tended in recent centuries to emphasize the statement of outer beliefs, questions of ritual as well as of social action, in contrast to becoming involved in personal spiritual disciplines. When we view the full range of Western religious history, however, we see things in a larger perspective; we are then able to appreciate how much is contained in the West as well as in the East.

We find that the religious experience of human beings, whether it is in the East or in the West, is much too complex and varied to be understood in terms of categories that are either/or. It is not a question of being either introverted or extroverted. Neither of these alone can possibly suffice as descriptions. At all levels of culture, even while human beings are acting to meet the needs of physical survival, they are also engaged in seeking an inner meaning for their lives. They seem to have an inherent need to reach out for meaning whether they live in a simple, primitive culture or in a complex, technological civilization. And further, they have the need to represent their perception of that meaning in some specific form, in mythological symbols or in rituals that are religiously performed.

These representations of meaning appear in forms that are marked by their virtual infinity of numbers as well as by the ingenuity of their imagination. As a result we find that mankind has accumulated in the course of its history a multiplicity of beliefs, concepts, symbols that reflect man's varied intimations that there is a significance and purpose to human life. These are stated as doctrines and professed as faiths of one kind or another. But all through history, parallel to the beliefs in the various faiths, there is an awareness of a further truth, the recognition that there is a knowing beyond words, a depth beyond the doctrines. This is not in contradiction to the doctrines themselves, for it accepts them, whichever doctrines they may be. But it reaches to a further interior truth that is contained within them. It is seeking that inner quality of knowing of which the doctrines that are stated and believed are only the outer expression.

Because of this double need, the history of religion moves on two perceivable levels. One is the external statement of beliefs that can be used by the society to establish easily recognizable guidelines for codes of conduct and group action. The other concerns the inner ways of knowing, by which believers reach toward the mysteries of truth beyond the doctrines. It is on this inner level that the various forms of meditation are practiced. In the context of the history of religion, meditation serves to carry the inner experiential side of the quest for meaning in human existence. In a multiplicity of ways it provides the methods, the *how to*, for finding and experiencing the larger significance, the cosmic and spiritual connections, of individual life and destiny. And it is by means of these practices in each society that those individuals who have a strong enough motivation can embark on a path toward deeper wisdom in order to attain a direct experience of it.

One characteristic of the major religious traditions is that they are large enough to be able to provide space and content for both the inner and the outer aspects of human life. They provide the externals as these are necessary for social functioning, and they provide the means for inner experience as these are needed for the regular renewal of spiritual contact. It is probably a fair statement to say that those religions that do not include both of these aspects and do not fulfil them in sufficient degree tend not to have a strong staying power in history. If they have only the inner, they tend to become esoteric and lose their rootage in society. If they have only the external, their contact with the sources of spiritual experience dries up and there is no inspiration for periodic renewal.

Viewed in the perspective of time, the great religious traditions seem to move in cycles in which now the inner, now the outer is dominant. In recent Western history, religion has passed through a period of heavy external emphases that have drained its sources of spiritual contact and led to a visible thinning of religious life. This has been especially true of the first half of the twentieth century, but the changes during recent decades have given us evidence that historical societies are subject to the same self-balancing principle that operates in individual life. An over-extension in any direction produces its own opposite, thereby correcting itself in time and bringing about a new situation. This self-adjusting process seems to be taking place now in Western culture. The external emphasis seems to be reversing itself and is stimulating a new exploration of inner experience, as we see in the renewed Western interest in meditation.*

It is interesting to note that the counter-trends to materialism which we are currently seeing in the West are being paralleled by an opposite movement in the East. In the Orient it is the emphasis on the inner that is being reversed, leading there to an increased involvement in material development. As Western technology is being incorporated into Oriental society, the people become more and more ambivalent about their ancient religious practices. As they seek to overcome the poverty and disease among their vast populations, they turn to modern technology as their best means of success. Appreciating the value of Western techniques, it becomes increasingly necessary for them to learn to speak the language and to think the rationalistic thoughts of Western science. They find also that the archaic rituals, the numerous Holy Days, of their religious orthodoxies tend to distract them from solving their material problems. Two worlds of conflicting values are thus placed before the Oriental persons who live in modern times. The conflict is embodied in the pressures of their historical situation. As the necessities of social existence build the tension, there is a tendency for the old observances and doctrines to drop into disuse and increasingly to be regarded as anachronisms.

At the same time that this is happening in the East, many persons in Western civilization are brought to an opposite conclusion. They see the fruits of science and technology as having passed their optimum point of being helpful to life and as now clouding the meaning of human existence. Increasingly, modern persons are rediscovering an ancient truth, one that is now restated in the language of our economic

---

* This self-balancing principle plays a very important role in the *Intensive Journal* method as a whole. See *At a Journal Workshop,* Chapter 20. The principle has been noted and described analytically in various systems of thought. Alfred Adler dealt with one aspect of it under the term *Compensation.* C. G. Jung spoke of it as "the principle of opposites," drawing on Heraclitus and certain aspects of Oriental philosophy. Leibniz, Hegel and Bergson emphasize other aspects of it in their individual ways. The *process* that is set in motion by the structure and procedures of the *Intensive Journal* workbook endeavors to provide room for all their special points of emphasis. Thus the *Intensive Journal* process is holistic in the sense that it enables each aspect of life to establish its own self-balancing process within the context of its own content and movement. The larger, encompassing process is thus *life-integrative* in that each aspect establishes its balance in its own terms.

society. They are finding that man cannot live by Gross National Product alone. Realizing this, they feel the need of a new spiritual resource. And because of their lack of spiritual inspiration in the past they assume that they cannot find this resource in their own heritage of Western culture. Thus they turn to the civilizations of the East, and there they learn of an ancient wisdom. Those old doctrines then become newly discovered teachings, many of them the very same doctrines that are dropping into disuse in their native lands. A constructive interchange of philosophy and technology is thus taking place, but it is not without its ironies.

In both East and West a process of historical adjustment is occurring, proceeding from opposite directions. Each is incorporating into its cultural life a factor to which it had attached little importance in the recent past. We see here an instance of the self-balancing principle operating in the life-cycles of civilizations. Projecting into the future, we may anticipate that in generations to come it may well be the Oriental societies that will have a predominantly materialist and technological interest, while Western civilization will develop an increasingly spiritual orientation to life. We can even predict that, if significant new spiritual advances are to come in the future, they will take place first in Western society. The reason is simply that at the present time the Oriental cultures are self-satisfied with their spiritual attainments, while Westerners are struggling and searching out new possibilities in their spiritual lives. We shall be seeing once again at work in history the principle by which opposites balance one another as they move through the cycles of time.

Whether in the East or in the West, we have the question of what is the relationship between meditation and religion in the life of civilization as a whole. The best approach toward answering that question comes from understanding the significance of these two contrasting factors that are found to dominate the history of religion. As they have been interpreted by social historians and scholars of religion, these factors have been described in various terms and divided into various categories. They have been called the outer and the inner, the surface and the depth or, in the classic language of Henri Bergson, the static and the dynamic.* Beyond the varying points of emphasis, however, there is a perspective in which the large and fundamental nature of meditation

* See Henri Bergson, *The Two Sources of Morality and Religion,* University of Notre Dame Press paperback.

presents itself to us. It enables us to see the unifying and ever-renewing role that meditation plays in the continuity of religious life.

In each historical religion there is the system of beliefs, the structure of doctrines that is its identifying content. This is the statement of faith and philosophy with which it presents itself to the world. It also contains the symbolism known and shared by the believers, the rituals, ceremonials, modes and occasions for worship, the varied paraphernalia and regulations that establish the religion as a social institution. This is the outer aspect of the religion, the face it shows to the world. It is the fixed form in which it serves as a stable social vehicle for its believers.

The second aspect of religion is quite different. This is a further level of perception, an *inner reality* of spirit that carries the deeper meaning beyond the stated doctrines. Here there are mysteries of veiled truth to be known. The doctrines that are taught at this level are often couched in esoteric symbolisms that need to be studied long in order to be understood, and longer still in order to be experienced. This second level of religion requires an additional intuitive sensitivity, a developed capacity of spiritual perception in order to be fully comprehended. It deals with a subtle area of truth that needs to be entered into intimately in order to be known. This is the depth beyond the doctrines, the inner wisdom that underlies the outward statements of socially accepted religious belief.

To reach this depth, each historical religion has developed special practices and esoteric teachings which it transmits with careful protections and restrictions to its adherents. These disciplines and instructions are of many kinds. They may be of greater or lesser profundity, sometimes in harmony with orthodoxy, sometimes labeled as heresy by the light of the dogmas of the time. The Western religious tradition, as well as that of the East, has carried many such disciplines, presented sometimes in easily understandable terms, sometimes in the context of obscure and esoteric symbolism. They may take a variety of forms, as prayer, fasting, ascetic practices, intense and specialized study, ritual observances, vows, penances, ceremonies and tests of initiation that are particularized to convey an occult symbolic teaching or a mysterious and paradoxical wisdom.

In one form or another, although they often rely on external modes of experience as their vehicles, all of these teachings, with their special practices and requirements, have to be understood as *interior* disciplines.

This is because these religions' eventual goal is to train, develop and test individuals to the point where they know and experience the religion's special truth from within its own terms. As spiritual disciplines they serve both to prove and to strengthen the individual's ability to know and to enact the doctrines of the religion while reinforcing the commitment to the system of belief as a whole.

The function of meditation in the history of religion is to provide the methodologies by which these inner experiences can be strengthened and sustained. Taking a historical perspective, we must therefore include in our conception of meditation the full range of spiritual disciplines that give access in any form to the depth dimension of religion. This casts a larger light on the relationship between meditation and religion. It also enables us to answer the question whether meditation is always a necessary part of the religious life.

The fact is that meditation is not necessary as long as people are content to participate in their life and in their religion at a surface level. The outward observance of holidays, ethical behavior, good fellowship in community, even social action can take place without the practice of the interior disciplines of meditation. But if outer life is to be participated in with a depth of meaning, and especially if it is to be connected to the larger spiritual reality that underlies social morality, whether in terms of religious belief or a personal philosophy, some degree or aspect of inner experience is necessary. Some methodology of meditation is necessary then to provide a means of reaching the sources and inner meaning of outer behavior. Without it, ethical conduct and religious belief certainly can continue. But if they do not have a means of interior renewal, they soon lose their contact with their source. In time, then, they become dry and blow away like leaves in autumn.

Meditation as a means of spiritual practice is indeed necessary if individual experience is to be connected to the deep sources of meaning and energy in life. A person may make strong statements of faith, but it eventually hinges on a question of fact which no rhetoric can disguise. That fact is the question of the person's experience. What validation does it have? What is its range? What is its depth? Through what cycles of variation and testing has it passed in the continuity of time? How profoundly does this person know the things that he or she thinks or claims to believe? Is he merely echoing what he has heard others say, merely repeating dogmas he has been taught to believe? Or is he among those who have themselves experienced their spiritual knowledge so that their faith is based on a foundation of interior fact?

This is one of the criteria for those who would be the wisdom teachers within a religion or a philosophy. If their knowledge has merely been learned, it will be meager and weak. But if it has been formed in the course of their disciplined practices, they will have gained access by direct experience to the esoteric depth of their religion's message, and that will be the foundation of their spiritual strength. This quality of experience is true of the great leaders and teachers of a religion, but it applies as well to all who aspire individually to reach a profound inner communion, a private and intimate relationship, with the truth that they have found. For each person, a capacity of inner knowing is essential. It is a capacity that requires more than intellect, and more than conscious desire. It requires a sensitivity to the interior symbolism of life, whether within a particular religion's doctrines or beyond them.

The central point of these spiritual capacities and sensitivities is that they involve more than intellect and more than conscious desire. They can be brought about only by the practice of disciplines for the development of greater abilities of perception and response in the dimension of spiritual reality.

The nature of religious beliefs is such that, on the surface level, they can be stated by the rational mind and interpreted by means of intellect. But an inner experience of direct, non-rational knowing is essential in order to open the capacities of awareness at the deeper levels of reality to which the beliefs ultimately refer. And these experiences take place only along a track of consciousness that by-passes the intellect. These are the experiences that yield the kind of elusive knowledge upon which spiritual understanding is based, but only to a very limited degree do they follow the styles of reasoning that people are accustomed to use in their everyday life. The experiences of a religion or of a depth philosophy thus require us to have access to an additional aspect or capacity of consciousness. Since it seeks direct knowledge and a heightening in the quality of one's inner being through the immediacy of experience, capacities of consciousness additional to the rational mind are needed to bring it about. That is the reason that a program of profound and effective techniques whose trustworthiness has been proven by time is necessary as a support for spiritual experience. It may use a single approach or a combination of techniques and disciplines. Whatever specific approaches it uses as its means of cultivating inner experience, those are its ways of meditation.

This takes us to the heart of the conception of meditation with which the work of Process Meditation proceeds. Meditation is the area of human experience that draws on the multiple methodologies developed during the history of religion to provide a means of reaching and deepening the experience of meaning in life. Primarily these are the methods of spiritual experience that move beyond intellect. They comprise the various disciplines and techniques for strengthening the inner capacities of individuals so that they can test, validate, renew and extend by their own direct experience the depth and degree of truth of the doctrines of religion and philosophy.

In its varied forms meditation provides the means of reaching the depth beyond the doctrines. It does this by giving access to the elusive and intuitive knowledge that lies implicit in the deep levels of wisdom where it may be covered by layers of symbolism that have accumulated through the centuries. This is what the practice of meditation is for. It is the inner side of religion at the practical level of strengthening the interior muscles of spiritual awareness. Its purpose is to build the necessary capacities for spiritually meaningful life, especially the ability to reach the depth beyond the stated doctrines—the mystery, the paradox, the symbolism, the wisdom beyond the doctrines—whatever the teachings of the religion or the philosophy may be.

This definition, broad as it is, is sufficient to give us a criterion for what meditation is and what it is not. We have to look not at the content of any particular technique but at its context and especially at its range of purpose. The criterion of whether a particular method is in fact meditation depends upon whether the goal of the work is to deepen the experience of meaning in life, and whether its procedures move in that inner direction. If the techniques used are helpful for individual purposes but are not related to a deeper inner experience, then they are whatever they are, but they are not meditation. There is no judgment involved in saying this. It is simply that we need to be able to distinguish for ourselves the forms of practice that can serve as spiritual disciplines.

It has been found, for example, that certain methods derived from ancient or Oriental spiritual disciplines can be helpful in meeting some of the physical problems that arise in modern society. They seem to work very well when they are taken out of their original context and are used separately to meet particular needs. In specific cases they provide a means of dealing with difficulties in blood circulation, breathing, body tensions, nutrition and more. When allowances are made for differences in culture and environment, these procedures are often found to be valuable both for their healing effects and for the new body understanding that they bring.

While we may examine and use such techniques at appropriate times, it is important that they not be confused with the larger purpose of meditation. Insofar as they seek to bring about control of the blood flow, or of the breathing apparatus, or of the autonomic nervous system, they might more properly be referred to as methods of body conditioning. Where their purpose is to bring about control of the movement of thoughts, suppressing certain ideas and affirming others by manipulating the subliminal mental processes, they should be understood as methods of mind conditioning rather than as meditation. Their pragmatic goals are important, and it is valuable to use such methods in their proper contexts. But meditation itself has another purpose. It is to develop the capacities of inner knowing that will take us deeper into the realm of spiritual reality where, without fixed preconceptions, we can participate with the great religions and philosophies of the ages in the enlarging search for truth by our personal experience.

In this operational definition, meditation includes all the possible methodologies that we may call upon as we proceed with our interior practice. We may try one and then another, for our commitment is to no single doctrine or method. Our commitment is rather to the deepening contact with spiritual reality in whatever form it presents itself to us as we continue our open-ended work. Whichever techniques we may be using, whatever framework of beliefs we may follow, the essence of meditation lies in its intention, in its commitment to work inwardly to reach into the depths beyond the doctrines of our beliefs.

In this conception of it, meditation is a supremely empirical approach to the inner life. It deals with subjective experiences, and yet it proceeds in the spirit of science. We see this expressed as early as the fourteenth century in the classic volume of mystical spiritual direction, The Cloud of Unknowing. The anonymous monk who wrote that book was describing to a student the procedures he had found to be most helpful in his effort to achieve unitary experience and to be, in his medieval language, "oned with God."

The monk was there dealing with a very specific set of teachings and techniques, but at no point did he speak in a doctrinaire tone. He described his methods always in a tentative, experimental way. Given particular problems—for example, how to deal with unwanted thoughts—he described two alternate methods. Try each one, he tells the student, and see how it works for you. Then you can choose between them and use either one as new situations arise.

Or again, how shall the student judge the validity of particular experiences that have come to him? The monk again counsels an empirical approach. Allow time to pass, and meanwhile observe all that happens. Does the experience recur? Do new experiences come? Let your observations in the course of time guide you to your judgments and your decisions.

And then there is the practical side of applying the dictum of Saint Gregory that "All holy desires grow by delays." Again the monk adopts a very cautious, empirical approach. He advises the student not to prejudge any difficulties that may arise in the course of his work. They may be painful disappointments when they happen, but they may also be the carriers of unwanted *delays* that have a valuable and constructive purpose. Only by waiting and by careful observation will the student be able to know what its meaning is and what action he should take. And then, that action will depend on whatever new "stirrings" will arise in him out of the depth of his "naked being" as he is waiting and is observing his inner experience.*

When I first studied his text many years ago, I was exceedingly impressed by the factual attitude which the monk of *The Cloud of Unknowing* followed toward spiritual experience. He has the mind of a modern empiricist, I thought, but he applies it to spiritual facts. At that time it was for me a striking discovery to find that a person classified as a mystical author would follow an empirical approach. Since then I have found that to be much more common that I had thought.

Studying the history of religious thought has demonstrated to me that individuals who work committedly with spiritual disciplines have no alternative but to proceed in a careful, empirical way. They have to deal realistically with the changing conditions of their inner lives. Oth-

---

* See Ira Progoff, *The Cloud of Unknowing, A Modern Rendering with Commentary*, Julian Press, 1957; Delta paperback, 1975.

erwise the experiences that come to them as "stirrings" from within will not give them a more profound awareness of meaning, but will only build in them fantasies and delusions of knowledge. This consideration is one of the reasons why it is common among conservative religious groups to believe that those who seek truth along arcane or occult paths run a great risk of psychosis along the way. Since the path along the razor's edge is very narrow, one has to proceed with great caution. Great dangers may be present all along the way, often hidden behind the strangeness and the symbolism of the esoteric doctrines. The dangers may be all the greater because the subject matter is very subtle and subjective and may arouse unconscious emotions. A new seeker for truth who is earnest but inexperienced may be unprepared for the side effects of spiritual seeking, and may be especially vulnerable if he or she is engaged in an individual search for truth without adequate social supports or protections.

The dangers that arise along esoteric paths are real indeed, and individuals who seek to find their way there should proceed with care. It is also true that there is a validity to the spiritual knowledge that may be found and experienced at the depth level to which individuals may come in their privacy. There are persons whose intuition tells them that the validity of spiritual experience is so great as to make it worth while facing whatever dangers may lie along the way. Such persons have no alternative but to proceed with their quest. It is essential, however, that they proceed slowly, progressing by delays, and that they exercise sufficient respect for the facts of inner experience which they may encounter. They must be able to maintain a firmly empirical attitude so that they can proceed experimentally as they work with their various spiritual disciplines.

As we consider the way of the contemplatives and mystics like the monk of *The Cloud of Unknowing,* it is interesting to compare their trial-and-error approach with Jacob Bronowski's description of science. "Science is experiment," he writes in *A Sense of the Future.* "Science is trying things. It is trying each possible alternative in turn, intelligently and systematically; and throwing away what won't work, and accepting what will, no matter how it goes against our prejudices." *

In a comparable spirit, one important strength of the *Intensive Journal* program lies in the fact that it provides a large and flexible range of

---

* Jacob Bronowski, *A Sense of the Future,* The MIT Press, Cambridge, Mass., 1977, p. 2.

experience in which individuals can try now this, now that, and can be free to fail without prejudice. An especial value of the *Intensive Journal* workbook is that its structure provides a means of gathering the facts of inner experience empirically so as to make them accessible for our continued inner work. Some are meaningful at the time we first experience them; others will be valuable later on. Therefore we do not reject any, but keep an open, empiricist's mind toward all the contents of our inner life. In addition, the exercises for using the sections of the workbook, especially the procedures for practicing Process Meditation, enable us to touch inner levels we may not have been in contact with before. Thus, as we proceed with our work of Process Meditation, we increase the number of facts of inner experience that are available to us for our personal spiritual work.

Whatever form it may take, in the broad variety of methods by which meditation reaches the depth beyond the doctrines of religion and philosophy, an empiricist's respect for facts of experience is a primary requirement. It is merely that in this case the facts at issue are facts of inner experience. They are inner facts. But that is all the more reason to respect them, to observe them neutrally, and then to act toward them with caution and understanding.

In the empirical mode of spiritual discipline, there is a second aspect that is very important in addition to the respect for facts of inner experience. It is the sense of time and of timing where inner experiences are concerned. We have a good indication of this in the discussion of "delays" that is found in *The Cloud of Unknowing.** There the monk refers to the various phases, the "times" of the inner life. First there is the time of seeking and desire for spiritual knowledge. At that point the interior experience has not yet happened and it is only an intimation of things that may yet come to be. Then there may be "stirrings," images and understandings by which a grace of understanding seems to be coming to "young spiritual disciples." It fills them with enthusiasm, and with an exalted self-opinion. Thus their next problem arises in the form of their pride, for they are experiencing pride with respect to their past experiences, and pride because of their expectations for the future. Thus for inner reasons there needs to be a "delay," and soon the delay comes.

Stirrings of imagery and understanding may still continue to ap-

* See Chapter LXXV.

pear, but their quality, their tone, and their quantity also, are now different. The grace of awareness seems to have been withdrawn. When a person perceives this lack and recognizes its reality, new emotions and fears arise, and they cause the condition to increase. The inner sources seem then to dry out, and the stirrings no longer come spontaneously. A fallow time arrives in the life of the spirit. Increasingly it becomes one of those delays that seem more like an ending than merely a delay. Grace seems to have been withdrawn, and one does not know for how long. Then anger and resentment replace pride. At such times, the monk tells us, "It is often the case that young fools think that God is their enemy, when He is completely their friend." The fallow time was intended merely as a delay to serve a good purpose. And it still can do that if it is properly understood.

A perceivable movement of cycles takes place in the life of the spirit. We find it not only in the earlier, religiously oriented centuries but in our modern culture as well. The cycles of inner experience form a process that seems to be generic to the quest for truth, wherever persons seek that truth individually at a depth beyond the outer statement of the doctrines.

We can identify this inner process as it moves with its characteristic rhythms and dynamics. It appears that the similarity in the cycles of the process reaches beyond the differences in historical circumstances. The quest for meaning by personal experience is the central factor whether that quest is taking place in a religious society or in our modern secular culture. The spiritual essence of human experience involves an inner process whose effects reach beyond the differences in social conditions. This fact of observation provides us with one very important starting point as we seek to find a method of spiritual discipline that can be practiced effectively in the modern world.

Chapter 3

Process and Inner
Experience

HYPOTHESES OF PROCESS FOR CREATIVITY AND SPIRIT

Of the two words in our basic term, *Process Meditation*, we now have an understanding of one. We see *Meditation* as the multi-aspected spiritual activity by which human beings seek in many forms throughout history to discover and experience directly the meaningfulness and the validity of their lives. Meditation is not limited to any system of beliefs. It encompasses all the disciplines and methods that we may call upon in order to deepen our inner awareness so that we can know by our own experience the depth beyond the doctrines.

  The other word, *Process,* involves a concept of which we have become particularly aware in modern times, in part because of the impact of the natural sciences and the numerous philosophers who have studied the implications of science. The content or *way* of process is not restricted to modern times, however, but has been observed and taken into account in philosophies and spiritual disciplines that reach far back into history. Lao Tse's ancient teaching of the *Tao,* for example, can be translated in many of its usages as *process.* And the sense of inner timing, which involves process in spiritual experience, is apparent not only in the lives of the Biblical prophets but in the contemplatives and the mystics of the European Middle Ages. The understanding of process in its broad range of meanings and with its lived applications is important for us to have in the background of our thought as we come to work in the practice of Process Meditation.

Fundamentally *process* is the principle of continuity in the universe. In recent generations it has developed into one of the most important concepts available to modern persons for understanding the world in which we live. In one framework of thought, the idea of process gives us a means of conceiving what takes place in the cosmic world, the physics and chemistry of natural evolution. On another level it gives us a means of approaching the history of civilizations and the changes that take place within societies. And now we find that, as we adapt the conception of *process* to the *Intensive Journal* methodology, we also have a means of working with it in the inner world of our spiritual experiences.

In its role as a tool for modern thinking, the conception of *process* serves primarily a unifying function. It helps us see the relatedness and the ongoing connection between phenomena that look dissimilar when they are viewed externally. When we see them from within a conception of process, we are able to understand that their differences reflect their position at changing points along the path of the process, and that a connective unity underlies their apparent disparity. When many diverse phenomena are approached with the idea and hypothesis that a single line of process can be found to be connecting them, a great economy of thought and study becomes possible. Once the individual process has been identified so that its specific contents can be marked off, what was an amorphous mass of information can be quickly integrated. Things fall into place as though by themselves.

In any area of study, even if our first hypothesis is not exactly correct, as long as it is relevant enough to serve as a starting point it suffices to draw together in meaningful ways a large amount of otherwise undecipherable data. And when this is done with respect to the events of a person's life, a rapid integration of experience can take place. The use of hypotheses of process, it may be worth noting, describes the sequence of events by which the *Intensive Journal* process was originally developed. The process as a whole, and the individual processes which are embodied in the sections of the *Intensive Journal* workbook, were established first as *hypotheses of process.* Each section of the *Intensive Journal* workbook was in effect providing the space in which to test the hypothesis that a particular process of experience would move effectively through it. The experiences at the early *Intensive Journal* workshops then served as an empirical testing ground where these hypotheses could either be confirmed, altered or refined. When the hypotheses had demonstrated their validity, the *Intensive Journal* program could be set into motion as a resource in any community.

When we use it as a conceptual tool for purposes of research, we find that an hypothesis of process has an integrative effect. It draws things together in such a way as to give us leads to the next steps that can fruitfully be taken. This fact of our experience is probably indicative of a more general principle, namely, that the nature of process in any area of study is that it leads toward integrations. Or, in another way of saying it, a process of continuous movement tends to balance itself and to form new units that are an integration of the contents within the process. Jan Christian Smuts was referring to a principle of this kind when he described what he perceived as the holistic movement of natural evolution. He saw the evolutionary process as bringing about ever more refined holistic units, new forms of life, new species, coming into existence by virtue of the inherently integrative process in evolution.

The significant fact about these new holistic units is that they were not contained within the factors of the process that brought them forth. Essentially they could not be predicted. They were altogether new in the clear sense that they had not been in existence before but were brought forth as a *further result* of the process. This is the kind of event for which the philosopher of evolution, Henri Bergson, used the term, *emergent.* He meant by that the situation in which the sequence of cause-and-effect within a continuous process leads to an outcome that is more than was contained in the cause-and-effect components themselves. It is an unpredictable *extra.* An integration has taken place and it has brought forth something that is not only new but that is more than simply the result of a cause-and-effect process.

The holistic view that Smuts and Bergson have given us is a fruitful way of viewing evolution. In describing how new *emergents* are brought forth by the processes of nature, it enables us to see them as creative events in the life of the universe. Numerous creative persons have indicated their empathy for this point of view, Nikos Kazantzakis, Teilhard de Chardin, and Arnold Toynbee among them. It may be that one reason why the Bergsonian holistic philosophy rings true to persons who have themselves been creative in their lives is that, with its view of bringing forth emergents from evolution, Bergson's view of Nature's creativity is in many ways a prototype for creativity in human experience. Creative persons therefore recognize a reflection of Nature's creativity in their own lives. They are seeing process in its creative aspect.*

A working conception of process is especially valuable in dealing with the subjective materials of inner experience where elusive factors of personal belief and break-throughs of inspiration play an important role. That is why the hypothesis of process has been so productive in forming the *Intensive Journal* method. It enables us to give a tangible form to the intangible factors of personal experience. Our subjective feelings and experiences become accessible to us as a definite movement. We can identify each phase of them as particular processes, however we eventually describe their details; later we can bring them together in larger contexts of process.

By means of the *hypothesis of process*, what was elusive becomes graspable and knowable. It is not that we catch it like a fish in a net, cut it up, dissect it, analyze it, and conclude that it is nothing but this or that. To do that is the way of intellectual analysis. Working with the *hypothesis of process* enables us to draw together large amounts of subjective and intangible material while they are still in their living movement. Since, by definition, process does not make anything come to rest, nothing that we identify by means of process stays inert long enough for us to cut it up and analyze it. It is moving, but we perceive its motion, and we can relate our inner awareness to the form and vitality of its movement.

A specific and practical example of the *hypothesis of process* in action can be seen in the way we relate to our own lives. One way is to think of our lives as a mass of facts and conditions that we can study and analyze. Holding ourselves in a static position so that we can analyze ourselves, we come to the conclusion that "This is what I am" and "That is what I am." And thus we hold ourselves in our past. An alternate way of approaching our lives, which is the *Intensive Journal* way, is to regard life as an ongoing, living process and to ask of it: Where is my life trying to go? What does my life desire to become? What does my life require of me?

Asking those questions does not call for a definite or final answer. It

* See Jan Christian Smuts, *Holism and Evolution*, Macmillan, New York, 1926, and Henri Bergson, *The Two Sources of Morality and Religion*, University of Notre Dame Press, 1976.

cannot have a final answer because, being a process, it is becoming. It is not final until we are dead, or until we surrender our vitality. When we conceive of our life as a process, we conceive of it as being in motion. We do not analyze it but we relate to it in its continuing movement. Conceiving our life as a process, we can have a continuing relation with it. We can dialogue with it. We can evoke latent capacities contained within it, and we can help develop them. We can work together with our life as a process, reconsidering with it what it wishes to become, and helping it arrive at the place where together we decide it should go.

The hypothesis of process seems to be an approach that is especially congenial to creative persons. One reason for this is that it enables them to establish and maintain an ongoing and intimate relationship with the actuality, and especially the movement, of their subjective experiences. We find this to be true of novelists and artists as well as those who are engaged in the performing arts. And it is equally true, with a slightly different emphasis, for those who have committed their lives to a spiritual quest.

Consider in this regard a person like Dostoevsky. His life was a particularly eloquent embodiment of the fact that the spiritual and the creative are ultimately two sides of a single coin—or better, two sides of a single process. They cannot, or should not, be separated from one another, but should be allowed rather to feed into each other. In Dostoevsky's life they did feed into one another, and thus the intensity of his spiritual concerns became an important source of supply for his creative activity. Correspondingly, his creative work became a means of working out some of the knotty conundrums that arose in the course of his spiritual quest. Given what we know of the tremendous emotional pressures that Dostoevsky experienced on the personal level, it may well be that the interplay of the creative and the spiritual in his life was what provided his energy and enabled him to function. With its back-and-forth movement, it was a sort of interior teeter-totter by which Dostoevsky could keep his inner life in a dynamic, if precarious, balance while he did his constructive work.

Within Dostoevsky there seems to have been at every moment a burgeoning aggregation of thoughts, images, fears, ideas, plans, visions, stories. We may well wonder how a person with such a mass of subjective material within him could keep from being overwhelmed by it. We know that one elemental step that he took, which proved to be very helpful to him in several ways, was his writing things down in his notebooks. It was not that this enabled him to sort things out rationally. Not at all. That was not its purpose. Its purpose, which Dostoevsky understood, was to provide a channel, many channels, for the movement of process within him so as to have a means of carrying his multiple inspirations. In that way each could follow its own continuity and come in its own time in the course of his novelistic work to an inner integration that would show what it was trying to become.

There were many small processes constantly beginning and growing in the prolific, unconscious areas of Dostoevsky's psyche. Including them all, however, there was one over-arching process working within him. It was a many-sided movement that would not stay quiet long enough to have its contents analyzed and classified. The entries in his notebooks were only the first step in giving form to that process, for an unstructured notebook will, by itself, go no further than collecting data, and it runs the risk of going around in circles after a while.

Dostoevsky was able to take another step that moved beyond the data-gathering functions of his notebooks. It was most likely because of the strength of the creative thrust in him that he was able to draw together, out of the mass of process within him, portions that became distinct units of process and could move toward their own resolution. These were the stories that took shape within him and that came together to form his novels. As the writing of each of his novels became a definite process within him, Dostoevsky could have a personal relationship with them. As small processes they could be persons to him, and therefore he could ask them in his mind where they wished to go, what they wished to become. And the answers took the form of the further development of his writing.

In the life of Dostoevsky we see the close relationship between creativity and the spiritual quest for meaning. We see it again in the life of St. Augustine, although here the emphasis and the form are slightly different. Beyond his writings, Augustine's life itself was his artwork, including many works within it, organizational and philosophical as well as spiritual.

Like Dostoevsky, Augustine contained much puzzlement as well as intense commitment in his life. There were so many questions within him, so many desires, ideas, urges, dreams drawing him in opposite directions. A life like that is a process of opposites. The mass of it taken together is overwhelming. As the issues and the possibilities of the life mark themselves off, however, they show themselves to be moving as distinct, smaller processes within the encompassing process. Augustine could relate to these, and he could also describe them. Even while he was contained within these moving processes of his life, he could be in a dialogue relationship with them, asking what they wished of him and where they were seeking to carry him in his life.

We see repeatedly in the lives of those who have reached creative and spiritual attainments that where questions are asked in terms of the inner process of the life answers are received. And the answers often come in the tangible forms of new artworks and new conceptual understandings. This has important implications for our perspective of how process operates when its contents are the flux of subjective thoughts and feelings that comprise the inner life of a human being.

In the physical world, if we follow the holistic thinking of Bergson and Smuts, we see the processes of life being carried by an elemental energy. Each process moves through its cycles, its phases of change, until it comes to a point of integration. That is to say, a process continues through its variations until the disorganized contending parts within it come together and form a whole. That is the difference between confusion and clarity. When the jumble of things settles and forms an integral unit, that is the holistic process of life taking its elemental step. It is forming a new *holos,* an integral unit.

All the elements that have been part of the moving process can now come into balance and form a new unit. Those contents that can find no place for themselves in the new whole drop away, perhaps to reappear in another form at a later time. A new integration is taking place. In one sense this integration is the ending of a unit within the larger process. It is the end of the phase of chaos and turmoil. The new integration that replaces the confusion with a core of clarity serves also as the starting point for the movement into the future.

When an integration is formed in the life process of a person's experience, *something extra,* something additional to the process itself may come into existence. At the moment when the integration is happening, as things are coming together to form a significant new pattern, something more than all the contents of the process may come into being. The word that is of prime importance in that last sentence is *may,* for the *something extra* is an unpredictable element. It cannot be counted

45

on, but sometimes it happens. When it comes, it is the *emergent* of which Henri Bergson spoke.

In the context of physical evolution, we may regard the occurrence of an emergent as another instance of the curious and remarkable creativity of the natural world. In the context of human experience, however, it leads to questions that open a number of possibilities with respect to the factor of creativity in our inner lives. Some of these are large and profound questions with far-reaching implications.

How does a *process* proceed when its contents are subjective rather than objective? Is there a difference, then, in the nature of its phases, its rhythms and cycles? What is involved in its *integrations* when the contents are subjective and when the movements of process take place in a framework of symbols and images? How does this affect the possibility that emergents will come to pass? Does it increase the possibility? Or decrease it? Or does it set up the requirement of specific conditions? And are we able to take steps toward meeting those conditions?

These large questions open for us when we extend the holistic principle of integration from the physical level to the level of human experience. Their contents will be intangible, elusive, difficult to grasp and define. That will be very inconvenient. We may then recall that the main contents of creativity and spiritual experience also are intangible. Considering that suggests to us a further intriguing possibility: May it be, when we carry over from the physical realm to the human realm the holistic principle of integration as Smuts and Bergson understood it, that we open a way of entry to the dimension of creativity and spiritual experience? To the degree that that may be so, we should note that the methodology of Process Meditation derives ultimately from Smuts' holistic principles, via Holistic Depth Psychology.* Its practice, therefore, especially in relation to the *Intensive Journal* system, gives us a means of testing the holistic hypothesis as a way to creativity.

The main point of difference between the human and the physical realms is that there are definite, measurable factors of chemistry and biology moving toward integration in the physical world. For the most part these can be visibly traced and measured. But the mass of thoughts and desires, fears and visions in a human person, in a Dostoevsky or an Augustine, or in anyone who is passing through the confusing cycles of

* See Ira Progoff, *Depth Psychology and Modern Man*, Chapter 4.

inner experience, are intangible. They are very difficult to catch hold of and describe. When these confusions lead to difficulties so great that a psychiatric approach is called for, the accepted way is to try to identify and analyze them. If we suspect, however, that the confusions are part of the necessary difficulties in moving toward a further level of development, it is better not to analyze the contents but to evoke and extend the process as a whole.

Beyond pathology, we soon realize that there is no point at all in trying to catch and hold the contents of our creativity and spiritual experience. If we catch a fish and take it from the water in order to dissect it, the fish will die. The same happens to our thoughts and visions, emotions and inspirations. They can live and thrive as long as they are free to move about in their native atmosphere. We find also, with respect to the fish swimming in our inner sea, that when they are encouraged in their moving about they come together in combinations that are altogether beyond our imagination. They form new integrations, new holistic units, that we could not possibly have directed them to make. We would not have known what instructions to give them. And yet, in the expression of their freedom within us, they come together by their own spontaneous guidance to establish an inner balance where we thought we had only confusion before.

There seems to be a principle at work in our "inner sea" that draws our disorganized subjectivities of thought and emotion and image into meaningful integrations, into new holistic units of consciousness. But how shall we recognize that such an integration is taking place? Where shall we look for it? One observation I have made of this process in people's lives is that when things seem to be starting to come together, there is immediately a sigh of relief and a flush of enthusiasm. But it is premature. Usually those first signs are ahead of time. The integration may have started, but there will be further delays before it can be carried through. It may also be that the excitement of the enthusiasm breaks the continuity of the process, and therefore delays it further. This possibility should be borne in mind when, in a little while, we consider the cycles of experience that are described in the Psalms.

Where shall we look and how shall we position ourselves in order to be in favorable contact with the integrations that may be trying to happen at the depth of our inner life? The place to look for the integration and the place to be with it is where the confusion and the life-disorganization is at its fullest. Look for the integration in the depths of the darkest moment. That is where it is beginning to form itself.

We can test this principle for ourselves and apply it at many points in our *Intensive Journal* work, especially in the practice of Process Meditation. When you feel yourself to be in a situation where confusion or the bleakness of your prospects are drawing you into panic or despondency, an essential step to take is to establish a relationship with the process as a whole in your life. Then you will be able to place yourself at the depth where the crisis is, and you will be in a position to move with the integration when it is ready to start, proceeding from the ground up.

There are a number of ways of placing yourself in such a position, especially within the framework of the *Intensive Journal* program. The goal of the various techniques that we may use in this regard is to establish a point of meeting for ourselves with the process as a whole within our life. We do not need to analyze that process nor to try to understand it. We need simply to establish an ongoing relationship with it, like two persons who are friends. Two friends know one another. They do not necessarily understand each other, but they know one another at a point of inner meeting in their lives. That may be the model for the relationship that we require between ourselves and the inner process of our lives.

Is there a direct way to establish that relationship, whether in a time of difficulty or in a time of creative activity? Yes, the *Intensive Journal* method provides a number of points of entry to begin the relationship. As we proceed into the practice of Process Meditation we shall see the means of connecting ourselves at a depth of our inner experience by the various ways of working in the *Meditation Log* section. In the basic work dealing with the personal aspects of our lives we can achieve a comparable connection by the way that we work in the *Period Log* section. Other sections of the workbook can also be valuable in this regard, notably the *Inner Wisdom Dialogue.** Later in this book you will come to *Peaks, Depths and Explorations.* The use of these sections depends on the individual's level of familiarity with the *Intensive Journal* methodology as a whole. We need not discuss here the details of using these *Intensive Journal* sections, particularly since they are described in their respective chapters. But we should note that the process of which we are

---

* See the chapters with these headings in *At a Journal Workshop.*

speaking here has been known, at least intuitively and on the level of direct experience, in cultures other than our own. We see instances of it expressed in the Psalmist style of experience both in the Old Testament and in the Dead Sea Scrolls.

A number of the Psalms were written as spontaneous, unself-conscious expressions of emotional process in the midst of crisis situations. They reflect the unedited movement of the process as it was passing through the cycles of experience, from confusion and panic to integration.

Often the Psalm begins as an outcry. It is written out of the pressures of personal necessity, much as an entry would be made in the *Intensive Journal* workbook at a time when the circumstances of life have become exceedingly difficult. It is an expression of desperation and especially, as the tone of it in the Psalms indicates, it is an unpremeditated call for help.

The beginning of Psalm 13 is characteristic of the searing complaint, the desperate outcry.

> How long, O Lord, wilt Thou forget me forever?
> How long wilt Thou hide Thy face from me?

The Psalm begins in hopelessness. The difficulties in life have multiplied until it seems that one is at the very bottom of things. The feeling at that moment is that one has been cut off from the constructive forces of life, disconnected from the abiding Power to which one had looked for support. Thus there seems to be no hope, for there is no visible resource on which to draw. It hardly seems to be the person who is speaking but the hopelessness itself crying out, "How long, O Lord?"

The subjective feeling that makes the outcry is one of despair based on the conviction that one's life has come to a dead end. The difficulties of life have sent the energies downward, and one's whole existence now seems to be at the bottom of the valley. As the movement has been going downward steadily, there is no way to know, and no reason to believe, that a change will take place. That is the reason for the panic, and the pressure that sends forth the outcry. The atmosphere at the low point in the valley is burdensome and oppressive. The person becomes fearful.

> How long shall mine enemy be exalted over me?

The movement of the emotional process is deeper into the valley. There seems to be no end to it. And that is reflected in the tone of the statements that are made in the Psalm. Hope seems to have been surrendered altogether. Then suddenly, unexpectedly, the mood changes. There is a toughening of outlook. Unaccountably an attitude of resolution has entered the situation.

> Behold Thou, and answer me, O Lord my God;
> Lighten mine eyes, lest I sleep the sleep of death;
> Lest mine enemy say, "I have prevailed against him";
> Lest mine adversaries rejoice when I am moved.

How shall we account for this change of tone, for it is indeed inherent in the movement of the process?

The movement downward into the valley of our emotions is like a chaotic retreat while it is taking place. The structure that had previously given us support is now breaking apart. It has lost its strength, and with that its validity is gone. Our various abilities had been drawn together and given direction by this inner structure. Its unity had carried our beliefs with respect to the meaning of our life. Now, as it is breaking apart, everything within us is segmented. This is the source of the confusion, of the panic, and of the outcry.

In one aspect the outcry expresses the intensity of the fear that is generated within the person through the awareness that an inner disintegration is taking place. But it is also a spontaneous attempt to stop the rolling downhill. Things are breaking apart, but the outcry is like a person awakening from sleep in the midst of a fire. All the faculties are mobilized. Whatever resources are available to the person are instantaneously drawn together and called into action. It is an inner integration taking place under the pressure of events. When there is not the outer stimulus of a fire but only the inner stimulus of despair, the necessary sequence within the process is the same. It draws together all that is available to it.

The panic is assuaged. The tension is softened. It may be that not nearly enough has yet been drawn together and given form, but the mere fact that some integration has taken place carries with it an affirmative emotion. The downward movement seems to be halted and what feels like a constructive development is taking place. Thus we find a toughening of outlook. The person feels stronger, for a source of support seems now to become available.

> But as for me, in Thy mercy do I trust;
> My heart shall rejoice in Thy salvation.
> I will sing unto the Lord
> Because He has dealt bountifully with me.

The process has now gone almost full circle. Beginning in despondency, it has become an affirmation of faith.

It is important for us to note that this transformation in attitude has taken place altogether on the level of inner experience even though a serious difficulty in outer life was implicit in the background of the despair. The transformation in attitude came about through a cycle of experience that passed through a discernible series of stages. At the start there was the outer difficulty together with the sense of anxiety that it generated. As the fear enlarged and became despair, an inner deterioration was set into motion. That was a falling apart of beliefs and knowledge, a loss of inner strength. Incapacity increased, until at virtually the last possible moment and at a primal level of perception, there came a realization that a major danger was at hand.

That is a moment both of panic and of life-preserving action. The inner resources that have fallen apart are now brought together. The integration that takes place may not be the best that is possible, and it may not even be adequate to save the situation for very long. It may be capable of lasting for no longer than the time of the emergency. But if it does only that, it may save the day—at least for the time being.

That first integration of a person's resources is brought forth by the intensity of a danger that has been instinctively perceived. In the moment when the calm arrives, there is a tremendous feeling of relief. One may sigh a sigh the size of a hosannah. But the subjective feeling of relief at having a heavy burden lifted may be greater than the objective facts warrant at that time. Difficulties may remain, for the full cycle of the experience may not have been completed. Further, the enthusiasm at believing that one has already been saved may have the effect of drawing one's attention away from the difficulties that still lie ahead. It may, in fact, be necessary to move through several cycles of integrative experience before one can gather together sufficient inner resources to meet a major life difficulty.

When the pain and despair have been very great, however, and have persisted for a long time, it is difficult to restrain the exaltation that arises when one believes salvation has unexpectedly come. The first experience of integration will very likely not be sufficient at all, and the person knows that in his heart. But what he has also recognized intuitively and with great joy is that the tide has turned, or is about to turn, in his life. The cycle is moving in another direction. The painful descent into the valley need not continue long. There is the hope that an ascent into a brighter place will soon begin.

Sensing a change in the direction of life, a new attitude begins to establish itself. That is the next phase in the cycle. The manner of the Psalmist is to express directly the feelings that arise in him in the terms of his symbols and beliefs. Thus we find a Psalmist of a later century, one who composed the hymn in the Dead Sea Scrolls, saying:

> I give thanks unto Thee, O Lord,
> For Thou hast freed my soul from the pit
> And drawn me up from the slough of hell
> To the crest of the world.

He was acknowledging the movement of the cycle within him, sensing himself to be borne up from his suffering as on a wave. Out of hopelessness he recognized hope, and that led to the exhilarated feeling that his life was being reestablished on the "crest of the world." We realize that the symbolism of his language serves as a vehicle by which he could acknowledge the working of a profound principle at the core of his being. He might affirm that principle in the language of his beliefs as "Lord God," but he empirically dealt with it as a process moving through his life. Both perceptions are expressed in the experience which the hymnist recorded in saying:

> So walk I on uplands unbounded
> And know that there is hope
> For that which Thou didst mold out of dust
> To have consort with things eternal.*

* Theodor H. Gaster, *The Dead Sea Scriptures,* Doubleday, New York, 1956, p. 138.

ASPECTS OF SUBJECTIVE PROCESS:
CYCLES, INTEGRATIONS AND EMERGENTS

Setting the experience of the Psalmist side by side with the experience of persons in other periods of history gives us a perspective of the range of process in individual lives. We have seen the general role of process as an underlying factor, the principle of continuity in the universe. Now we have to look at it more specifically, especially as it is expressed in the lives of individual persons.

Process in the physical world takes place in terms of tangible, objective, largely measurable factors. Most important, the contents of process in the physical world do not have opinions about the process that contains them. They do not seek to interject their opinions or attitudes as part of the process. If the winds seem to blow with fury, that is our emotion that is being read into them. The actual cause of their velocity is something much more objective. On the other hand, the subjectivity of our thoughts, emotions, and the decisions that lead to our actions is the very essence of process as it moves on the level of human experience. The consciousness of self, the tangible effects of subjective feelings and judgments, the degrees of freedom in thought and action, the possibilities of individual creativity are among the factors that mark off the phenomena of human experience and distinguish them from the phenomena of the physical world.

Subjective process is so distinct a realm of experience and observation with its inherent principles and phenomenology that it deserves the attention that would be given to a full field of study. It should be regarded as its own branch of science. One of the empirical foundations of the *Intensive Journal* system is, in fact, closely related to that idea. Originally it was the research into life histories, especially of creative people, that provided the source of the data for the various *hypotheses of process* with which the *Intensive Journal* system was constructed. That work was first undertaken, not with the *Intensive Journal* concept in mind, but to provide source material for a full systematic study of the phenomena of *subjective process*, and thus to fill out some of the broader concepts of Holistic Depth Psychology.

As things turned out, those early studies led directly to the conception of process that suggested the specific formats of the *Intensive Journal* system; and the *Intensive Journal* work, once it had taken shape, proved to be a tremendous source of exactly the type of data that the study of subjective process requires. Proceeding with its own momentum, the study of that material has been taking the shape of two current projects that are side by side with Process Meditation: the *Intensive Journal* study of life histories, and the applied field of the Humanic Arts.*

Each of these fields is a special area and extension of Holistic Depth Psychology with its study and applications made possible by the unique manner of functioning and outreach of the *Intensive Journal* system, especially the way that it helps people function in their lives at the same time that it provides a resource of data for further knowledge of human process. There are a number of implications for social and research applications that come from these lines of work, but I must leave that story for another volume.

The primary quality of process in human experience, as in the physical world, is its *continuity*. Forms change, but the process continues. And yet there are differences that we must note in the forms of continuity in the physical world and in the human world.

In the world of physical evolution, when a species dies that is the end of it. It lives on only in the neutral form in which its chemicals return to the earth. When, on the other hand, within our human experience a context of thought or belief, a set of ideas or a project of activity breaks up, comes to an end and seems to die, that is not the end of the component parts of it. The wishes, images, thoughts, emotions that were part of it no longer remain together, but they do not disintegrate. They retain their individual forms, but they are no longer directly involved in the active experience of the life. They drop back into the bank of memory within us where their existence continues, but on an inactive status. They are on reserve, waiting for a new situation to arise so that they will be called back to the surface where they can be combined with other factors and resume their active life in a new context. In the meanwhile they are waiting. But the continuity of their existence is maintained.

In the *Intensive Journal* workbook there is a section that embodies

* I first published that term and concept in Forum, ICIS, New York 1968. Both the further formulation of the Humanic Arts conception and the use of the *Intensive Journal* method in the study of lives have been waiting for further formulations within the *Intensive Journal* system as a whole, of which this book is a part. Further publications in both of those areas may therefore be expected in the not-distant future.

this aspect of continuity in human experience. It is called, *"Intersections: Roads Taken and Not Taken."* The conception behind it, stated simply, is that there are more desires and possibilities present in certain situations of life than can be carried to the level of actuality. The possibilities that are pursued are the roads taken; the others are the roads not taken. But the roads not taken do not thereby drop out of existence. They are gathered into the bank of memory—of the individual, of the community, of the civilization—where they remain as a resource waiting to be called upon whenever their appropriate time comes. Continuity is thus maintained on the level of human experience, but it is a qualitative continuity rather than merely physical. That aspect of continuity has implications for our inner experience that will become important for some of us at a later point in our practice of Process Meditation.

In one sense, process in the universe is formless. It simply continues, and we cannot say that it has a predetermined goal, or that it has any direction, or no direction at all. Sometimes process seems to be following a definite rhythm or pattern or style, and sometimes no pattern is visible. The continuity of process may be harmonious and constructive, and it may be discordant and disintegrating. It may be pleasant or unpleasant, ethical or immoral, civilized or barbaric.

We see that while process is continuous as a unity, it moves in opposites. It combines contradictories. Does that mean, therefore, that the principle of continuity is self-contradictory? No. It means that the continuity of process moves by means of cycles. And the nature of cycles is that they are a combination of opposites in motion. One way to define a cycle is as two opposites set in sequence, with the necessary time of transition intervening. Thus the movement from noon to midnight is a cycle, as light and dark are opposites combined in sequence.

A cycle of that type is easy to perceive because it is tangible in the physical world. It is more difficult for us to discern the movement of a cycle when the contents involve movements of inner experience. Nonetheless, it is probably true that the cyclical style, going from opposite to opposite, is the primary mode by which process moves on the inner level of experience, as we could see from our reading of the Psalms.

While the continuity of process moves in pairs of opposites, it also does the opposite of that: it draws diverse factors together to form units of experience in which an integral connection is developed among the parts. The parts thus become identified with one another, and their participation in the new holistic unit becomes their prime characteristic, over-arching their original differences.

The formation of a unit in a human requires a directive image within it to set the tone of it and to provide a measure for which life-contents will be drawn into it. For example, young persons are living amorphously in their early years, trying this and trying that, when an image comes to them in which they see their life being lived as a musician or as an artist, or as a businessman, or as a mother. Or perhaps their image is concerned with the beliefs they will follow in their lives. Perhaps they have a vision of themselves as making a vow of commitment to their religion and living devoutly within it; or perhaps they envision themselves as living like an angry prophet fighting social injustice, perhaps joining with one or another ideology; or they may have a Spinozist vision of living the philosopher's life in tranquility, or a Bachian vision of living amidst the profundities of music. Whatever that image may be, it comes as an interior experience. It may not actually be visual, but for the individual it is a visionary feeling. It is felt inwardly, but on the inner level it is only a possibility. It needs to be taken out into the actualities of life to see whether it can be filled with specific contents.

Will it in fact be possible to live out the image of being a musician in the world? Will the fervor of religious commitment last long enough and be strong enough to provide the basis for a life? Whatever the nature of the image, it sets the goals and chooses the contents for that area of the person's life. In itself it is only a possibility; but if, in practice, it fits together well with other persons and activities so that it proves to be livable, it becomes the basis for a new unit in the person's life. The combination of a subjective inner experience with outer contents that are more tangible in nature forms the basis of a new unit of life experience.

In this unit the image that carried the original visionary feeling of possibility increasingly becomes dominant as it sets the direction for the events that take place within that unit and spreads a sense of purpose through all its parts. Thus the dominant image serves an integrative role in the unit of experience.

In the course of this, persons may experience many fluctuations in their life, going through external changes which will be experienced subjectively as uncertainties and anxieties; but eventually a sufficient number of outer experiences will fit together with the inner image and a unit of life experience will be formed. At that point the visionary intimation of a type of life to be lived will become an actuality of existence filled in with the details of business or politics or music or family life, whatever it may be. The integrating image places its mark upon all the components of that unit of experience, and it draws that unit toward an ever more finely honed condition of wholeness or integration. The diversity of the person's experience becomes unified as all the contents are drawn together toward a common purpose and move in a single direction.

Once a unit of experience has been formed around a dominant image in a person's life, the new unit begins to move toward its goal and to develop its characteristic style of movement. As the unit of experience achieves its first purposes and builds its energy, it moves straightforwardly in a single direction. It builds a core of integration within itself. It then can go ahead with its activities, progressing in a linear way, onward and upward. Once the unit of experience with its inner, integrating image has been established, a continuous forward movement can be established.

At this point the development of the unit of experience begins to show signs of having a life of its own. It has passed through a period of amorphousness, of confusion, and now it has crystallized and found its direction. As its early tentative aspects drop away, it comes into a time of maturing when its various lines of experience come together. They seem to be consolidating themselves, as though they are marshalling their forces for a further advanced phase of development.

This is the plateau phase in the process of a unit of human experience. It is the time of stabilization, when the vision and the actualities of life come together so that the achievements which were the goals or hopes of the governing image when it began can now be brought to fruition.

From the plateau phase, movement can go in either of two obvious directions. Either downward, in diminution and toward disintegration, or upward in further development. In either case the unit of process is brought to an end, for it now has formed a full cycle of movement. This is the sense in which we speak of a *cycle/unit* of process. Naturally there are great portents for the personal life of the individual hinging on the question of whether the ending of the cycle comes about in the course of a disintegration or the launching of a further stage of development.

The plateau phase of the cycle/unit is its critical point. It may be that the unit of experience has now fulfilled all that was possible or valid for it, and that it now should come organically to a close. Some-times, when that is the case, it is difficult for individuals to recognize such factors of timing at the subjective level of their experience. It may happen then that a situation is carried beyond its plateau point so that its ending comes about not as the harmonious completion of a unit but as a breaking apart. The other possibility is that at the plateau the quality of integration is so developed that it becomes a further point of renewal, a starting point for a further cycle/unit of experience.

In terms of individual lives the essence of process in human experi-ence lies in the continuity of its movement toward new integrations, the formation of new holistic units. Of the various factors that enter our life experience, some fit together in a complementary way that adds a quality to each. Components that had been separate may come together so that they are contained within a new whole. They now belong within a context of form that did not exist before. The unit is new and they are changed within it. That is what is meant by an *integration*.

When in the course of a cycle/unit such integrations are brought about, they are the fruitage of that unit of time in the individual's life. They are the artwork that embodies its fulfillment, whether in a field of the arts, or science, or business, or sports, or religion, in whatever area of commitment and interest the work has been carried through. In itself, the achievement of an integration is an act of creativity; but something more is possible. Beyond the creativity that brings forth new integra-tions, there is the possibility of an *emergent*.

In the process of natural evolution, as we have seen earlier, emergents come about as the great unexpected and unexplained leaps when something altogether new enters the world. The mind itself and the human capacity of creativity are striking examples of emergents that have entered the world out of the evolutionary process as *something extra* beyond any combination of components that could have caused them or brought them into being. In the physical world emergents are the extras that come about whenever they do and if they do. Since they are additional to causality, emergents cannot be planned for and brought about deliberately on the physical level. Equally, on the level of human life and experience, emergents cannot be brought about on purpose. And yet it is a fair observation that emergents tend to come about in the experience of individuals who have put special effort and commitment into their lives. The *something extra* of emergents has no specific cause, but it seems to be related to something that is part of our inner experience.

One way of understanding it is that an emergent is the *something extra* that comes about in the course of forming a new integration. It is not the new integration itself, and it is not caused by nor brought about by the new integration. It is not a result of it, nor even a by-product of it. But it comes about while the integration is taking place within us as something additional that accompanies the process by which the integration is happening. There is clearly no inherent causality bringing it about. It is *something extra*.

The theoretical question of how emergents happen can be set aside in favor of a more pragmatic question: what disciplines and practices can we carry out that will increase the possibility of emergents breaking creatively into our experience? To achieve that is not specifically a goal of Process Meditation, but it is often one of its accompaniments. In observing the process of creative and spiritual experience, a fair hypothesis is that when an integration has taken place it establishes a congenial foundation on which an emergent may follow and to which an emergent may be drawn. An emergent may take place or, equally, it may not take place. But the integration that has occurred sets a base and opens a possibility.

When an emergent does come to us, we may welcome it as an evidence of good fortune. In past generations when emergents have come to individuals as part of their spiritual lives, theology and philosophy have had appropriate names and explanations to apply to them. Beyond labels, however, we may regard emergents as a mysterious bonus that has been granted to mankind from time to time through the experience of especially fortunate individuals. One of the purposes of Process Meditation is to increase the chances of that good fortune taking place in modern times by providing practical methods and opening channels so that the experience of emergents can become a greater possibility among all of us.

BUDDHA, FRANCIS AND THE TWO CREATIVITIES

Considering, as we have been doing, the phases of process in the inner experience of human beings, we see that emergents are off to one side and that they place the whole subject in a special light. Emergents raise the question—more, the possibility—of freedom and creativity and further evolution in the process of human experience.

The mere use of a concept like process implies a regularity of law and principle, even an inherent determinism. Considered in a context of process, all creativity appears to be conditioned and controlled to some degree by the circumstances in which it takes place. Emergents, on the other hand, imply a freedom, and yet not an arbitrary freedom separated from the regularity of nature's processes. We can speculate philosophically about the dialectic here, but the question has direct consequences for our experience. Do we have, in actuality, freedom of will and mind and spirit and the possibility of bona fide creativity in our lives, or is that only an intellectual conception and an illusion? It is not a question that can be answered in the abstract, but only specifically in terms of each individual's capacities of experience.

It is not only a question of whether a person has the potentiality of freedom and creativity. It must be that a great many people have that potential. But the further question is whether an individual has practiced to a sufficient degree the disciplines that develop the inner capacities for spiritual creativity in personal experience, as that is an expression of freedom. Our *Intensive Journal* program as a whole is intended to provide a vehicle for such disciplines and development, and Process Meditation is the particular means of integrating that range of experience. As we prepare to work with its practices, therefore, we should consider the questions of freedom and creativity in specific and practical terms.

If we think back to Gautama, the great teacher of Buddhism, we realize that the creativity in his new awareness gave him a substantial measure of freedom, but there were certain freedoms he did not have. He did not, for example, have the freedom to be a Christian nor to hear the words of the Lord God of Israel. By the same token, St. Francis did not have the freedom to become a Buddhist, even though he would most likely have understood very well the things that Gautama was saying. The life of Francis took place in the time of medieval European Christianity, and that provided the context and the limits of the understanding that was available to him. Equally the experiences of the Buddha were bounded by the framework of knowledge and belief of his time in history.

As human beings we feel a freedom in our inner life that reaches beyond determinism, but that freedom cannot be arbitrary. We do not have the freedom to recognize truths or to receive inspirations that are not within the process of that part of history in which our lives are rooted. Each of our lives follows a thread of inner continuity that is individual and unique to us alone. But it also contains a core of necessities that derive from society and that set the requirements and limitations of our life. Depending on the circumstances of personal destiny and the fortunes of time, the life of any individual person may have been one that could be lived only in the ancient world, or within a Christian worldview, or within a Hindu worldview. Whether it is chance or predestiny, those are the limits set by the larger movement of process as it establishes the context of life as a whole, as well as the specific contents and circumstances of an individual existence.

It has often been observed in history that certain individuals enter into the inner process of their lives with so strong a commitment that it brings forth something much more than might have been anticipated. It is in such lives that we observe freedom and creativity occurring as actualities in a way that sets those individuals apart. No good purpose can be served by our trying literally to imitate the lives of such persons, since each human existence is unique in its conditions and requires its own integral development. We may, however, discern the movements of process and the quality of involvement within those lives; and that information can be incorporated in the inner disciplines which we ourselves will practice.

As we follow the process of life experience in such persons as the Buddha Gautama and St. Francis of Assisi we perceive a sequence of events that is predictable in certain directions and degrees, and then becomes altogether unpredictable. Reconstructing the legends of the life, for example, of the man who came to be called the Buddha, we trace a cycle of experiences beginning with his innocence as a sheltered prince living in his father's court. This is followed by the shock of his discovery that pain and disintegration are conditions inherent in the physical existence of human beings, his realization that death will come with the passage of time. There then follows a period of crisis and personal breakdown in the life of Gautama. He can no longer accept the pleasant and superficial doctrines he had been taught to believe, but he knows of no other truth with which to replace them. This, therefore, becomes the time of emptiness for the Buddha, corresponding to the time of despair in the valley for the Psalmist. It is the time when there is no longer the old belief, and not yet a new one.

In the legends of the life of Gautama the shock of discovering that there is pain in human existence led him to surrender all the protections and the pleasures of his life as a young married prince. He left his home, his possessions and, implicitly, his old beliefs behind, going forth in search of a new truth that would enlighten him. But he did not go directly to the experience of enlightenment. When he left his wealth and family he went first to the ascetic life of a mendicant monk, begging his food and meditating. During that time there was no way to know when enlightenment would come, or if it ever would. That was the time of treading day by day the long, dry path of the desert in the valley, and with no end in sight.

It is a fair assumption that during this time the glimmerings of a new understanding were beginning to take shape for Gautama. When they finally came together in the form of a new truth within him, that *integration* was the experience of enlightenment that came to him beneath the fabled Bo Tree. After that transforming experience which completed the major *cycle/unit* in Gautama's life and led to his recognition as the Buddha, the movement of his life was renewed in a further cycle of experience. In this unit of his life he was teacher, the articulator of a new doctrine of spiritual understanding, and gradually the founder of what was to become a world religion.

Parallel to this is the process that moved in the life of the thirteenth-century merchant's son, Francis of Assisi. Francis was not sheltered from life as Gautama had been, but his youthful years were given to the license of sensual pleasure and to the adventures of soldiering in the affluent days of Italian history. In those years his main personal characteristic seems to have been a flamboyant self-confidence, but a sharp shift took place during his early twenties. Francis was a military prisoner for a while and there was a period of illness as well. These may have made him aware of the mortality and finitude of human existence in a way that is similar to Buddha's experience of shock at seeing an old man's disintegrating body. Without knowing the details, we have evidence that Francis passed through a confusing period of transition during which he recognized that the goals of his earlier years did not constitute a worthwhile purpose for living. But he was not yet convinced of any other beliefs or values for his life. It was therefore a wilderness time of psychological wandering.

During those years Francis seems to have become increasingly sensitive to the pain human beings suffered through the various plague-like illnesses that were common in that day, particularly leprosy. He felt the incapacity and the poverty which such illnesses brought, and his active nature seems to have sought a means of doing something more than merely sympathize. But the weaknesses of the human condition presented a problem too large for him to overcome.

In those years of no longer holding his old beliefs and not yet having new ones, Francis expressed his depressed and confused condition in the silences of prayer much, perhaps, as the Psalmist had done in Old Testament days. In the course of kneeling in prayer one day his doubts and his searchings came together in an inner experience that became the transforming event of his life. It was an inner event of *integration* that seems to have crystallized on a level deeper than his consciousness, his old concerns and confusions, and his desire for a new direction of life. Francis was alone in a broken-down old chapel when he heard the words spoken to him, "Francis, repair My church." With our advantage of knowing in retrospect the Franciscan role in Catholic Christianity, we can now recognize the broad symbolic reference of those words. At the time, however, Francis understood the words he heard only in a specific and literal sense. He was to repair the broken-down old church in which he was praying.

Acting on his calling, Francis became the organizer of what today might be called a corps of volunteer church repairmen. He drew together the funds, the material, and the labor. And one thing led to another. His new course of action precipitated a break with his father and family. It led him to articulate further the theological ideas that had been developing within him regarding humility and poverty and service. And as an increasing number of persons joined him in his work of physical repair, the combination of his teaching and his commitment brought about the formation of a new Order. In a few years Francis was meeting with the Pope, and his group was a recognized force working for the spiritual "repair" of the Christian Church as a whole.

Even though we are outsiders to his life looking at it from this distance in time, we can see a continuous process moving through the inner and outer events that Francis experienced. The words that he heard as a commandment redirecting his life were an image that carried an *integration* of the doubts and searchings in his past. They became the point of renewal that enabled his life energies to embark on a new course of activity which became and remained the meaning of his life. In that sense it can truly be said that the inner experience calling Francis to "repair the church" was an experience of renewal that began a new cycle/unit in his life, one that was to last until his death some twenty years later.

As the continuity of process moved through his life within that cycle/unit, Francis experienced a great many highs and lows, both of outer and inner events. Out of the flux of the contending forces, a core of integration gradually took shape. Primarily this was the Franciscan Order that formed around him, giving organization to the purposes of his work and a tangible expression to his teachings.

But *something extra* came about as well. While Francis was striving to live a life that would be meaningful in the sense that it would make a contribution to human existence, he found himself asking fundamental questions. What is the significance of pain and suffering? What is our relation to animals? To death? To the sun and the moon and the rest of the natural world? Struggling through his cycles of experience that alternated humility and forceful purpose within him, maintaining a physical poverty and yet with a sense of inner richness and conviction, Francis experienced the tension of many small cycles in the course of that major unit of his life. Its tangible results were numerous. These were the various integrations that came about as his religious order formed about him and as its works and teachings reached into many lives. While he was working at this, however, a further process was taking place within Francis. From it unexpected *emergents* came forth, *something extra* and additional, unpremeditated and yet somehow related to the process working in his life.

What were these emergents, these extras that came into existence in the course of Francis's life?

One of them is his "Sermon to the Birds." That was a simple event that happened one day. Contrary to their usual behavior, a flock of birds did not disperse as he approached them. So Francis stayed and talked to them. "Brother birds," he said, "you ought to praise and love your Creator very much! He has given you feathers for clothing, wings for flying, and everything you need. He has made you the noblest of his creatures, for He has appointed the pure air for your habitation. You have neither to sow nor to reap, yet He takes care of you, watches over you and guides you." And it is said that the birds remained in place to listen to his sermon attentively, fluttering their wings while Francis stroked them and blessed them.*

Another emergent of his life is *The Canticle of the Sun,* which might well be called the Psalm of St. Francis.

> Praise be to Thee above, Most High, for all thy creatures,
> Especially for Brother Sun who brings us the day and sheds
> > his light on us;
> Lovely is he, and radiant with great splendor,
> And he speaks to us of Thee, O Most High.
> Praise be to Thee, my Lord, for Sister Moon and the Stars
> Whom Thou hast set in the heavens, bright, precious and fair
> Praise be to Thee, my Lord, for Brother Wind,
> For air and cloud, for calm and all weather
> By which Thou sustaineth life in all thy creatures
> Praise be to Thee for Sister Water,
> Who is useful and humble, precious and pure
> Praise be to Thee, my Lord, for Brother Fire,
> By whom Thou lightest the night;
> He is fair and merry, mighty and strong
> Praise be to Thee, my Lord, for our Sister Mother Earth
> Who sustains and governs us
> And brings forth varied fruits, bright flowers and plants
> Praise and bless my Lord, and thank and serve Him with
> > great humility.

And perhaps the most important emergent of Francis's life is the prayer that is known by his name.

> Lord, make us the instrument of Thy peace
> Where there is hatred, let us sow love
> Where there is injury, pardon
> Where there is doubt, faith
> Where there is despair, hope
> Where there is darkness, light
> Where there is sadness, joy

* See Stephen Clissold, *The Wisdom of St. Francis and His Companions,* New Directions, New York, 1978. The *Canticle* and *St. Francis' Prayer* are also from this volume.

May we seek not so much to be consoled as to console
Not so much to be understood as to understand
Not so much to be loved as to love.
For it is in giving that we receive
It is in pardoning that we are pardoned
It is in dying that we awake to eternal life.

Given the problems of communication and record-keeping over many centuries, there is some question as to whether Francis himself is actually the author of these three emergents that we have cited. But the fact is that they are in the world, and that they have added strength and compassion to many lives in the course of the centuries. The further fact is that they express the spirit that was embodied in the activities of Francis and of those who shared their lives with him. By virtue of that, these creations have become over the centuries a means of contact and inner identification for those who are reaching toward the same dimension of reality. As emergents, that is undoubtedly their most important quality.

Parallel to Francis, as we think back now to the process moving through the life of the man, Gautama, we recognize that many *integrations* were brought forth as the visible results of his life. A body of doctrine capable of many enlargements and schools of interpretation was a result of the life of Gautama; and the formation of an organized religion capable of reaching into many lands was also a result of his life. But in addition to these, there was also *something extra*. There was the silent "Flower Sermon." There was the "Diamond Sutra." And like these, there were the additional emergents of poetry and wisdom teachings that came forth in the course of his life. There was the special quality of being that is the ineffable but lasting mark of the Buddha's presence in the world. Beyond the products of creativity which are the results of *integrations,* these are among the *emergents* of his life.

Something of great value which had not existed before they lived has been in the world as a result of the lives of St. Francis and Gautama. That is one criterion of effective freedom and also of the reality of creativity. One sign by which we can know that a creative act has occurred is when we find a human life that has served as a vehicle by which something distinctive and of lasting value has entered the world.

That there are important spiritual messages in those lives is apparent. But we have another question here. What can we learn from their lives about the nature of creativity, the process of creativity in itself, and its relation to spiritual experience?

A first step in learning from Buddha and Francis is to perceive the two kinds of creativity that took place in their lives. They each passed through a crisis experience that marked their transition first to a life of spiritual quest and then to a spiritual dedication. Those events encompass a cycle/unit of experience that covered the major period of their lives. In the course of that time various projects were undertaken, both on the inner and the outer level. As that period moved toward fulfilling its possibilities, some of these tasks were achieved in ways that were innovative as well as constructive in the circumstances of the time. These were creative aspects within the cycle/unit, fulfilling its goals and drawing it toward wholeness.

Each unit of experience in a human life contains certain desires and goals that define that period. As the person achieves those goals, a basic act of creativity takes place. The possibilities of the period are being actualized, at least to some degree, as the work that is done draws them into the shape of tangible results and products. As the achievements begin to approximate the possibilities with which that period began, we can speak of an act of integration taking place in the sense that a unit of lifetime is being rounded off. A unit of experience is being completed in terms of its potentials, and this opens the way for additional units to be started.

In the course of this integration various acts of creativity are carried through, primarily the achievements and products that belong to that period of time. Qualitatively the results of this creativity may be of greater or less degree, but this is the *Core Creativity* that accompanies the successful completion, the rounding off, or integration, of a unit of experience in a person's life. In this sense, each cycle/unit in a life has its acts of Core Creativity to the extent that the primary goals of that period have been fulfilled. We can think of a number of acts of core creativity during the main cycle/units in the lives of Buddha and Francis, the disciplines they developed, the teachings they articulated, the students and supporters they drew around them who thus formed the base of an organization. These were achievements that were inherent in their work as persons who lived successfully through a cycle/unit of experience in their calling as spiritual teachers.

Acts of core creativity take place in terms of the needs and context of the main cycle/unit of a person's life, whatever the goals of its activity may be. The creativity involves the act of bringing into existence something that meets the requirements of the cycle/unit, thereby helping to bring about its integration. Acts of core creativity are those that tangibly fulfil the goals in a person's life, whatever those goals may be: the painting of a fresco, the writing of a novel, the management of a farm, the nurturing of a child, the conduct of a business.

In this sense the criterion for the achievement of an artwork is mainly subjective to the person. The test of its success is objective to the degree that it has observable results. The management of a farm, for example, cannot be considered to be successful if it does not produce usable crops; nor can the conduct of a business be considered successful if it goes bankrupt; nor can the nurturing of a child be considered successful if it does not help the welfare of the child. Within those limitations, the ultimate judgment of an artwork is the person's own judgment of it, insofar as it is that judgment that determines whether it fulfils the goals of the cycle/unit. If the person feels satisfied with it, he or she may then feel free to close off that cycle/unit and move on to another unit of experience. Thus the core creativity need only be sufficient to meet the standards and demands of a particular cycle/unit in a person's life.

For some individuals, the criteria for that judgment will be very high. For others it will be more flexible. The judgment that is made of the artwork by other persons as to its qualitative value, especially if it is in the realm of the arts or science or religion, is quite another matter. The judgments made by others are relevant to the works of core creativity only to the degree that their lives also are affected by the artwork. It may be that many persons are involved in the work of a single individual, perhaps because, if it is a political work, they will be affected by its outcome; or perhaps, if it involves a group project, they will participate in it actively at a later stage of its development as an organization or a business; or perhaps they will share in it esthetically as members of the audience for a composer or a novelist. Essentially, however, the works that are the products of core creativity express each individual's attempts to fulfil those goals that are meaningful and valuable with respect to the cycle/unit through which that person is living. The works fulfil the goal and possibilities of that unit in the life, and as such they are steps toward integration and wholeness.

While this core creativity is taking place, something additional may also happen. While Buddha and Francis were doing the day-to-day work in carrying out their personal callings, the work that brought about the core creativity of their lives, *something extra* was taking place in and around them. This was not something on which they could plan, or something they could deliberately seek. It came about while they were engaged in the purposive work of their cycle/unit, but it came as an additional and unannounced factor. Beyond the purposes of their conscious goals, it carried a quality, a tone, and sometimes a content, that could not have been thought of in advance and therefore could not have been the purpose of the experience. These were the events of Emergent Creativity. They were the unplanned extras of the life. And yet, in persons like Buddha and Francis, they are the essence of the life. They are what the life was *for*.

Most of the time the acts of core creativity are relevant and valuable only to the individual persons who carry them out, and to the small group immediately around them with whom they share the fruits. Sometimes, however, an act of core creativity seems to strike a chord that sounds throughout the universe, speaking a truth that resonates to a great many persons over the generations, or expressing beauty in a form that all can recognize. When that happens, *something extra* has taken place. An act of emergent creativity has come about while an individual human being was engaged in carrying out the works of core creativity that were necessary for the life.

Such acts of emergent creativity add to the common heritage of mankind. They contribute to the cumulative resource of civilization, building the qualitative dimension of meaning and beauty and spirit. The paradox that governs them, however, is that, though they are of the greatest value to human life, they cannot be planned for as purposive acts. They can only happen, seemingly of themselves. And yet we observe certain preconditions for their happening. One essential precondition is that a person be engaged in a line of activity that is integral to the development of his or her life. As that work is being done with commitment, it leads to acts of core creativity which have a validity within the framework of the individual life. That is the basic fact of experience that must be present before an event of emergent creativity can take place. First an act of core creativity must be engaged in with deep and substantial integrity. As a by-product of that, *something extra* may happen, either at the time of the original event or in subsequent years. That is the emergent creativity. It reaches out beyond the person who was its original vehicle. Having a life of its own, it then goes on to unfold and extend its own unpredictable destiny.

Since events of emergent creativity cannot be brought forth by deliberate planning, since they come about not by directed activity but by a kind of *indirection,* it would seem that there is nothing to be done about them. Either they happen, or they do not. In noting, however, that there are certain preconditions that must be met before emergent creativity can take place, we open another avenue of approach. It may be that of the necessary preconditions for emergent creativity, some offer greater possibilities than others do; and it may be also that there are ways of increasing the range of these possibilities. That is one application of our *Intensive Journal* work, and especially of the practice of Process Meditation.

Although it was not originally phrased that way, it can truly be said that the structure of the *Intensive Journal* system is focused toward bringing about larger achievements of core creativity. This happens naturally because of the fact that the *Intensive Journal* workbook and its accompanying procedures follow the structure and contents of a cycle/ unit in the life of an individual. The basic format of the *Intensive Journal* work * is designed to bring about a larger clarification of all the contending factors within a given cycle/unit of a person's life. It then works to draw those factors toward integration at a level of achievement and personal wholeness. In the course of this process, the development of various artworks is stimulated and brought to fruition. Thus the *Intensive Journal* work supports and enlarges the products of core creativity in the context of the person's life as a whole.

The basic precondition for emergent creativity, that persons be engaged in a committed activity that is authentically connected to the unfoldment of their life, then has additional implications. One further aspect of the preconditions is that the individual's activity not be oriented primarily in a pragmatic way. Emergent creativity seems to be drawn toward individuals who are not engaged in the opportunistic seeking for advantage in the conduct of life. Its precondition seems to require that the commitment with which the life is lived be directed

---

* As described in *At a Journal Workshop.*

toward the finding, the development, or the creating of something that is of inherent value for mankind, something that conduces to the meaning of life itself. If there is an advantage to be gained from this activity, it should be an advantage that is more than personal. It should tend toward a connection with realities of life that are of a larger than personal significance.

As we consider this series of preconditions in the context of our *Intensive Journal* work, we see that it places a particular emphasis on the experiences within the cycle/units of a person's life. It directs the attention toward the side of life that deals with the depths, better in the French phrase, the *profondeurs*, of human experience. The more-than-personal profundities of human existence, the underlying meanings of the universe and our connection to them, are essentially the subject of the Process Meditation dimension of *Intensive Journal* work. In the course of our practice of Process Meditation we may well discover that, as we are expanding our relation to the *profondeurs* of life, we are increasing the possibility that events of emergent creativity will one day unexpectedly take place in our personal experience.

We may thus see in perspective the relationship between the *Intensive Journal* method and the two creativities. The basic personal use of the *Intensive Journal* program is directed toward balancing and strengthening the varied contents of the cycle/units in our lives and providing the means for developing them further. There are sequences of exercises specifically directed toward evoking more imaginative possibilities for our work projects and leading them to a creative outcome beyond their original goals. In this way the *Intensive Journal* program as a whole can make a helpful contribution to core creativity.

The achievements that are the works of core creativity become the base point for much of the deepening of inner process by which emergent events may break into the area of one's creative work. That involves an opening to a further level of experience, an expansion of understanding and awareness that is essentially a spiritual capacity of knowing. For this a form of spiritual discipline is needed that speaks to the condition of modern consciousness, and that is one purpose of Process Meditation.

An important aspect of Process Meditation in this regard is that it enables us to establish a closer relation to the emergent events that have transpired in the experience of other persons in earlier periods of history. We can thus encounter and begin to know by means of their lives the dimension of spiritual reality that can become present in ours. It is a means of gaining entry to the "house with many mansions" so that we can gradually learn to find our way along its complicated corridors. As we become more familiar with the dimly lit and twisting passageways in that vast house, we are able to recognize many more mysterious truths, including the fact that its deepest paradoxes and mysteries are reflected in the depth of our selves. At that point the inner process in each of us begins to disclose its messages and its possibilities. We shall experience the varieties of this as our practice of Process Meditation proceeds.

As we consider the possibility of emergent creativity entering our lives we are reminded of the paradoxical role that inner process plays in human experience. It is a dynamic reality that moves in the depth of us, and we are able to understand many of its facets. Nonetheless we do not have the freedom to use it nor to direct it according to our conscious will. We have knowledge of our inner process, but we do not have the power of creativity over it. The experiences and the awarenesses that have begun to be gathered by means of Process Meditation do, however, give us reason to believe that we can eventually have much greater access to this dimension of experience. While we may not be able to control or to direct new events of emergent creativity in our spiritual lives, there are practices we can follow that will increase the possibility of such events finding their way into our experience.

The key lies in the relationship that we establish with the inner, subjective process of our lives, and the resources with which we maintain and deepen that relationship. Some persons in history have had experiences of emergent creativity in the spontaneity of their lives. They were simply going about their regular activities when *something extra* happened. We know that emergent events cannot be brought about on purpose. To sensitize and deepen our relation with the inner process of our lives may, however, increase the possibility of their happening. It will give them more congenial soil in which to take root. We have just a little more preparation before we proceed to the practical discipline of doing that.

Chapter 4

Practicing Process-Plus-One:
A Methodology
for the Inner Life

Having a fuller perspective of its two main elements, meditation and process, we are in a position now to view the range of Process Meditation and its role in our creative and spiritual lives.

As our discussion of subjective process has proceeded, it has enabled us to see more clearly the significance of the definition of meditation that we are following. When we speak of meditation here we include all the forms by which human beings reach toward meaning in their lives. It is not valid to identify meditation with any limited set of techniques, since fundamentally meditation is a way of reaching out to make personal contact with the infinity of life. Meditation may include, but it is not limited to, techniques for becoming quiet, methods for controlling the autonomic nervous system, concentrated reflection on ancient metaphysical doctrines. All of these may be included in our definition of meditation, and much more as well, provided that they are being used to find or to deepen the person's connection with meaning in the larger contexts of life.

When we study the life histories of many individuals, we find that some spend a great deal of time experimenting with a variety of beliefs and teachings. This is particularly true of modern times when communication and education have made available a broad knowledge of beliefs and doctrines drawn from the major traditions. It is not uncommon nowadays for individuals to take a spiritual journey through both Eastern and Western doctrines seeking a thread of truth among the pluralism of teachings. In this way some exceedingly interesting and adventuresome spiritual histories have been compiled over the past generation.

Other persons in modern times follow a simpler path in that they seek their contact with truth within the framework of beliefs that come from the main traditions of their society. These people do not experiment with many different doctrines, but they try to establish as deep and satisfying a connection as they can within the tradition in which their life is rooted. For such persons a single set of symbols provides not only the framework of beliefs but also the context for doubts and wonderings. A great deal of inner experimenting can take place in this way with much spiritual struggling, searching and changing, even though these are primarily variations on a single theme. Most of the great spiritual figures of history have reached their experiences in this way, as we saw in Buddha and Francis.

An interesting fact emerges as we consider these two opposite types of spiritual lives. We find that, whether a person seeks truth by exploring a diversity of many doctrines, or by working with commitment within a single framework of belief, the result is a process of inner experience in either case. Each builds a spiritual history that is unique to the person, moving through phases and cycles and integrations of experience. In one person the process of change is explicit, as the movement proceeds from one doctrine or group identification to the next. In another person the process of change may be less visible because the external observances of ritual and ceremony remain the same throughout. Only the inner relation to the structure of beliefs changes, and this may take place secretly in the privacy of an inner struggle. Such a person, remaining within a single context of belief throughout a lifetime, may give the impression to others of having a static and unchanging spiritual life. Many dynamic developments, however, may have been taking place in the depths of his or her inner experience, and these are the contents of the personal spiritual history.

We can see that in both of these opposite types of persons a process of spiritual continuity and development takes place. Since its contents are primarily spiritual experiences, the movement and intensity of the inner search may not be visible to others, except for changes in religious allegiances and external group identification. The fact is, however, that in both a process of continuity and change is operating and is as real in its effects as the natural process by which seasons change, or animals grow, or chemicals affect one another. The process that moves through the varieties of meditation is _subjective process_ since its contents are formed by individuals in their personal inner experience. The movements or rhythms of subjective process are definite and discernible, but they have to be understood in terms of the intangible realm of inner experiences in which their energies and principles have their effects.

Once the implications of this fact have been appreciated, it becomes possible to mark off the specific qualities of movement that take place within subjective process. Even in the brief space of our introductory overview we could see the forms and rhythms in which subjective process moves and changes. It passes through regular phases which we can mark off in the _cycle/units_ of individual experience. Within these units of subjective experience we can also discern a definite style of movement in the direction of _integrations_ which draw together the potentials of the period and its achievable results. Both on the inner and outer levels, integrations round off units of life experience and bring forth the fruit of the work, the planning and activity, that have taken place during the cycle/unit. These are the products of the core creativity that carries the basic achievements of the period. And beyond the integrations, there is the occasional good fortune of an _emergent_ event that brings a special quality of creativity and adds to the qualitative total of human experience.

The step between the cycles of subjective process and the _extra_ of emergent events takes us to the question of the reality of freedom and the possibility of creativity in our lives. We have to acknowledge that process has a deterministic effect. The fact of physical process places limits on our physical life, and the same is true of our inner experience. Therefore we have to ask ourselves what the reality of freedom and creativity actually is in our lives, considering the limiting effects of both physical and subjective process. And further, if we do find an entrance to the freedom of creativity, is there a method by which we can keep the door ajar, and even open it wider from time to time?

We should first consider the conditions of creativity in our world of outer and inner process. When we were outlining the sequences of subjective process, we saw that the heart of it lies in the cycle/units within individual lives. That is where the main contents of existence are conceived and matured; the desires and plans, the projects, relationships and beliefs. All the goals of a person's life are worked through within the framework of a cycle/unit of experience. Certain projects are of central importance to the unit, and when they come to culmination they carry the cycle/unit into its *integration* phase. That is the time when the parts of a person's life that had seemed to be disjointed can finally come together. After what may seem to be interminable delays they form new integrations as the outcome of the cycles of experience through which the individual has passed. Possibilities which at an earlier stage had seemed to be hopeless now combine with others to give a constructive result. It may not be the outcome that was planned or desired, but it is directly related to the efforts that have been expended in the course of the cycle/unit. It is the fruit of the work that comes in the time of *integration*. These are the results of the core creativity that fulfils a unit of process in a person's life.

Moving beyond process, we saw the events of emergent creativity that seem to happen as though of themselves. In that sense they are acts of freedom, especially since each act of emergent creativity brings something new and valuable into the world in whatever area of experience it takes place. It is freedom in a paradox, however. The person in whom an event of emergent creativity takes place cannot say that it is his creativity or his freedom that is expressed in it. The fact is that it was not within that person's power to bring the act of emergent creativity to pass nor to determine its contents. And yet, without the individual's willing participation, the acts of emergent creativity would not have happened. It seems that somewhere in between the achievement of core creativity in the process of our lives and the *something extra* of emergent creativity there is an area of paradox and mystery where our spiritual freedom may be found. It is perhaps the ultimate conundrum of our existence. It is the riddle within which we live as finite human beings in a world of regular and deterministic process, having the intimation that there is freedom and meaning just beyond the edge of our present existence.

In reaching into the midst of the paradox of process, there seems to be one doorway by which we can take a step into it and occasionally beyond it. That is by establishing and maintaining a special kind of *relation with process* in its various forms as subjective experience. This is provided by our practice of Process Meditation. Our *relation with process* at deep, inner levels is the foundation of the practical work that we can do. We can indicate some of the basics here and consider their implications further after we have experienced the main body of Process Meditation work.

The first and fundamental relation to process is: _Knowing_ process. In this relationship process is an object of knowledge to us. We step outside of it in order to scrutinize it, study it, know it as something separate from ourselves. In this act, whether it is physical process or subjective process that we are studying, it is objective to us. We know it factually as we know the given data of the natural world.

The second relation to process is: _Being_ process. We consciously accept the fact that continuities of process are moving through us, through our physical lives and through our qualitative lives. For us to _be_ process involves an act of voluntary unification. It is voluntary, but it is an acceptance of what already is. There is the paradox again. As a tree grows unself-consciously, a person eats when hungry, sleeps when tired, works, mates, ages through the cycles of physical process, fulfils the changing roles that social process requires, and moves through the cycles of experience. That is _being_ process, moving with the rhythms of it, allowing the cycles of life to happen through us and not inhibiting them by our rational self-consciousness.

Like _knowing_ process, this second relation of _being_ process is good and valuable in itself. Both of these can be very helpful in bringing about integrations within the cycle/units of life and in stimulating the core creativity that accompanies them. We have to note, however, that neither _knowing_ process nor _being_ process leads to emergent experiences of creativity. Something further is needed.

Seeking this additional factor, we may look more closely at those persons whose lives have been a special source of information to us. Persons like Buddha, Francis, Dostoevsky spontaneously lived in such a way that not only acts of core creativity but also emergent events took place. What was their effective relation to process?

One quality that we observe in them is that they worked consistently and with commitment toward a single goal. Whether this purpose was in the arts or in religion or whatever it might be, there was a single dominant process in which their energies were channeled. In the lives of such persons we often find experiences in which a life-crisis and a new inspiration have come very close together.

The first part is in some form a rejecting of the old aspects of one's life, a clearing of the field even though one does not yet know how it all will be used in the future. The second part is an experience of intimation in which the individual has an image of something he or she may eventually do or may become. This *image of intimation* contains an intuitive perception, a generalized vision of what is possible in the future, and it also carries a large resource of energy. The combination of these, placing the purpose in the future and providing the strength with which to get there, gives the person an affirming and unitary feeling of the process as a whole by which the goal can be fulfilled. In the language we have used, they intuitively *know* the process, sensing it before it has actually taken place; and they *are* the process because they are committed to being and doing it. That totality of commitment seems to be an essential of creativity whether in the arts or in the life of the spirit.

Possibly a main reason why commitment and energy are so important is that the goal that was shown in the *image of intimation* is seldom fulfilled quickly. The intimation is of the future and the distance is traversed a little at a time. The old spiritual truth seems to apply in all areas of creativity: one travels by delays.

When a large creative project is undertaken, it proceeds well for a certain distance and then it comes to rest. The process moving within the work has then completed a cycle. In order for the work to move on to its next phase of development, another cycle must be started. To do this, the person must re-enter the process of the work, be within it, and begin to do the work once again. In that way, as we re-approach the work from within its own process, letting the process take itself forward another step and still another step at a time, the work builds its strength again and again. In each unit of experience it moves through a further cycle in its development.

Large works may require many such cycles of starting, stopping, and re-entering the process from within, again and again. Certain persons of whom we know, like Dostoevsky and Francis, did this spontaneously and with great commitment, although not without many emotional struggles. Most persons, however, find great difficulty in re-entering the process of their work, delay after delay, as they seek the goal which they glimpsed in their *image of intimation*. They require tools that they can use, and methods that will enable them to maintain the continuity of the process within them so that it can renew its strength and begin new cycles. They need a means of *practicing the process,* and this is where the procedures of Process Meditation within the structure of the *Intensive Journal* program have a special role to play in creativity.

A key to the role of Process Meditation in creativity lies in our understanding the distinction between what an artwork is and what is merely a work.

A work is a task that we do in order to get it done. It may be done honestly and adequately, even done very well, but it is simply carried through to its necessary completion in order to get it done. An artwork, on the other hand, is worked and reworked, done and altered and redone, seeking always a qualitative improvement. An artwork, in whatever field of life it is carried out, in literature or painting, in business or politics or raising a child, is not done only in order to be done, but it is "done as well as may be." *

It is done and redone so that it moves further and further toward being brought to its best possible form. That phrase, "best possible," has subjective overtones, and we know that no two people may agree on what is precisely the best possible form to which an artwork can be brought. When an artwork is begun, however, there is an intuitive perception of the potentials of the artwork. It is an intimation given ahead of time of the possibilities of what may be achieved, similar to the *image of intimation* that may come to persons indicating what they may do and what they may become in the future. That intimation of the possibilities of the artwork becomes a personal criterion by which the artist, in whatever field of life, can judge how close the artwork is coming toward fulfilling its possibilities. There may be the realization as the work proceeds that the artwork is capable of going far beyond the original vision. Then the standard is readjusted, and the work proceeds.

The question of how closely the artwork is being brought to fulfilling the seed of its possibilities is answered privately by the person each step of the way. Each unit of involvement of working with the artwork changes its relation to its original possibilities. It comes closer to it or goes further away. Perhaps the cycle of experience has been an advance. Perhaps it has been only a delay. Either way, it is an addition to the continuity of the process. The commitment of the person to the integrity of the artwork requires that the process be continued unit by unit. After each cycle of experience, the implicit question is asked: is the

* This phrase is from the classic work of the American philosopher/economist, Thorstein Veblen, *The Instinct of Workmanship and the State of the Industrial Arts,* New York, 1914.

artwork now "right" in relation to the seed of its potentiality? The answer may be subjective but the honesty of the judgment and the commitment to remain with the process until the artwork has found its true form will say a great deal about the person as an artist in life.

There is a fundamental parallel between this practice in creativity and the meditative quest for meaning. The artist re-enters the process of an artwork in order to work and rework it from within its process. With respect to the experience of meaning in our lives, many persons are like an artist without an artwork. We know that something is missing but we do not know exactly how to obtain it. Individuals may live for many years without being consciously concerned about the meaning of life in general or the purpose of their life in particular. If they feel that something is lacking, it is only a vague feeling which they can easily cover over by submerging themselves in the pressing issues of everyday life.

Sooner or later, the question of meaning in life forces itself to the forefront of one's attention. In earlier generations it was mainly in the so-called "second half of life" that the question was articulated. In recent decades, however, young persons have increasingly raised the question and taken active steps committing their lives to the quest for finding answers. There can no longer be any doubt about it in psychological quarters: the question of meaning in life may be validly raised at any point in a person's life as a legitimate issue and not as the starting point for a psychiatric diagnosis.

The question may be talked about superficially and given the conventional answers that are current in one's social environment. Such casual or conventional talk may take place for a long time without the issues really being raised. By the word "really" I mean with strong feelings and concern. But then one day, or night, an inner experience spontaneously takes place, perhaps in a symbolic form, and it draws the question of meaning to the forefront of consciousness in a way that cannot be ignored.

The primary awakening comes as an *image of intimation,* an intuitive feeling that there is a truth that can be found and known personally, if one can only make contact with it. That *image of intimation* corresponds to the intuition with which an artwork announces itself. From that point onward in our life, the experience of meaning is an artwork that draws us on, calling upon us to fulfil it "as well as may be." Sometimes, after an *image of intimation* has been experienced by a person, the pressures of outer life push it back out of view, and it may remain in a state of abeyance for many years before it is reawakened.*

In other lives, the inner experience that carries the intimation of meaning in life is so strong that there is no choice but to make a life decision and commitment with respect to it. After that we may pass through many phases and cycles of experience, finding, losing and finding again. The intimation of truth that first comes to us may awaken our awareness and desire for meaning as it does in the fairy tales where it is love's first kiss of the spirit. But the first is seldom the last, and many further emotions, experiences and realizations follow the first intimation of truth before it is fulfilled. After the enthusiasm of discovery there may be a period of excitement, then doubt and ambivalence, rejection and forgetting, renewals and rediscoveries that are different from the first experience and yet curiously recall and extend the original intimation.

Through the continuity of these varied experiences, doubting and rejecting as well as discovering and affirming, a personal spiritual history is being built. As it passes through cycles of experience, it is moving progressively toward the artwork that it had intuitively previsioned. It is reaching persistently toward meaning as the artist reaches toward the perfect form of an artwork that will embody truth and beauty, that will be whole unto itself.

Recognizing the parallelism between the creative and the spiritual life, our work of Process Meditation follows the spontaneous practices of the artist-at-work as the model for its systematic procedures. It recasts these into their equivalent in terms of subjective process so that they can be used in regular and practical ways by means of the *Intensive Journal* workbook and its continuous program.

Our basic procedure is to re-enter the process by which our individual spiritual history has been moving toward meaning. That is the continuity of our meditative life in all its forms and variations. It includes the diversity of contexts in which we have reached toward meaning at different times in our lives, sometimes in the sacramental forms of religion, sometimes in the secular forms of modern culture. All these inner and outer events, including the variations in the cycles of

* For an instance of this see "The Dream of the Luminous Child" in *Depth Psychology and Modern Man*, Chapter 3, p. 64.

81

experience through which they have passed, constitute a single process. We re-enter that process so as to reconnect ourselves with the inner principle of its movement, and especially so that we can take a further step toward the artwork that is our personal sense of meaning. We do this by using the *Intensive Journal* workbook as our instrument, especially the Process Meditation sections with their exercises. We do the work both privately and at a workshop with others, depending on the circumstances.

Through all our procedures we keep the perspective of being artists who are working at the artwork of meaning in our lives. We take into account that this is an artwork in which we have been personally engaged from time to time over the years, sometimes with deliberate activity, sometimes with spontaneous experiences. Now we are re-entering the flow of the process as a whole so that we can position ourselves within its continuity in the perspective of our life history; from that base, using our methods of evoking a deep quality of consciousness, we shall seek to move organically into further experiences. Each time we work at it, we seek to take the process one step further. This holds true, and shows itself to be possible, regardless of what the contents of our individual process have been in the past.

The principle that underlies Process Meditation is that we re-enter the continuity of our whole spiritual history as we have personally experienced it, and by means of our methodology we add to it one further and deeper experience at a time. We are working in our inner process plus one further experience. We move forward with process plus one further experience at a time. As these experiences accumulate, they reconstellate themselves, establishing new patterns, giving new points of emphasis, even setting new directions. Whatever changes and new developments take place come from within the process itself. That is an essential protection to assure the integrity of our artwork of meaning. It will always be drawn from the continuity of our own spiritual process plus the one further experience that is our next experience.

We know the past of our spiritual process, or we may believe that we do. But we have no way to know what the plus-one experience will be. Since our next inner experience in Process Meditation will come out of the context of our whole spiritual history, that should be assurance enough. It is true, however, that we do seek to open ourselves to our next experience with no predeterminations. Practicing the process in

Process Meditation gives us a means of deepening our relation to whatever beliefs are now important to us. If that leads to experiences which in turn lead to changes in our beliefs, that belongs to our development in the future. Process Meditation by itself does not bring changes, and in no way does it suggest what those changes should be if they do occur. It only takes us into our individual spiritual process—*plus one experience,* that next deepened experience, whatever it shall be. And it opens the way for that.

On one occasion at an *Intensive Journal* workshop I was speaking about the open perspective of Process Meditation, and I was describing how the various procedures lead to something more, to process-plus-one experience at each point in our spiritual life. One man participating in the workshop took some exception to this. He was apparently a person of strong Fundamentalist views within his particular religion, and he said that he was not interested in finding something more in his religious life. He was convinced that at this point he had found the truth, and he was therefore content to remain with it. He did not want a method for finding something additional.

I, in turn, had a question for my questioner. I asked him first whether he had newly discovered his present belief, or whether some time had passed since he had found it. He said that some time had passed. I asked him then to recall the state of his understanding at the time of his conversion experience. And I asked him further to consider the present state of his inner life. Was the latter different from the first? Had issues arisen since his original experience that he had needed to clarify, and that had led him to extend or to deepen his understanding?

He replied that a number of issues had indeed arisen in the course of his holding his present beliefs, and that he had sought to resolve them by prayer and religious consultation and especially by serious thinking within the context of his beliefs. And yes, he agreed, in response to my further question, there certainly was more now in his religious life than there had been when he had his first experience. Apparently a continuous process of development had been taking place at the unconscious levels of his spiritual life.

This discussion enabled him to see the purpose and the potential use in his life of the Process Meditation procedures. Its function would be to give him a methodology, a set of procedures for deepening inner experience in the context of his whole spiritual life. He would be able to use it to enlarge and extend his religious life by working with the contents of inner experience that presented themselves to him. If new experiences came to him by using these procedures, they would be in the context not only of his present beliefs but of a generally reverent attitude toward the inner life. In our discussion he then stated to me what is the basic orientation of Process Meditation, that it is more important to affirm the reality of spiritual life than to prescribe any system of thought as final truth. Our faith must be not that we begin with the truth but that continuing inner experience will lead to a larger recognition of truth.

On another occasion a Catholic priest was participating in a workshop, very actively involved in the *Intensive Journal* procedures. As I later discovered, he was a very learned theologian. He was also a person of East Asian background whose roots were in a religion other than the one in which he was now achieving some eminence.

About midway in our Process Meditation work (as we were preparing for the Mantra/Crystal practices which come further in this book) he raised an objection to the work, saying that he had already had the spiritual experiences that were necessary for him and that he did not need any others. Therefore why continue with the exercises?

In return I had a question for him. I asked him whether there had been only one spiritual experience in his life or whether there had been many. He said yes, there had been, as a matter of fact, quite a number. And he agreed with my further comment that where there had been many, there might very well also be at least one and perhaps several more.

The priest then volunteered the information that there had been a qualitative development in the course of his various spiritual experiences in the past, and that each experience had added a further content to his inner life. We then found that we agreed that a method that would open the possibility of still further inner experiences could only bring an additional benefit, and would in no case present a danger to a person. On that basis we proceeded with the exercises.

As it happens, the new experience that took place for the priest on that occasion is indicative of one of the possibilities that open to us in the course of the Process Meditation work. Using our Mantra/Crystal procedures, he found himself drawn back to the time in his youth when he was practicing an Oriental religion, not Christianity, in another cultural context in another language. Now, in his experience at the workshop, the language of his childhood returned to him and he heard himself chanting and singing religious materials from both religions in his original tongue. It was an intensely emotional experience for him on the personal level, but on a deeper-than-personal level it was a step toward drawing together the past and the present of his spiritual life.

The priest was glad to acknowledge that a further experience had indeed been given to him. He explained that for many years the two historical strands of his life had been separate and had not seemed to have a possibility of uniting. Now he felt that the basis for a dialogue relationship between them had been spontaneously established at a deeper-than-conscious level. This feeling, he said, gave him a sense of harmony and peace. He made the further comment that he drew from his experience more than an implication, a virtual promise, that there would be more connections and experiences reached by him through this approach. It enabled him to give recognition to the process that had already been operating in his religious life over the years and to have a means of systematically evoking it further in the future.

It is interesting to reflect that, when we consider the various approaches to spiritual experience that are available to us, our customary impulse is to choose among them. Soon we realize, however, that it is not necessary for us to affirm some and reject others. Each spiritual discipline possesses its own validity within the context of its principles and beliefs. Each has its own integrity. It is thus not even appropriate for us to compare and judge, to affirm or reject one or the other. We have, rather, to establish our individual relationship with each spiritual approach that is personally meaningful to us. Whether it is a discipline of practice or a system of belief, there are various levels on which we can explore what it has to say to us and by which we can evoke within ourselves new experiences in relation to each of them that will deepen the quality of our spiritual awareness as a whole.

As a methodology for the inner life, Process Meditation provides a context of principles and a variety of procedures for opening channels of connection between our inner processes and the spiritual teachings and traditions of our past. In the course of our life they may have become estranged from one another, but we wish now to open the possibility of renewal and a deepening dialogue. Whatever they are, Process Meditation rejects none and is intended to replace none. It is not an alternative to any belief or spiritual practice to which you may be committed. Process Meditation does not compete with any doctrine but rather provides the means of moving deeper into each teaching or symbol so that more of its possibilities can be experienced. It complements the beliefs to which you find yourself drawn by providing additional contexts of experience and new angles from which they can be approached. Given these new perspectives you are better able to consider what valid place a particular doctrine may have in your future beliefs and in your spiritual life. Especially because of its active procedures, Process Meditation often serves as a catalyst so that many people find that it stimulates fresh experiences within the framework of old beliefs that had become routine.

These two qualities, first serving as a complement to other spiritual disciplines by opening new paths to them and new ways of relationship; and second, by serving as a catalyst to evoke a fresh vitality of experience within them, indicate the role that Process Meditation can play in modern consciousness. We are at the point now where we can begin its practice.

PART II

Working with the
Meditation Log

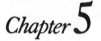

Chapter 5

Assembling Our Inner Data

Now we come together to begin our practice of Process Meditation.

Using our *Intensive Journal* workbook, we turn to the Process Meditation division with its purple dividers. There are five sections for us to work with here, and together they will establish a unified field for our inner experience. The names of the sections may seem strange to us at the start, even esoteric. But gradually they will become familiar to us as we work with them. And we shall feel comfortable in using them.

The names of the sections reflect the contents and the special kinds of entries we make in them. The sections are: *Meditation Log; Connections; Mantra/Crystals; Peaks, Depths and Explorations;* and *Testament.* As we proceed, the experiences we have will enable us to understand the principles that underlie the structure of these sections. The five sections carry a progressive interior movement so that what we experience in the course of the exercises of one section leads to and sets the basis for the exercises and entries that we work with in the other sections. In some cases the movement will take us back and forth among the sections of the Process Meditation division itself. In other cases it will take us to other sections of the *Intensive Journal* workbook.

This is the dynamic of the *Intensive Journal* work, that it evokes new experiences, new understandings, and especially that it generates new energies by its cross-fertilizing, back and forth movement among the

Journal sections. This Journal Feedback method provides the means of connection between the Process Meditation procedures and the rest of the *Intensive Journal* workbook. By means of it, what we experience in Process Meditation can be fed into the personal aspects of the individual life. And by means of it also the contents of our personal life can be brought into the larger perspective that is provided by spiritual experience.

The section with which we begin our Process Meditation work is the *Meditation Log*. The first thing we notice about this is that it is a *log* section. In the context of *Intensive Journal* work this means that it is essentially a recording and fact-gathering section. Altogether there are six log sections scattered at strategic points throughout the *Intensive Journal* workbook.* Each of these sections serves to collect the data of our life experience as seen from a particular point of view.

The log sections are those in which we gather the subjective facts of our inner experience, our feelings, thoughts, symbolisms, awarenesses. Here we describe what has taken place within us as objectively as we can. These sections are the collectors of the varied facts of our inner life recorded and drawn together as much as possible without censorship, without repression, without judgment or interpretation. We simply gather our inner data as objectively as we can like reporters, not editorial writers. We are collecting the subjective facts of our life experience so that at a later time we can explore and extend these entries by means of the Journal Feedback process. The log sections are the suppliers of the raw data with which we build the dynamic of Journal Feedback in the *Intensive Journal* method.

Each of the log sections has its special function in gathering the factual data of a segment of our lives. Some of the material relates to our past and is known to us consciously. Some of it comes through unconscious media like dreams and imaging. Some of it involves facts of outer life that are objectively verifiable, and much of it involves inner facts that we only perceive subjectively. Whatever their nature, objective or subjective, we have a place for all of them in one or another of the log sections. Taken together they contain the raw, uninterpreted contents of an individual life and they give us the starting point for our active Journal Feedback work.

* See Model of *Intensive Journal* workbook in Appendix, page 317.

The Meditation Log, however, is different from the other log sections in a very important regard. Where they are collectors and gatherers of the data of personal life, the Meditation Log not only gathers the data that pertains to the meditation dimension of our life experience but also carries it forward in an active way. Bearing in mind our broad definition and understanding of meditation as all the forms and methods by which we reach toward meaning in our lives and by which we seek the depth beyond the doctrines in religion and philosophy, we can see that there is a large range of entries to be made in the Meditation Log.

We have already seen from our definition and perspective of it that meditation is not limited to any single type of religious practice. It is a generic human activity, for the reaching toward meaning is inherent in our lives. The experiences of meditation are taking place to some degree whenever human beings stop the mindless movement of their individual life experience in order to reflect on its significance, refocusing their relationship to its contents and its movement. Meditation includes all the forms by which we may turn our attention inward, first to consider our personal life within its own terms, and then to place it in the larger context of the universe. We are engaged in a form of meditation whenever we participate in a practice or an observance or a discipline that seeks either to explore a truth or to develop our capacity for greater awareness in any context, whether it be religious, philosophical, or our personal sensitivity to spiritual issues in everyday life.

We find that we can discern a variety of forms in which our inner experience presents itself as we proceed in the process of our meditation. Sometimes we experience our meditation in a dualistic form, sometimes in a unitary form, sometimes in an integral or holistic form that seems to draw the two together. Sometimes meditative experience comes to us in the midst of the activity and the turmoils of our life. Sometimes it comes in times of rest or in times of emptiness when nothing seems to be present and operating in our lives.

The movement of meditative experience has a paradoxical and often misleading appearance when looked at from the outside. One observation, however, that helps give perspective is our taking note of the fact that, like phenomena in the rest of the cosmos, the processes of our inner quest also move in cycles. In the course of our experience we touch highs and we touch lows, and we move back and forth through the gradations of expectation and disappointment. Understanding this adds a resiliency to the philosophy with which we can approach our life. Since neither the high nor the low is permanent, neither is necessarily to be preferred to the other.

The integral movement of the whole process of our inner life requires both of the opposites. Just as the sun cannot remain fixed at noon but has to set before it can rise again, so we must expect and prepare ourselves for a continuity of opposites to pass through our inner lives. We know in advance that we shall experience it with a sharp diversity of intensities, of fulfillments and frustrations. To meet it we require a method that will enable us to move through the continuity of inner change in a way that is harmoniously related to it even when the momentary message that it carries to us is so unpleasant that we wish to reject it.

One way to express it now at the outset of our work is that the deep process of meditation requires us to accept all that transpires in our lives. But the word *accept* is too strong here and is not really correct. It is rather that we must learn to *acknowledge* whatever occurs in our lives, whether at outer or inner levels, so that it can move without being prejudged through the cycles of our life experience and eventually find its proper place and meaning in the continuity of our life as a whole.

In this context, a primary function of the sections in our *Intensive Journal* workbook is that they provide us with a tangible, flexibly structured place in which we can record and describe the outer and inner events of our lives. Once these are recorded and thereby acknowledged we can proceed to work with all the variations of our subjective life in an objective way. Then we can relate to them and see how the continuous movement of the cycles of life wishes to unfold within us. From that we can discern the message that our life holds for us, and we can form our response to it in the course of our meditation.

In this way our individual destiny is shaped progressively as a deep dialogue with the messages that life gives us as we acknowledge and relate to the many levels of reality in our existence. To carry this through is for each of us a large, probably illimitable, enterprise. But it is an enterprise that is fulfilled by degrees. Thus we can know that if we work at it we shall find some measure of fulfillment as we proceed, even if it is never complete.

For such an interior undertaking, it is necessary that we be willing to work from a position in which we are freed from our personal and habitual opinions. That is the requirement that Socrates set in his day, and he used his method of questioning (Maieutics) as his technique for achieving it. There can be little question of the fact that Socrates defined his goal correctly and that his method was a valid as well as a noble one. My experience in working with modern persons, however, has led me to conclude that it is too much to ask of human beings that they overcome their opinions to such a degree that they can actually be freed of them. There is simply not time enough in our finite existence. And yet it is necessary that our false and partial opinions be overcome.

The alternative is to move *with* our opinions in order to move through them to a place beyond them. In this way we avoid the difficult task of subduing our opinions. We let them be, but we place them in the position of serving our larger knowledge. Beyond their truth or error we let them be the vehicles that carry us to our next level of awareness, whatever that turns out to be as we continue our movement through the opposites of our life experience. In this context the whole of the *Intensive Journal* process and especially our present work of Process Meditation may be understood as an instrument for meeting the goal that Socrates set. And our use of the Meditation Log to collect and acknowledge the unfolding facts of our inner reality is the step with which we launch the process of our work.*

* In the course of writing *The Symbolic and the Real* it became clear to me that Socrates perceived in his time a truth of the human condition to which Holistic Depth Psychology addresses itself in our day. See Chapter 2 in Ira Progoff, *The Symbolic and the Real*, Julian/McGraw-Hill, New York, 1963, 1973. The later chapters of that book were my first attempt to answer the Socratic question in a form that would be practicable for modern persons. From that starting point I consider my second attempt to have been much more successful. In the course of my second try, I developed the concepts and methods that eventually became the *Intensive Journal* program. As that program has developed in social use during recent years in the form of the National *Intensive Journal* Program, it can be seen to be an extension and a democratization of the basic Socratic approach to life and knowledge.

Chapter *6*

Entering the
Meditative Atmosphere

We begin our work in Process Meditation by establishing an atmosphere of quietness and depth. We do this whether it is a private workshop experience that we are giving ourselves alone or whether it is a workshop that we are participating in with many others. We begin by establishing a quiet atmosphere whether we expect to be engaged in our meditation for a short or a long period, whether we are setting aside a whole day or two days, or whether we are allotting it only a half hour at a time.

The units of our work in Process Meditation may be thought of as atoms of time. They are holistic units—as Jan Christian Smuts used the phrase—each entire unto itself with its own nature. The needs and the potentials of such a unit are inherent within it, and they must be honored equally regardless of the length or the duration of the unit of experience. Each is whole unto itself, an atom of time. Thus even when we are allotting only a brief unit of meditation time, we must take care not to skip the step of establishing a meditative atmosphere. That first step is essential, and without it any unit of meditation, whether brief or extended, will begin by being off balance. And it will then be difficult for things to come into harmony.

One lesson that our varied experience with Process Meditation has taught is that the essence of meditation is not to be found in its content, nor in its doctrines or concepts or teachings. Its essence lies rather in the quality, the spirit of its experience.

The quality of meditation establishes an atmosphere that has a clear and discernible effect with respect to both the energies and the tone of the awarenesses that are brought forth. The atmosphere is like the space around a person, but not a physical space. It might better be described as a space that is within the person. It is important for our Process Meditation work that we place our experience within that space as an atmosphere that will nurture and sustain the inner process of our meditation.

Over the years in our *Intensive Journal* workshops we have evolved a means of drawing ourselves into that atmosphere. We do it by means of *Entrance Meditations.* These are readings of inner experiences that have themselves been brought forth by the procedures of Process Meditation and have been collected into a sequence of units for publication. We have three such sequences currently available, and we call upon them to draw us into an atmosphere that will be conducive to the process of our meditation. We use *The Well and the Cathedral, The White Robed Monk,* and *The Star/Cross;* we may also use any other texts that fulfil for us personally the special criteria of an entrance meditation.

What do we look for in an *entrance meditation?* One of its essential qualities is that the reading of it serves to quiet and center us. But it does this in a neutral way, postulating no particular doctrine of belief. The entrance meditation may describe a specific inner experience even to the extent of drawing us into that experience, but it does so only in order to take us inward. It uses the experience only as a means of securing for us a path of entry into the realm of meditation. It takes us through the entrance, and then it lets us go. It does not seek to mold us or predispose us toward any particular content of experience or commitment. It does not seek to suggest to us or implant in us any doctrine or concept, nor to have us follow any particular path of symbolism or imagery. It only seeks to take us through the entrance into the inner realm so that the atmosphere we find there will assist the process of our meditation and enable it to proceed unfettered. Unencumbered by external concepts, it will have the freedom to find and form its own profundities.

In the following pages are three passages of entrance meditations excerpted from the sequences that we use in the workshops. Each is a unit of experience, and they are given here so that you will have a convenient means of moving into a quiet atmosphere. Read them through briefly, and decide on the one that you wish to use as the starting point for your first experience. There is no great commitment involved in making this decision. Whichever one you choose is merely to serve as a temporary vehicle for you, and it will in each case be a thoroughly neutral vehicle. You are merely choosing a short unit of entrance meditation to help give you passage inward. Choose whichever one feels congenial to you now, and then we can proceed.

From *The Well and the Cathedral:* *

The Center Point Within Me

1. We are resting,
   Physically quiet,
   Breath and body
   In gentle harmony
   Holding the stillness within.

2. Holding the stillness within,
   Thoughts fit into place.
   No longer spinning,
   They come together;
   No longer disputing,
   Our thoughts
   Are friendly with each other.
   The quality of wholeness
   Replaces
   The discord of the mind.

3. Mind and body
   Together,
   Thoughts and emotions
   Revolving around
   A single center point.
   Varied movements
   Actively churning
   Form a quiet center.
   A quiet center forms
   In their midst.

* See Ira Progoff, *The Well and the Cathedral,* Dialogue House Library, New York, 1971, 1977. The complete text is also available in a cassette recording by Ira Progoff.

4. We feel the center of our Self,
    The inner center of our Self,
    It is neither body
    Nor mind
    But a center point
    Not this, not that,
    A single center point,
    The inner center of the Self.

5. In the midst of activity
    Soft, slow breathing
    Sets a balance.
    An inward stillness
    Becomes present.
    The center point within me
    Establishes itself.

6. For each of us it is so.
    A center point within
    Forms itself.
    A center point is present
    Not in space
    But in our being.

7. A center point within me.
    My whole attention
    At that center point,
    Present there in the stillness,
    In the stillness of the Self.

8. Through this center point
    We move inward,
    Inward and downward
    Through a single straight shaft.
    It is as though we go
    Deep into the earth,
    But within our Self.
    Through the center point within

We go inward,
Deeper,
Deeper inward.

9.   My life
Is like the shaft of a well.
I go deep into it.
The life of each of us
Is a well.
Its sources are deep,
But it gives water on the surface.
Now we go inward,
Moving through our center point,
Through our center point,
Deeply inward to explore
The infinities of our well.

10.   Long enough
We have been on the surface
Of our life.
Now we go inward,
Moving through our center point
Inward,
Into the well of our Self,
Deeply,
Further inward
Into the well of our Self.

11.   We move away
From the surface of things;
We leave
The circles of our thoughts,
Our habits, customs.
All the shoulds
And the oughts
Of our life
We leave behind.

12.   We leave them on the surface
While we go inward,
Into the depth of our life
Moving through the center point
Into the well of our Self
As deeply
As fully
As freely as we can.
Through the center point
Exploring the deep places.
Exploring the deep places
In the Silence . . . In the Silence.

From *The White Robed Monk:* *

Standing at the Altar/Tree

1.   I am standing before the altar
Of the underground chapel,
The stump of an ancient tree,
Massive,
The power of ages
Compressed within it.
Ancient,
Alone,
It stands self-contained.

2.   The altar/tree
Is centered in itself.
I feel the primeval depths
Of the beginnings of life
Move through the rings
Of the aged wood.
How far back they go,
How present they are.

* See Ira Progoff, *The White Robed Monk*, Dialogue House Library, New York, 1972, 1979. The complete text is also available in a cassette recording by Ira Progoff.

3. I feel myself entering
   The center of the rings
   Of the aged wood.
   They quiet me,
   They focus me.
   I feel myself to be
   At the center
   Of the circles of time
   There in the circles
   Of the altar/tree.

4. I feel the movement of time
   There in the circles of the tree,
   I feel the movement of time
   In the center of my Self.
   I stand before the altar/tree
   Centered in its circles,
   Swirling inward
   In the rings of time,
   Time before time,
   Time beyond time.

5. I go into the swirling circles,
   Into the timeless circles
   Of the tree of life,
   I stand before the ancient remains
   Of the tree of life,
   The altar/tree
   Of the underground chapel.

6. I am standing before it now
   Feeling my life.
   Feeling my life
   With all else that lives
   And has ever lived,
   There in the rings of time
   At the center of the altar/tree.

7.   I stand before the altar/tree
Entering its circles,
Moving into it,
Feeling time beyond time
Present now,
Here
In the movement of my life.

8.   Feeling the years of my life
Passing through time,
Feeling the timeless in my life
Present
In this moment.
Feeling the timeless in time,
Knowing it,
Being it . . .
In the Silence . . . In the Silence.

From *The Star/Cross:* *

Letting the Self Become Still

1.   We are sitting
In a place of quietness
Letting the Self become still,
Letting the breath become slow,
Letting our thoughts come to rest.

2.   Letting the Self become still,
Energies that were moving about
Can go inward now,
Can come to rest
In the stillness
Of our quiet being.

---

* See Ira Progoff, *The Star/Cross*, Dialogue House Library, New York, 1981. There is also a partial cassette recording by Ira Progoff.

3. Breathing becomes quiet now,
    Not breathing
    By the tempo of outer things
    But by an inner tempo
    Breathing at an inner pace
    The breath moving in
    And out
    Of itself,
    Carried by its own rhythm
    Adjusting itself
    To itself.

4. Breathing at an inner pace.
    Our thoughts let go
    Of our breathing.
    Breathing at an inner pace
    The breath is free
    To come and go
    In its own timing.
    The breath is slow
    And regular,
    Moving in and out
    By its inner tempo
    Carried by its own rhythm
    Adjusting itself
    To itself.

5. Breathing at an inner pace
    Thoughts become quiet,
    Restless thoughts
    That have been moving about,
    Restless thoughts,
    Dissipating their energies,
    Can come to rest now,
    Can bring their energies together
    Into one place
    Resting
    On the steady breathing.

6.   Excess thoughts drop away.
We become still.
Thinking becomes quiet,
Thoughts fitting together
And settling into one place
By themselves
Without our thinking them.
Many mixed thoughts
Become one whole thought
Contained within itself,
One whole thought
In the mind at rest.

7.   Letting the Self become still,
Letting the thoughts come to rest,
Letting the breath become slow
Breathing becomes quiet,
Breathing becomes slow,
And slower;
Breathing becomes regular,
Regular.
The unevenness
Of nonessential thoughts
Drops out of the breathing.
It becomes
The breathing of the Self.

8.   Breathing at an inner pace,
The breath moves
At the center of my Self
At the center of my Self
In regular rhythms.
My body is quiet,
Holding its place.
The breath is moving evenly,
Inward,
Outward,
Evenly

In its own rhythm.
The breath moves evenly
At the center of my body,
At the center of my Self.

9.   The breath is moving
At the center of my Self
In a regular rhythm.
The breath moves at the center.
The breath moves at the center,
Breathing at an inner pace.
As the breath moves at the center,
Quietly,
Evenly,
The self becomes still
Like quiet water.

10.   The self becomes still
Like quiet water.
In the stillness of the Self,
In the quiet of the water
My inward ear hears,
My inward eye sees
Signs and words and visions
Reflected in the quiet waters
In the stillness of the Self,
In the Silence . . . In the Silence.

When you have chosen a unit of entrance meditation to set the atmosphere, we are ready to begin. You will have your *Intensive Journal* workbook before you, open to the Meditation Log section. By way of preparation for the exercise write at the top of a fresh page the phrase "Entrance Meditation." And write beside it the date.

Take a moment to sit in stillness, doing nothing, letting your breathing become slower . . . and slower. When you feel ready, begin to read the passage of entrance meditation that you have chosen. Read it in whatever way feels most comfortable to you. Read it aloud or silently, repeating lines you need to repeat, phrasing it as fits your feeling. Presently you will come to the cue words, the phrase, "In the Silence . . . In the Silence." That is the point where we each go into our own silence. We have been carried by the reading through the entry way, and now we move further by ourselves in the open, inward spaces of our silent being.

As we go into the silence our eyes are closed. Our thoughts are quiet and our energies are not moving outward but inward. External phenomena do not distract us now, for our attention is directed to the events of our inner space. We perceive by sight, by sound, by each of our senses. All the senses by which we are accustomed to perceive things outwardly are available to us for our inward perception. Observations are presented to us, and understanding of an inner, intuitive kind comes to us as well when our eyes are closed and our energies are turned inward. We do not seek to control or direct what takes place in this interior space. We let it unfold out of its own nature. And especially we pay attention to what transpires. We observe it, and we record it.

*   *   *

This is the first use we make of our Meditation Log. As we move inward by means of our entrance meditation, we observe whatever comes within the span of our inner attention. Sitting in silence, it may be words that we hear, not words heard by the ear but words spoken inwardly. Or it may be sounds of music that come to us. It may be symbols that take shape as visions that we see, that we see not outwardly but inwardly. It may be symbols that are not visible and not audible but that we perceive intuitively and that we know by a direct inwardness. It may be sensations that come to us in our body, memories, anticipations, anxieties, joys. It may be ideas or inspirations that suggest projects we had not thought of before.

Perceptions of many kinds may be presented to us when our eyes are closed and we have turned our attention inward in the silence. Some are literal perceptions of things we know about from our past experience. Some are thoughts that now flow more freely than our ordinary thinking does. Some give new knowledge, but only indirectly by means of symbols. And some, being symbolic, seem to be intimations of things to come. Whatever form they take and whatever their message seems to be, we observe them as they come; and we take note of them without judgment, and especially without censorship.

It is of the greatest importance that we do not consciously and deliberately add to what is presented to us, that we not embellish it and thus inadvertently distort it. We must be careful that we do not unintentionally create an inner scenario with an outcome that will artificially satisfy our desires. That would be inauthentic and self-deceiving. It is essential that we not manipulate nor contrive any of the perceptions that present themselves to our inner attention. We merely let them proceed by means of their own self-contained process while we observe and record what takes place. We describe as briefly, as cogently, as impartially as we can all that comes before us when our attention is turned inward in the silence. We try not to censor or screen out what we do not like; and we try not to encourage and enlarge consciously the things that please us. We are equally accepting of whatever presents itself, and we record it impartially.

In thus taking our first step in Process Meditation we are placing ourselves in the atmosphere of inner experience. In the conceptual principles of the Holistic Depth Psychology that underlie the *Intensive Journal* method, this is termed the *twilight range*. It is the range of experience between sleep dreaming and the directed conscious activity of wakefulness, and it is here that many of the experiences take place which, at a later point, lead to the enlargement of awareness. Here, at this point in our work, we are learning to gather the raw data of these experiences as they take place at the twilight level. It is a first step in our learning by practice how to work objectively with the elusive and often symbolic contents of the twilight level. In the Meditation Log we are gathering the raw materials of inner experience so that we will have them in a form and in a readiness that will enable us to feed them into the active process of our meditation at a later, appropriate phase of the work.

To recapitulate: in order to establish a meditative atmosphere and to enter the twilight range of experience, we begin by choosing a segment of an entrance meditation. Reading that to ourselves, we allow it to carry us into its atmosphere, eyes closed in the silence. We let ourselves feel the inner atmosphere of the twilight level as we observe the varied types of inner happenings that come to pass, being formed as though by themselves.

Sometimes the field of inner experience is very active, sometimes it is simply a quietness. In either case we record impartially all that we observe as our attention is focused steadily and inwardly in the silence. We should bear in mind that at this point in our work our task is not so much to stimulate new experiences as to establish an atmosphere of quietness at the twilight level. We are therefore interested less in an active imaging experience—although we record whatever takes place—than we are in perceiving the depth and fullness of inner space and of experiencing ourselves as being there. Relaxing our conscious control, we let ourselves be absorbed into the stillness. That is the atmosphere in which we wish to enter the process of our meditation.

Chapter 7

Spiritual Positioning

When we have recorded our entrance meditation experience, we re-main in quietness. Specifically, we do not read our Journal entry back to ourselves at this time. I mention that here because an elemental step in the Journal Feedback method is the reading back to ourselves of each entry that we have made in our *Intensive Journal* workbook. Especially if we read it back soon after the original experience, while we are still in its atmosphere, it often has the effect of re-activating the process that was at work within us. It then draws us back into the movement of the experience and stimulates the flow of its content so that the experience is renewed and extends itself.

At the present point in our work, however, our immediate purpose is not to stimulate further experience but to establish an atmosphere of stillness. Therefore we do not follow our usual Journal Feedback pro-cedure of reading our entry back to ourselves. Rather, when we have completed our writing, we let ourselves rest in quietness. We sit in stillness, and it is out of the midst of this quiet atmosphere that we take our first step of *Spiritual Positioning*.

To set the stage for this exercise which actively launches our work of Process Meditation, we take a fresh page in the Meditation Log section and write the phrase, "Spiritual Positioning" at the head of it. And we write the date beside it. We are thus setting up a second sub-section in the Meditation Log for our present and our future use.

We are sitting in stillness. Now we are sitting with eyes closed again, encouraging the further inner movement of our thoughts, our feelings and images. We are allowing them to move freely so that they can reflect any of the aspects of our life. We ask ourselves: How is it with me now on the spiritual level of my life? On the creative level of my life? On the believing level?

Spontaneously as it comes to us without considering intellectually or analytically, we write a few quick sentences to record and briefly describe the situation of our inner life at this time. Two or three sentences—four at the most—is all that we want to write now. Just a brief entry to record what we find when we look at our inner situation at this time. No censorship, no judgment, no interpretation. And above all, no self-reflection. As spontaneously as we can, we record what we find when we look within to see and to describe our inner condition during this recent period of our life.

For example:

This has been a time when I have been wondering about many things. Things I used to take for granted are doubtful to me now. Perhaps it is because I don't see Mary any more that I don't go to church now. I seem to be spiritually in between things.

Or, the present spiritual position may be:

I find myself alone a lot and wondering. Reading many things is good and interesting, but it seems to increase my unsureness. I start to meditate, but I don't keep it up. I wish I could pray, but I don't think I know how.

Or it may be:

The experience I had with Rev.——in April has brought sunlight into my life. I understand now why they talk about being "born again." That is exactly how it feels. But it does not answer all my questions and it has not solved all my problems. I still live where I live, in the same place with the same family and with the same job. I feel I am at a plateau of my life, but I feel that there is a lot more for me to do, and there is a lot more for me to know. And I don't yet know what it is.

Or it may be:

My political beliefs are my spiritual life. At least they have been. My ideals and my ethics have been there and I know that my commitment to political action has had a religious quality. But right now I am hanging loose. I miss the need for action, but it gives me a chance to look at things.

Or it may be:

I feel much more centered and less edgy since I am with Swami——. Maybe that is because I can be off drugs with him. I think he has more to teach me and I hope I will be able to learn.

Or it may be:

I remain true to the religious commitment that I made when I was in my teens. I know that truth is there and God is there. But quite often I cannot pray the way I should, or even the way I used to pray. And lately I have not felt the steadfastness in love that I should, or even that I used to have.

The entries can refer to any content or emotion. Whatever presents itself to us as the facts of our inner life is what we should record here. If we find that we are judging ourselves, that is a fact; so we record it. Often we are unduly harsh in our judgments of ourselves when we say what we "should" be feeling or what we "should" be able to do; and by the same token we may be over-quick in our self-praise or in our rejoicing at experiences that have come to us. But the fact is that we are feeling those self-judgments, invalid or premature though they may be; therefore we record the fact that we feel them. That is how we take the first step in establishing our spiritual position.

Sometimes in making this brief entry of spiritual positioning a metaphor or simile will come to us. Quite often these are especially valuable since they provide an expressive, non-literal way of stating our inner condition. In the course of this work, because of the elusive quality of spiritual experience, we often have reason to remember that one symbol may be worth a thousand words. A symbol from a dream or an image that comes to you in the course of twilight imaging, or perhaps one that presents itself during the entrance meditation may convey a great deal in a few words.

When Leo Tolstoy, for example, was drawing together the spiritual journal that he called, *My Confession,* he recalled a dream in which a fledgling bird fell from its nest. He felt that this expressed his inner condition at the time when he lost his faith. If Tolstoy were attending a Process Meditation workshop at that time in his life, an appropriate entry under the heading of "Spiritual Positioning" would have been: "I feel like a fledgling bird that has fallen from its nest and cannot fly." With just another sentence or two to indicate the details of the circumstances, Tolstoy would then have placed himself in the spiritual movement of his life. That is what we mean by Spiritual Positioning.

Bearing this in mind, we let ourselves rest in the stillness that was established in our entrance meditation. Our eyes closed, we let ourselves feel and consider the present situation of our inner life. What is the atmosphere, the sense of meaning, the tone of our inner life at this time? What are its main contents? What are the messages we have had about it from our dreams or other spontaneous experiences that have come to us? What are the beliefs that are holding strong within us? And what are the doubts, the wonderings, the explorations? What are our involvements in outer activities? What are our concerns about social or political issues? And what are our concerns about the ultimates of truth in human existence? What are the commitments of our life? And what are our hesitations?

Describe the contents and the condition that you find there when you look inside yourself, experiencing your feelings and awarenesses but recording them as an impartial observer of your inner life. Simply record what you perceive there, briefly, objectively, non-judgmentally. Describe it just as it presents itself to you before you give yourself a chance to reflect upon it or to think of a comment about it or an interpretation to place on it. Put it on paper quickly, spontaneously, concisely—even if you write it ungrammatically, even if it is misspelled. We do not have to write the whole thing now, but just a few sentences.

Just enough to give ourselves a starting point for the next steps that are to follow in our meditative work. We take the first step with the brief statement of our spiritual position, writing it now, in the silence.

*　　*　　*

Writing this short, spontaneous summary of our present spiritual position has the effect of recalling many awarenesses and memories to our minds. But we do not let them intrude into our statement. We wish it to be brief and succinct, expressing the primary elements in our present inner situation. We find that, if we can hold the details to one side, the essentials are drawn into sharper focus, and this gives us the kind of starting point we require for our further work. That is why just three or four sentences written directly and unself-consciously is the best way to proceed.

Although we do not include them in it, the thoughts and memories that come to us while we are writing our statement of spiritual position can be of great value to us. We certainly do not wish to by-pass them and lose contact with them now that they have been recalled to us. They may contribute to our understanding of how we arrived at our present position and the issues that are involved in the contents of our beliefs. More than that, those memories and awarenesses may contain energy and ideas that will be drawn upon in a later phase of our inner experience. In the background of all our practices in Process Meditation is our awareness that we are cumulatively gathering data that will serve as an inner resource for us in the continuity of our work.

With this in mind, we now take a step to incorporate in our Meditation Log the various pieces of information that were recalled to us but that we did not include in our basic statement. At this point it is worthwhile for us to give them as much space and range of expression as is needed to record all that they suggest to us. We take a fresh page for this, so that the descriptions we write here will be separate from our statement of Spiritual Positioning. We want to let that remain by itself so that we can return to it in a little while, read it back to ourselves, and perhaps add some further thoughts and comments from another perspective.

We now begin to write what may become a flowing and open-ended description of the recent development and contents of our inner life. How did we arrive at our present beliefs and opinions? What questions were we asking that called those issues to our attention? What questions are we still asking? Who were the persons who influenced us and played a role in our inner experiences? What was the chain of circumstances, what were the outer events and pressures of life, the book we happened to find, the speakers we happened to hear, that led to our present state of belief?

We wish to recapitulate here and describe as fully as we can whatever has taken place in the recent period of our experience. We are retracing the presence, and also the times of absence, of a sense of meaning in our life, personal and more-than-personal. We want to recall and record as much as we can of the changing phases of our beliefs, our doubts and intuitions, our certitudes and our confusion, our intellectual ideas, our symbolic understandings, our participation in rituals, our agreement with others and our arguments on doctrines and beliefs. We want to reconstruct it all so that we can see our inner picture as a whole, and re-experience it in the depth of ourselves.

To do this work we begin by sitting in quietness, our workbook open to the new page following the statement we have written regarding our present spiritual position. We focus our attention on the present condition of our inner life, however full or empty it may currently seem to be. We let the controls of our intellectual mind drop to a relaxed state at the twilight level so that memories and thoughts can move within us as a free-flowing stream. Whatever comes to our mind, we record. Just brief entries are sufficient here. Just a few words. Just a phrase or two. It does not need to be a complete sentence or a grammatical construction. Just enough to convey the thought or feeling or memory or idea that has come to us. And the memories need not be complete. Do not postpone writing it down until you can remember the whole thing. If you remember only a small bit, start with that. As you are describing it, more will come to your mind. It is a self-stimulating process, but it has to have a starting point in order for the evocative effort to be set in motion. As you put your pen to paper you will find that the act of recording one item, however insignificant it may seem, tends to stimulate the thought of something else.

As you recall events or experiences, describe all that comes to you. Write down more than you need to. Describe more than you feel is necessarily relevant. It is easy to eliminate or pay no further attention to things you recorded if, later on, when you read them back, they do not seem to be important. But if you do not write them down, you will not be able to make that evaluation. And perhaps they will become important in a later context. Furthermore, the act of describing them on paper will often elicit additional awarenesses you had not thought of before.

In describing the contents of this spiritual period in your life, it is good to open up as many issues as come to your mind. Do not restrict yourself to particular themes. You are not writing a school composition that has a beginning, a middle and an end. Describing this time in your inner life is an open-ended work. You want to stimulate and mention as many different facets of your inner life as you can. In that way you can bring them to your own attention and you can come back to explore them further at a later time. Here we are engaged in progressively loosening the soil of our inner life.

Many of us, having been brought up in a materialist culture or, alternatively, in a rigidly traditionalist culture, may find that thoughts and feelings of a spiritual nature are packed hard and tight within us because we have not given ourselves the freedom to experience them. As a result we do not have easy access to them. Some of us may even be led to think that they are not there, that we personally do not have such awarenesses and desires. Little by little, however, by loosening the soil of our inner lives, we will each find that an inner reaching toward meaning in life and toward a larger-than-personal connection is present in all of us, although in each of us it takes a different form. If we have thought that it is not present in us and if we are not accustomed to working with it, its presence may not easily become apparent to us. But entry by entry, in the delineation we make now or as it will be stimulated in us, and gradually build as we proceed through the exercises that follow, we shall touch and find what is spiritually present in each of us at the depth of our being.

It is most important that we get the process started, and we do this by describing any significant aspect of the present phase in our inner life. Once our description has begun, recollections, observations, even specific rememberings will come through to us in increasing abundance. It is a self-sustaining process once it is set in motion. We do, however, have a number of check-points to which we can refer in order to help get the process moving and to build its momentum. We may stimulate our capacity of recall, for example, by asking ourselves questions like the following:

What have been my primary beliefs during this recent period with respect to the fundamental issues in my life? For example, in religion, or personal ethics, my political philosophy, my involvement in social causes.

What doubts do I have about beliefs that I have had in the past? Do I still believe in the things I was taught as a child? Is it changing? Or deepening? What wonderings and searchings, what deep thinking is taking place in me?

Have I had any strong inner experiences during this period? In dreams or at religious services or in meetings of any kind, with drugs or meditation or in the midst of discussions?

Have I had any special awareness at times when I have been alone?

Have I had any important prayer experiences either in privacy or in a group? Have I had any striking experiences that were not exactly prayers but might be considered the equivalent of prayers?

Have I had experiences that led me to feel that they had to be expressed in some form of art, as a poem or a painting or a song?

Have I had any moments of changes in my consciousness, a sense of deepening or heightening? Have there been any moments when I felt that I was able to know something important and that I knew it in a special way?

Were there any times of really intense prayer, of spontaneously asking out of great need? Times of prayers being answered? Of waiting? Of being anxious and disbelieving during the time of waiting?

Considering these various factors and states of interior life, and many, many more that will rise to our consciousness as we are recalling and describing these, we go back over the path of our inner experience during this recent time and recall what has taken place within us. What were we seeking? What were we convinced of? Or wondering about? With whom were we sharing our concerns? Our acts of faith? Our acts of anxiety? Agreeing or disagreeing? Believing and disbelieving? These experiences that we did not expect, or those that we heard about and wondered at, that speech we heard, that book we read, that dream, that image, that idea?

We go back in our minds over what there has been in our inner lives that has led us to where we are now, no matter where it is that we are now. These recent months, these recent years, the events on the inner road, the road that we have traveled with all its turnings, its changes, with its unknowings, that led us here to where we are now.

Sitting in quietness, we record as much as we can recall, describing it in the Spiritual Positioning sub-section of our Meditation Log. We write it as it comes to us, without judgmental selecting or censoring. We reject nothing that comes to our mind but we describe it as objectively as we can, whether as the brief mention of specific facts or as the flowing recollection of contexts of circumstance. This is our delineation of the present period in our spiritual life. We write it in the silence.

*   *   *

Sometimes when we set out to write these elaborations of our interior experience, we find it difficult to get started. Nothing comes, and it seems that our supply of thoughts and memories has run dry. "Nothing is there," we think. But we should not make that judgment about ourselves. If we are accustomed to the psychological jargon of modern times, we may also be drawn to make a quick diagnosis of ourselves, saying, "I am blocked." But that is probably not the actual problem. More likely it is simply the operational difficulty of being unable to set the process into motion. With so many thoughts, partial beliefs and interior events from which to choose, we are not able to pick one on which to focus and begin. The difficulty lies in not having a starting point, for without a starting point we cannot begin.

Under such circumstances an effective way of setting ourselves into motion is to emphasize no single point in our experience but simply to proceed chronologically. Taking a general period of time as our focus, we simply recapitulate the sequence of events. Any event at all can serve as our starting point because we can describe the movement of time going forward chronologically, and also time moving in reverse. Starting at any point, we can list the events that followed it, and we can also move back into the sequence of events that preceded it. Thus where we begin does not matter. Being free to move chronologically both backward and forward in time, we can let the relevant facts of our experience fill themselves in without our having to predetermine what they should be. They also can tell us what the boundaries are for our present period of inner experience. If the memories move further back chronologically, that indicates to us that the relevant sources of this period in our life reach into an earlier time.

Taking any starting point and moving both forward and backward in time, we recapitulate, as directly and as objectively as we can, the sequence of events in our recent past with respect to our inner life. There is a distinct advantage to our proceeding in this neutral way, especially during the early phases of our *Intensive Journal* work when we are still becoming accustomed to its procedures.

Working with chronology backward and forward, we have an objective guideline that allows us to begin with any convenient point of focus. We simply refer in our minds to the sequence of events, and we make our descriptions accordingly. We record the beliefs, the experiences, the doubts, the questionings and seekings, the realizations and spontaneous awarenesses, the ideas and artworks we have contemplated, the studies and discussions and rituals in which we have participated. We list them without elaboration as the chronological sequence enables us to recall them without strain. We should bear in mind, however, that while chronology is helpful, the purposes of this part of our Journal work do not require that our listings be in precise chronological order: It is more important that we build a momentum that will increase our facility for recalling inner experiences.

When we work chronologically, we simply list events, experiences, circumstances, thoughts, imagery—whatever is possibly relevant to our inner life. Once we have mentioned the facts of this subjective data and have described them in a Journal entry, we have not only brought them into our range of consciousness but we have made them available to us for our further exploration. Now we have access to them within the context of our *Intensive Journal* methodology so that we can work with them further whenever the time seems ripe.

An important benefit of following a chronological approach is that it enables us to take note of the inner events in our life and to describe them with a minimum of judgmental censorship or interpretation. To recapitulate our experiences chronologically seems to assist the process of writing objective descriptions; and the very act of writing an objective description seems to have a corrective and self-balancing effect. In the course of our writing, the events and experiences of our lives reveal themselves to us for what they are, true or false, lasting or transient. As we chronicle an event or situation, including in our description of it the subjective emotions that it carries, our self-deceptions tend to be neutralized. There seems to be an objectifying effect in the act of writing a neutral chronological reconstruction of the inner events of our life. This takes us a long step toward self-honesty.

With practice in the *Intensive Journal* work we realize that a variety of approaches and techniques are available to help us carry through the particular assignments that are necessary for collecting the inner data of our lives. As we become more familiar with the possibilities, we also become more comfortable in making our choices, knowing how to choose the right approach at the appropriate time. One fundamental principle to follow is that we prepare for each time of writing by sitting in silence, closing our eyes, and letting ourselves move into the twilight range of awareness. From that inner place, memories and recognitions come to us as though by their own guidance and without our interference. We should not press but let our writings and rememberings flow naturally in their own timing. If we simply state the facts of our inner experience as they present themselves to us, one description will lead to another, compiling a picture and an understanding that we did not have before we began. That is how we can proceed now, reconstructing the development and the details of this recent time in our interior life.

*   *   *

When we finish this piece of writing, we know that it is not ended, but that our reconstruction can extend itself at another time when the material is ready. We therefore come to a pause. Not pressing but relaxed, we return to an atmosphere of stillness.

Very often people find that by the time they have carried through the exercise of recalling the recent period and have described some of its main contents, their perception of the situation as a whole has been changed. They realize that the meaning and implications of this time in their life are quite different from what they had originally thought them to be, and thus their evaluation and emotional response to it are different as well.

For this reason, when you have finished writing as much of the recapitulation as you feel is appropriate for you at this sitting, turn back to the page where you wrote your original brief statement of spiritual position. Read it back to yourself now, observing what further thoughts and emotions stir in you as you read it. What changes would you make in it? Perhaps there are some enlargements or modifications that you feel should be added to your original statement. Or perhaps you now feel that your entire statement of position should be refocused and presented from another point of view in the light of the perspective that has evolved in the course of your writing.

Read it back to yourself again slowly, thoughtfully, giving it full consideration. And now write your second statement, taking note of any additional thoughts or feelings or awarenesses that have formed in you in the course of the *Intensive Journal* work you have done so far. This second statement need not be brief. Let it be as full and as encompassing as feels appropriate and satisfying to you. Or, if you prefer, let it be another short statement, but with some further comments relating to your original statement.

Whatever its length, or its content, let it be a statement that expresses the beliefs and the issues that you most profoundly care about, as far as you are presently aware. Bear in mind that this is a statement of spiritual position intended for no one's eyes but your own. Once you have written it, it will be your base point, the point from which you will set your active experience of Process Meditation into motion.

Let us begin in silence, therefore, reading back our original statement and, as we are ready, adding our second statement to it. Together they begin to form a tangible record of the inner process working in our lives.

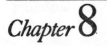
Inner Process Entries

When we have finished writing our second statement dealing with the present spiritual condition of our lives, we are ready to take the step that enables us to use the Meditation Log section continuously as an active instrument in our work. We noted earlier that the general role of the log sections in the structure of the *Intensive Journal* system is to gather the factual data of our lives. This is true of the other five log sections in our workbook, and it is true of the exercises we have carried through in the Meditation Log so far. But now we come to the point where the Meditation Log section takes on an active role. There are increasingly creative effects that arise from the way that we work with the third sub-section of the Meditation Log, the *Inner Process Entries.*

We begin by taking a fresh page and writing the name of this sub-section at the head of it. And we write today's date. The phrase, Inner Process Entries, has considerable significance for the principles that underlie the *Intensive Journal* work. It is the *inner process* of subjective experiences that draws a person's life together so that it can find its direction and eventually reach its meaning. That is why the sub-section of *Inner Process Entries* is especially important for Process Meditation. It is here that we gather the data of our inner process in a way that gradually forms and shows us the personal and transpersonal meaning of our lives.

As we pause to consider what we have done so far, we must realize that even at this early stage we have already taken several steps that have set an inner process into motion. By means of an entrance meditation we quieted ourselves so that we could enter the twilight range of experience. In that twilight atmosphere we wrote our first statement regarding our present spiritual position. Then we proceeded to recapitulate the inner and outer events in the recent period of our life as these have set the background for our present inner situation. This description could be relatively brief and cursory, or it could be a very full delineation. The degree of detail in which we found ourselves exploring and describing the interior development of this time in our lives may in itself be a significant piece of information for us. And the effects of that exploration may have been expressed when we wrote our second statement.

Each of these steps as we carried them out in our exercise is an interior event in itself. Viewed in sequence, they comprise an inner process. And we are now beginning to give tangible form to this inner process here in the Meditation Log.

Our next step is to record and briefly describe the inner experiences through which we have passed in our practice of Process Meditation up to this point. The details are already contained in the sections where we recorded the actual experiences, but here we want to build an overview of the continuity of our experience as a whole. With this goal in mind we go back over each of the steps that we have taken, listing them, describing them briefly if that is necessary, and summarizing what took place. It is especially relevant in this recapitulation of our inner process to describe what was taking place within us as we have proceeded from exercise to exercise. This is the place to take note of difficulties that arose and enthusiasms that we felt as we came to particular issues in our life.

What was the quality of our consciousness and the changes in it while we were engaged in the entrance meditation? What kinds of twilight imagery came to us? Writing now in retrospect, what observations can we make about the nature of the memories and the emotions that have arisen in us in the course of our experiences? We take note not only of the thoughts that came to us in the course of our experiences but the *lines of thinking* that were set in motion. Are we aware of new ideas and realizations that came to us now for the first time, interspersed with our emotions and our memories and our images? And are we aware of old ideas that we have thought of before and that we have pushed aside but that are now returning to us for reconsideration in new forms?

As we recapitulate our experiences, adding our observations and comments, we let the process of our inner perceptions continue and grow. We let ourselves extend the lines of thinking that bring old and new thoughts to us. We let them move of themselves so that we can eventually see where they are trying to go. We find that these lines of thinking and awareness tend to build while we are engaged in describing the inner experiences in which we have been engaged. That is why here in Inner Process Entries we recapitulate our experiences, describing our emotions and observations, and encouraging new lines of perception to be set into motion.

To prepare for this exercise, let us now return to our quietness. Sitting in stillness, we go over in our minds the sequence of interior events since we began our work, including our entrance meditation, our first statement of spiritual position, our delineation of the period, and writing our second statement of spiritual position. We go back over our experiences of each of these, recapitulating and describing them briefly, letting our perceptions move and flow as they come to us. In the Silence.

*   *   *

Each person's experiences are unique. For this reason no Journal entry can be taken as a model for someone else. Some examples, however, may help us see the issues and the possibilities that are involved. Consider, for example, this Inner Process Entry by S. J.:

> The silence of the entrance meditation was helpful, but it was not deep enough. I realize that I have to practice more at quieting myself. Not only for physical reasons, but spiritually.
>
> Reading back my statements of spiritual position, it occurs to me that they could have been written from another point of view. The facts are the same but I realize that I can look at those facts from two different angles. And they will both be true, at least in a sense.
>
> I mean, I have been following my conscience in political action,

and that is one important part of my spiritual life. And I have also been working out my religious philosophy, and sometimes this fits with my politics, and sometimes it doesn't.

And I have also been working out what my personal and sexual life should be; and sometimes this fits with my religion and philosophy, and sometimes it doesn't.

I realize as I am writing this that in this past year my different interests and different activities have all been trying to achieve a single integration. I have been trying to work out a single point of view with which to live my life. But it is complicated. It has so many aspects. That must be why I find myself thinking of it in more than one way. But I want it to be just one. I want it to be unified because I seek unity and consistency in my life. But perhaps that is not possible. Perhaps it is a wrong idea. It may already have caused trouble for me in my life. I have to find out more about this before I make further decisions.

In the entry just quoted we see a person placing himself in the midst of the movement of his life simply by stating the inner facts of that life. And we can see how his awareness is opening and expanding in the very act of the writing.

It would be correct to describe this as an example of "working in your life," especially as we take note of the fact that the "work" is clearly not self-analysis and not self-interpretation. The Journalist is writing a continuous statement that is conscious but is not self-conscious. It is an active consideration of the multiple contents of the life made in the midst of being engaged in the decisions of living. What we see here is not self-reflective thinking *about* one's life but, much more, the conscious act of living one's life by thinking through its issues. The Journalist in this entry was carrying forward the qualitative contents of his life not by thinking about them to analyze them, but by intensely thinking them through as the forward thrust of his life commitment. It can be said that he was *thinking his life* forward with the continuous recording of his Inner Process Entries serving as the vehicle for his movement.

We find that when there is difficulty or confusion in a life, the best way to proceed in making Inner Process Entries is simply by stating the facts of our experience. Do it as naturally and as unself-consciously as you can, and the process will begin to work for you. We see an instance of this in the following entry by R.N.:

> My first feelings when I went to describe my present spiritual position were confusion. I drew a blank, and I thought that must mean that I don't have a spiritual position. Other people do, but I don't. Then I decided to write about beliefs I don't have any more. In the present moment they are conspicuous by their absence. They are beliefs I used to have. I didn't think that I still had them on my mind, but when I went to write about them I became very teary. It was nostalgia, I guess. The tears took me by surprise. Otherwise I would have stopped them before they came. I realize that I have a lot of emotion tied up in those old beliefs even if I think I don't believe them any more. I think there's a lot of love blocked up in there too. It's love that I've been missing. I have opened something that I had hidden in a box. It scares me right now, but I feel warm where I felt cold before. I'll wait and see what happens.

In an entry like this, it is apparent that a process is beginning to move beyond the consciousness of the person. Something that had been dormant, perhaps lightly sleeping, has now been awakened and is becoming active again. We might have the thought that it would be better not to arouse it, but that possibility has another disturbing aspect. Following that approach, we might easily let a large part of the potentials of our lives remain asleep. In one frame of mind, when a person is in an atmosphere of anxiety and is fearful of whatever is not controlled, the impulse may well be to let sleeping beliefs and emotions lie dormant. As one begins to move into a more sanguine mood, however, as we see in R.N.'s entry, there comes the realization that those sleeping emotions have strong energies of life within them. The warmth of love is felt stirring in those emotions, and with it there is the intimation that something of wisdom lies latent there as well. It may well be worth working to draw them forth, as R.N. seems to feel. And it may be a great waste of potential if we let them sleep untouched.

We see an additional type of imagery described in the entry by D. F.:

As I write about it I realize that this has been a very active period for me spiritually and intellectually. I welcome the opportunity to get it all down, but it will require volumes. How can I say it all? I feel inundated by ideas that have to be sorted out and I can do that here. But when I looked into the lake in the entrance meditation, I saw a strange image that haunts me. I saw a tree reflected in the water with many leaves, but they all came off the tree and fell into the water as though it was autumn. Nothing was left but the branches of the tree except that at the top a group of leaves seemed to come together and form a star of some kind. And that star was exceptionally luminous. Very striking. I recorded it at the beginning but I didn't know what to make of it. Now, after the writing I've done, I think the falling leaves are all my intellectual ideas and the star is something new. I have an idea of what—but maybe I shouldn't say yet. I'll just wait and see. Perhaps my intellect is changing.

The Inner Process Entries that you write at this point in your Process Meditation work may be brief and simple. Or they may become quite complex as you reflect on the various implications of what has taken place in your experience. You may find that you are bringing into play old habits of interpretation and intellectual theories that long have expressed your point of view. The best way to begin is in a neutral, reportorial way, objectively describing what you observe. Start by saying simply that you find yourself to be loose or tight or relaxed or anxious—whatever may be—and proceed by describing the way the flow of thoughts or emotions came, or did not come. You may then find that your simple factual description has opened a stream of consciousness or perception or experience that is very complex and is moving in a direction you had not thought of before. In that case help it along, but try not to direct it or shape it. Let it move of itself, if it starts. But do not deliberately start it and do not prod it or manipulate it.

In writing your Inner Process Entries be natural, descriptive, factual; and above all, be as unself-conscious as you can. Just write as a fact-keeping entry for your own use. Remember that in this work there is no point in trying to impress yourself with exaggerations or vanities, and there is no point in trying to depress yourself with self-criticisms and breast-beating. Just say it as it seems to you to be. And then move on to say the next thing, the next thought or feeling or

experience or emotion or intuition or speculation. Let it come naturally. Do not force it. Remember that if it does not come to you now, it
may come to you later. This may not be the time when it is ripe to
come into written form. So you can wait.

The sub-section of Inner Process Entries in the Meditation Log
gives us ample space and leeway to explore and to work while we are
waiting for our experiences to crystallize. In fact, that is its special
function in the practice of Process Meditation. It accompanies us as we
work in each of the exercises in other sections. We record our experience in the section where we are carrying out the exercise; and we also
keep a running account of all our meditative experiences in the Inner
Process Entries. That is what we have done so far. We had our experience of entrance meditation, and then again our work of Spiritual
Positioning, each of which we recorded in its own place. And then we
made a recapitulative description of those experiences in Inner Process
Entries. That is a basic procedure for maintaining our sense of continuity and movement throughout our practice of Process Meditation.

Each of the sub-sections in the Meditation Log has a specific purpose and use. The segment for entrance meditation is the place where
we go in order to quiet ourselves so that we can reach inward to the
depth dimension. We go to this sub-section whenever we are beginning
a unit of Process Meditation work, for it is here that we can establish the
inward atmosphere that we require.

Spiritual Positioning is the sub-section where we can place ourselves
with respect to the movement of inner time. It also is the segment of our
workbook where we go when we are beginning a unit of Process Meditation work. Just as entrance meditation gives us entry to the depth
dimension of our experience, Spiritual Positioning places us in the Life/
Time Dimension. Thus these two sub-sections set a base at the beginning on which the continuity of Process Meditation can be built.

The sub-section of Inner Process Entries, in contrast to these, is used
throughout our practice of Process Meditation. It is the primary vehicle
by which new data and experiences can constantly be added and assimilated. While the other two sub-sections are used occasionally, especially at the beginning of a unit of Process Meditation practice, Inner
Process Entries is used all the time.

In practice, because of its active and continuing use, Inner Process
Entries is the main operational segment of the Meditation Log. As we

proceed in our work, we shall see how this becomes a matter of accustomed *Intensive Journal* usage, especially where we use this sub-section to accompany our other exercises. At those points, when we say that it is now time to make our entry in the Meditation Log, it will actually be the Inner Process Entries to which we are referring. If it is entrance meditation or Spiritual Positioning that we mean, we call it by its name. But when we are to make an Inner Process Entry in the course of the later exercises of our Process Meditation work, we find that we often refer simply to the Meditation Log.

Since we are now at an early stage of our work, we cannot yet see the culminating and integrative messages that the Meditation Log may be carrying and building for us. But they will appear in their time. In the meanwhile we shall be adding our entries there as we proceed in our work following each of the appropriate exercises in the other sections of our workbook.

PART III

Connections:
The Making of Our
Spiritual History

Chapter 9

Alienation and the Cycles of Connective Experience

A good way to approach the concept that underlies the work we do in the *Connections* section of the *Intensive Journal* workbook is to think in terms of its opposite. The opposite of connection is separation, and *alienation* is the special term that has come to be used in describing the experience of being separated from life in modern society. Alienated persons are those who do not feel a personal linkage to a group or to a tradition or to any established system of beliefs or behavior. They feel separated from the social and spiritual structures that ordinarily support individuals in the conduct of their lives.

Persons living in modern times are particularly vulnerable to alienation because our period of history is one in which old traditions have lost much of their acceptance while new values have not yet been securely established. Individuals are therefore left very much on their own with no clear standards to guide them. They are subject to the pull of conflicting urges and desires but, not belonging to a culture that provides a solid frame of reference, they have no criterion for decision when circumstances call upon them to make an act of choice or an act of will. They are left in the disconnected world of alienation, vulnerable to the disorientation that results from living with unstable values. They are subject also to the symptoms of emotional disturbance that inevitably accompany feelings of unresolved conflict.

Over the years I have thought of the problem of alienation in terms of a Tibetan teaching that remains in my mind from the period in my life when I was first exploring the world's religions. It said, as I recalled it, that a drop of water will instantly evaporate if it is left by itself, but that it will last forever if it is united to an ocean.

In the state of alienation, the modern individual is the drop of water that has become separated from the sea. Because of aloneness the individual is in a very precarious situation, and in that state feels the *angst* that is the general condition of modern neurosis. The question is whether we can have a viable means of countering this *angst*. Given the many factors that tend toward alienation in modern society, is it possible to have a method of strengthening in individuals their inherent sense of belonging to larger contexts of life in order to extend their capacity for living? Can we help the drop of water maintain its connection to its ocean?

Human beings naturally reach for larger contexts of belonging and belief. The history of culture as well as that of religion bears witness to this, especially in those periods of intense social transition when broadly accepted beliefs have lost their hold on a population. History discloses that when the experience of connection does not take place, it leads to an emptiness of feeling and a disorientation in life. This is a social and cultural phenomenon but the experience of it is personal. Individuals feel its pain privately and with such intensity that they often seek to overcome it at all costs. In fact, one point of view from which we can understand the religious ferment in the second half of the twentieth century, especially among the younger generations, is that it expresses the spontaneous, and sometimes desperate, attempt to leap over the alienation of modern society in order to establish a personally meaningful connection to life.

Our Process Meditation work seeks to provide a means of establishing strong inner connections while avoiding the dangers that come from leaping and jumping in the desperate quest for meaning. The life of the spirit is too important to be approached haphazardly, and the large energies contained within it make it too dangerous to be dealt with carelessly. That is why we proceed step by step and follow a systematic methodology in reaching toward the larger meaning of our individual lives. We begin with the contents of our life, including experiences of every kind, from suffering to exaltation. And we are especially alert for the small intimations that come to us from time to time giving us clues to the larger than personal meanings of human existence. We gather these intimations and describe them as fully as we can. We try to draw them into such a form that we can work with them as the raw material for new experiences and for larger realizations that will come to us, each within the context of our individual life considered as a whole.

To collect the data of inner experience that will enable us to work toward the meaning of our lives is the main function of the *Connections* section. As it happens, the Tibetan "drop of water" contains a number of implications that relate to the principle underlying this aspect of our work. It is in fact very helpful for understanding the various exercises that we shall carry out here.

At workshops in recent years I have referred to the "drop of water" metaphor on numerous occasions as a means of introducing this subject. While preparing this manuscript, however, I decided to check the original quotation. I located it, and found that I had marked it off in an anthology called *The Bible of the World*, edited by Robert O. Ballou and published in 1939. I probably read it in 1941 or 1942 during the time between college and my army service, when my spiritual life was engaged in a serious and unsettling struggle with the political events of history. The political facts were all too apparent, but spiritually for me it was a time of searching for resources. In those days a person interested in world religions had a much smaller number of publications upon which to draw than is available to us now. I remember feeling very grateful when I came upon Ballou's large collection of texts.

The statement that had made its strong impression on me occurs in a section entitled, *Tibetan Scriptures.* The actual lines are:

> A drop of water is a little thing,
> But when will it dry away if united to a lake.*

Reading the passage now I could not help laughing at myself for turning the Tibetan lake into an ocean. Tibet, of course, is landlocked and has no contact with oceans but only with beautiful mountain lakes. I, on the other hand, have spent most of my life near the ocean's edge

---

* See Robert O. Ballou, *The Bible of the World*, Viking, New York, 1939, p. 342.

and have always sought to be near it during times of contemplation. So the ocean is a natural symbol for me. Whether it belongs to a small mountain lake or to an ocean, a drop of water will in fact disappear if it is separated from the larger entity to which it originally belonged. But if it remains connected to it, the drop of water will continue its life indefinitely, or for as long as that larger unit continues in existence.

An individual human being can be strengthened and sustained by being connected to a larger entity that may be of many different sizes or types. The connection may be to a larger political unit as a nation, to a local group in a neighborhood, or by blood ties to a tribe or to an expanded family of kinfolk. The connection may also be by less tangible markers than blood or land. It may come through subjective feelings of connection like shared beliefs and loyalties. It may come by being part of a religious tradition, holding a philosophy of life, being identified with a social ideology or movement, even appreciating or participating in the arts in a particular way. The forms in which connection to larger units of life may be experienced are exceedingly varied, especially in modern culture where the pluralism of subjective values is constantly being increased.

In making these subjective identifications that will extend their connection to life, human beings are like drops of water seeking to be connected to a river or an ocean. They intuitively know that when a person is connected to a larger whole, the individual life is strengthened and sustained and extended. We must take note, however, of a special factor that is at work where human beings are concerned. Our human nature is such that we cannot be connected to larger entities merely by a simple physical joining. We are not like stones that become part of a pile simply by being added to it, nor like flowers that become part of a field just by being planted there, nor like raindrops that become part of a lake as they fall into it. Human beings become connected to a larger whole only through their subjective feelings.

Human connection has a physical aspect, but that is only the raw material. Even the blood connections of race and nation require the subjective feelings of identification and loyalty. Without them, such physical facts as birth and color have no relevance. The critical element in human connection is the *inner* experience of the physical facts. If they have no *emotional meaning* to the person, they have no power. But when they are perceived as having an inner meaning, either emotionally or intellectually, they produce a great energy that can have tremendous effects. It can build the pressures that bring about radical social changes in history. And it can set the context in which individuals can deepen their perception of reality, enlarging their spiritual awareness. In broad terms, _connective experiences_ are the means of _meaningful inner linkage_ between a person's consciousness and the outer realities of the world. They thus have great importance not only personally, but socially and spiritually as well. The exercises that derive from our connective experiences become an increasingly valuable resource as we proceed in our ongoing work of Process Meditation.

The need for connection leads to religious-type experiences and beliefs but is not necessarily limited to what we think of institutionally as religion. The individual person needs linkage to the various social and philosophical frameworks in which persons can recognize the meaning of their life.

During the early years of life it is usually more accurate to describe the contents of connective experiences as being learned behavior. Beliefs tend to be taught or absorbed from the culture and there is relatively little that takes the form of spontaneous individual experiences. During childhood the doctrines of religion are taught together with the various codes of prescribed behavior, rituals, social manners, ethics and the like. While these teachings are being inculcated by the authority figures of the culture, the young person is absorbing them, acquiring beliefs that are being imposed from outside the self. During this early phase, learning is a process that moves from outside in.

Soon, however, what has been absorbed from the authorities of the culture returns in new forms as the spontaneous awarenesses of the individual. These are the first bona fide connective experiences in a person's life. They are the occasions in which individuals discover in the context of their own life, and by means of their own capacities of cognition, the experiential reality of perceptions of truth which they had known before only as doctrines to be memorized.

Once connective experiences have begun to happen spontaneously and individually within the young person, the development of consciousness has moved to a new level. From that point onward, the process of learning has two main ingredients. In one aspect it is based primarily on information and beliefs that are drawn from sources outside the individual. In its other aspect it involves new recognitions and understandings that come by direct experience from within. The inter-relationship, indeed the tension, between these two modes of life-consciousness plays a major role in shaping the tone and style of the individual's growth.

The years of adolescence are replete with such mixed experiences of learning. There is much objective information to be absorbed. There is also a great deal that can only be learned when its basis has been subjectively accepted: for example, the groups to which one belongs, the acceptable activities for one's station in life, beliefs about the gods and other ultimates of existence. In those societies where a single set of traditions dominates the culture, the process of adolescent learning is much simplified. There it is a unilinear process, since the culture does not have competing doctrines and traditions that are being simultaneously taught from different points of view.

Even these simpler societies, however, do not consider it to be sufficient for a person simply to be taught the doctrines of the tribe. They must also have their own experience of it, at least in principle or symbolically, so that they will be connected to the religion of the tribe or to the secrets of the craft not simply by words that have been memorized, but by direct, inner experience. That is the significance of the type of initiation ritual that requires a young person to be alone for three days in the woods and to fast until a visionary or other revelatory experience presents itself.

In modern culture the need for connective experience is at least as great as in earlier periods of history, but the circumstances are much more intricate. The complexity comes primarily from the fact that modern society is not limited to a single tradition into which every young person is to be initiated. In our pluralistic, secular culture there are many traditions from which to choose. Furthermore, in modern times the choice of the belief or the version of truth into which the person is to seek initiation is not determined by the society nor by the authorities of the society. It is left open for the individual to decide.

This freedom is exactly as it should be but, ironically, it compounds the difficulty. Many persons, being young, are not prepared to choose. They are not yet in a position to specify to which philosophy they wish to be initiated, or to which religion, or social or political ideology, or to which way of life they wish to commit themselves, whether to the arts, or to athletics, or business enterprise, or pleasure seeking, or scientific research, or whatever other ways of life the modern world may make available.

In modern culture the age of adolescence is much too early to be making a lasting life decision; in earlier, one-tradition cultures, that was the natural time to do so. The result is that where the outer form of a traditional initiation is retained in modern practice, it becomes only the shell of a ceremonial. An example of this is the retention after centuries of the Jewish *Bar Mitzvah* at age thirteen with its famous "Today I am a man" speech. Whereas in earlier generations of traditional Jewish culture the young man might be married at age thirteen and fully inducted into the responsibilities of the society, that announcement of manhood in modern times is quite premature. The young man's actual experience of connection to life in its larger aspects with a commitment to specific life activities must wait for an additional number of years to pass, perhaps another thirteen, or more.

The central fact is that, since the experience of initiation has lost so much of its cultural support in modern times, the individual can reach an experience of connection to life only through his or her own resources. And the one basic resource we each have is our own life with our inner perception of its contents. It is now the individual life and not the culture that provides the framework and the content for initiation experiences.

The connective experience no longer comes at a specific, culturally-set time. It is no longer induced and protected by a ritual situation. Now it comes at the time, or times, when the vicissitudes of the individual's life, its pressures, its circumstances, and the self-directed seeking by the person, bring about experiences so intense that they are connective to the larger scope of life. Initiation to meaning now takes place in the midst of the individual existence, forced by the pressures of its evolving life-context. That is one important reason why our *Intensive Journal* work begins by providing a vehicle for drawing our whole life history into view. It is by this means that we get access to the raw materials of our life and establish a *life-context* for the various connective experiences that take us toward our own recognition of meaning.

The complexity of individual spiritual experience in modern times presents certain disadvantages but it also opens many new possibilities for us. For one thing, if modern persons are not able to have their full connective experience at the time of adolescence, they may nonetheless have a series of connective initiatory experiences in the course of the ensuing years. And since we have a much longer life expectancy now than in earlier centuries, there is the possibility that many modern persons may have connective experiences of their own in their later years that will be of significantly greater profundity than the ritual initiation they might have passed through in their youth. In some lives we can discern a definite inner process by which successive connective experiences, occurring from time to time in the course of a long life span, bring a cumulative deepening of spiritual knowledge.

There is also a process that operates within our connective experiences. It is a cyclical process with highs and lows that can be deceptive to us when we are caught up in the emotional intensity of our personal experiences. It is very helpful to have a perspective of the movement of the cycle as a whole. With it we can sense where we are and can understand which transient pressures are working upon us when we find ourselves in the midst of the fluctuations of a cycle of connective experience.

The cycle of connective experience begins with its opposite, with separation from meaning, with the consciousness of alienation. Painful emotions accompany this phase of the cycle, the negativity of feeling that there is no meaning to be found, the anxiety that it will never be achieved, that one is not capable of ever finding it. And there is the depressive lack of energy, a phenomenon that is seemingly physical but is mainly an indication of the absence of connective experience.

During this low phase of the cycle there will also be a variety of experiences that take place in the twilight range of cognition. Some may be visionary, some may have the quality of nightmare dreams, some may activate intense emotions, and others may carry an intuitive fore-knowledge. The experiences that come during this phase tend often to have a dark, unpleasant quality, and for that reason they are often by-passed, repressed or ignored. It is important, however, to realize that, pleasant or not, these are integral parts of the whole process, and therefore that they must be acknowledged in neutral terms. We make no judgment of them but we take note of their presence as we proceed.

In the latter part of this time of darkness there begins to be a more affirmative opening. Possibilities become more apparent and we are made aware of them at the twilight level.

Gradually there is an increase in the energy level and a more active seeking for new understanding. Presently we feel that a new discovery has been made, that a new awareness has been given to us. In varying degrees a new connective experience takes place at this point and it often has the quality of a conversion to a new-found truth. At first the atmosphere may be one of uncertainty as we are unsure of our new belief. Once the doubts have passed, however, we may find our emotions taking us to the opposite extreme. Soon we find ourselves feeling the unrestrained enthusiasm that is common in new converts to anything. We experience the enthusiasm of new discovery and express it, for all of this is part of the *entry* or conversion phase of a new connective experience.

Once the entry phase is over and we are within the new belief or attitude, our emotions can settle into a more stable condition. Now it is as though we are in a new country with a great deal of exploring to do. We may also feel that we are on a plateau of awareness where the light looks different because we are up on a height. Subjectively we feel ourselves to be on a *high* and this affects our perception of reality. During this time a variety of experiences may come to us in the twilight range, often visionary and symbolic, tending to confirm our new beliefs. At least, while we are in this atmosphere of convinced believing, we tend to interpret our symbolic experiences as confirming our new understanding. It is a time of confidence and self-congratulation.

After a while this feeling of being on a plateau begins to diminish. The situation as a whole starts to follow a cyclic rhythm as it moves into another phase. The dreams and other twilight perceptions that come to us now raise questions we had not thought of before. Our initial enthusiasm is beginning to wane. We have absorbed so much of our new experience that we are now wondering, with some new anxiety, about what comes next. We are on the other side of the hill and so we now see things from a different angle of vision.

We began by moving through the *entry* phase of our new connective experience but now doubts and questions give us another perspective. We are moving toward the *exit* phase of the experience. It may be that events have taken place that have the effect of disillusioning us in our beliefs. It may be that our new knowledge has led us to still further knowledge so that we are now considering other doctrines or ideas side by side with our present beliefs. We may not have come to the end and we may not yet be moving through the exit, but the atmosphere is now markedly different from the enthusiasm with which we began. We no longer have the certitude with which we moved up to the plateau.

As it comes to its closing phase, the connective experience may merely be changing its form. It may not be an ending. The time of exit from a connective experience can have many variations. Sometimes the end is abrupt and final. At other times it is gradual. Often the person does not make a specific decision to alter or drop the belief, but reaches a point of realizing simply that it is not believed in any more. That becomes a statement of fact. From that point on, whatever one professes, the fact is that one has already moved through the exit gate of that belief.

Because changes in belief often move gradually, there may be no single perceptible point at which belief ends. It may not actually end at all, but simply neutralize itself and move into an incubation period during which nothing shows on the surface. When the incubation period, which may also serve as a time of reassessment, comes to an end, the old belief may re-emerge. Whether it has been only slightly changed or totally transformed, we often find that the core of an old belief returns in a new form at a later period of a person's life. It seems, indeed, that beliefs have a life of their own, and that they move through their own life cycle across the decades of an individual's existence, disappearing and then reasserting themselves in new forms.

Sometimes the old belief is immediately replaced by a new one so that there is no period of emptiness intervening. At other times there is nothing to replace it and we are left with a void when our connective experience has dwindled away. That is when we feel we are in a valley once more, or lost in the wilderness, alone in the desert. It is a dark night of the soul, a time of waiting and not knowing.

At such times we are brought back to where we were before we made our entry into our connective experience. The experience has gone full cycle. We are returned to the emptiness and the unsureness once again. But it is not the same as it was. Something has been added in the interim. It is we ourselves who are different now. We have passed through a full cycle of connective experience, and that means that an additional number of *interior events* have taken place within us. They have left their mark. The quality and the capacities of our inner being are different now in some aspect and in some degree because of them.

What are these *interior events?* They are the many small units of experience that take place within us as we move through the cycles of experience by which we reach for, find, lose and find again in new forms, a contact with the larger contexts of life. These interior events are the doubts, the fears, the hopes, the awakenings, the new awarenesses, the faith that arises during times of strengthening and growth, and the confusions that come during times of weakening and decline. They are the many subjective perceptions and activities by which successive inner transformations take place in our lives.

These small units of interior events are the steps and phases that comprise the full cycles of connective experience. Often they do not seem to be of great significance in themselves, whether they are inner events of emotional intensity or intellectual events bringing new insight and awareness. As a whole, however, the context of the encompassing cycle of experience may be of great importance.

Each time a person passes through a full cycle of connective experience it is as though a cycle of life has been lived, although in miniature and on the interior level. Something of the past, some qualitative belief, has been lost or has been given up, has been allowed to die. And something new has been found. Something new has been brought to life and given form for as long as it can maintain itself. Until it too dies, or is transformed in some other way.

In the course of the interior events that comprise these cycles, many tensions and pains are felt, many hopes and plans, disappointments and renewed efforts. Because they are experienced with an inward pressure, individuals are forced each time to reach more deeply within themselves to draw on previously untouched inner resources. Moving through each cycle of inner experience, therefore, serves as a challenge to us. It exercises our inner being, creating a pressure that stretches us from within.

Since it is an unpleasant feeling, most people try to avoid such times of tension as when an old cycle of connective experience is coming to an end, or when a new one is trying to be born in the midst of anxiety and confusion. Times of spiritual transition are painful to bear, personally and psychologically. The fact is, however, that the process of continuous inner growth requires that we pass through cycle after cycle of experience, learning to absorb the pressures so that they may be transformed into unitary understanding. We require a sense of inner timing as we move through successive cycles of connective experience in our lives. And we require also a means of re-entering those cycles so that we can draw from them the seeds of our next experiences and our further awareness. To acquire the techniques for both of these, for developing an inner perspective and the ability to use our personal history as a profound spiritual resource, is the purpose of our next exercises.

Chapter 10

Gatherings:
Collecting Our
Inner Resources

We come now to the practical step of assembling our spiritual history in the *Connections* section.

We begin by setting up a sub-section, *Gatherings*, which will serve as the collection point for the individual events that have an inner importance in our lives. This is the place for gathering our spiritual data, the raw material for our developing work of Process Meditation.

To start, write the title of the sub-section, *Gatherings*, at the head of a page. And write the date beside the heading. We should make it a point as we continue our *Intensive Journal* work that we record the date each time that we make an additional entry. In that way we can track the changes in our perceptions of our life when we read our entries back to ourselves at a later time. In the case of the *Gatherings* sub-section there are two dates to be recorded. There is the date on which we are making our Journal entry, and also the date when the event that we are describing actually occurred, as best we can recall it.

The purpose of the *Gatherings* sub-section is to draw together into one place our awareness of all manner of events that may have an inner significance to us and thus play a role in our spiritual history. These events may be of many contrasting kinds. They may be interior events that transpired altogether within our subjective lives. Or they may be exterior events that took place in outer time and space. In either case, whether they are outer or inner events, the important question is whether they have an inner meaning to us either now or at the time they occurred.

How shall we recognize an inner meaning? We spoke earlier of the sequence of *interior events* that form the cycles of our connective experiences. These events may take place in the external world, or they may take place altogether within us. They are interior, however, in the sense that they have an importance to us in the terms of our private perception and feeling. They have an *inner meaning* to us; and it is thus that they have consequences at the interior, qualitative level of our lives. They become the building blocks for the larger units of spiritual experience that eventually comprise our spiritual history.

These interior events may have an importance to us that is personal, but they are not merely subjective experiences. The paradox, in fact, is that an event or a situation can be said to have an inner meaning when it arouses in us something deeper than a personal emotion so that we feel it connects us to a context of life that is larger than ourselves. The inner meaning of an interior event comes from the fact that it is felt to have a more-than-personal significance. We do not see it as an event that just haphazardly happens. We see it as a significant linkage between ourselves and the universe. Its inner meaning is at a deeper than personal level, and comes by means of the traditions or beliefs or symbols that carry it.

Every day of our lives, for example, we are aware that the sun is in the heavens, and we see it there. But one day we see the sun move toward setting in a way that enables us to feel that we know the ultimate principle behind the setting of the sun, and that, beyond intellectual knowledge, we are one with it. That is an outer event with an inner meaning. We become more than ourselves in such an experience because we are connecting with the larger context of the cosmos. We become in that moment the single drop of water reconnecting with the cosmic ocean.

Such an event has an *inner meaning* to us because it gives us an intimation of transcendence. The paradox is that, while we think of it as *inner*, it is actually taking us *beyond* ourselves. But it is a qualitative and not a physical *beyond* to which we are carried. It is a connection to a larger context of life.

As an example let us consider another connective event in relation to the world of nature. I learn of a major earthquake in which great devastation is wrought and many innocent people are killed. Far from feeling connected to the beauty of life, my mind is overwhelmed by thoughts of the disharmonies within the universe, of the discord and destruction in nature, and the seeming absence of God. As a result of this perception of the earthquake and the questions that it raises, much new thinking and exploration may be stimulated. The catastrophe sets in motion a process of search that opens many questions about the nature of the physical world, good and evil, the role of divinity and other riddles of human existence. Eventually it may lead us, like Job, to a new understanding and perhaps to a reconnective experience.

An historical instance of just such an event was the earthquake in Portugal in 1755. It came in the midst of the eighteenth century's deistic vision of divinely guided progress. That was a confident period in history. The essence of its philosophy was expressed in Alexander Pope's couplet:

> And, spite of pride, in erring reason's spite,
> One truth is clear. Whatever is, is right.*

In that intellectual atmosphere the earthquake sent spiritual shock waves through European culture, and it led many people to re-evaluate their optimistic assumptions. Our period of history has its own earthquakes, social as well as geologic. They are the outer events that raise questions in us of inner meaning, and thus they become *interior events.* Many people in our time, also, are jarred by them into seeking a more profound understanding of the paradoxes of human existence. We are beset by many unpleasant events that shock us into struggling to find an inner meaning that will ring true to us. The conflicts of our time, cultural as well as personal, set into motion varied questions in many modern individuals seeking the elusive goal of authentic truth. It is a quest that takes many forms and moves through many cycles of exploration. For persons in the modern world this quest often has a secular content, and yet the way it reaches for meaning recalls the symbolic search for the Holy Grail in earlier centuries. Whatever its content, it is in the course of this quest that we each build our individual spiritual history.

*Alexander Pope, *An Essay on Man,* Epistle I.

The events that may be included in our spiritual history are of many different kinds. Events may range from pleasant to unpleasant, connective to disconnective, secular to religious, high *"peak"* experiences to low "in the valley" experiences. But the one common quality which they all share is that they are part of our individual effort to reach an awareness of meaning that will enable us eventually to feel connected to a larger context of life. They are all aspects of this effort in its various phases, and that is why we accept and record them without judgment. They are all contributing to the whole. With their diversity and sometimes with their seeming diffusion, they are building toward the unity of meaning in our lives.

In each person's life there is a continuity of process in the course of which a core of meaning gradually forms itself. One purpose of the set of exercises we are now beginning is to reconstruct our individual spiritual history so that we can identify what that core of meaning is in our individual life. A key to that lies in the relation between the specific interior events that have happened in our lives and the full cycles of our connective experiences.

Experiences of connection all have the effect of linking the individual human being with the larger-than-personal contexts of meaning in life. That applies to the experiences as a whole, but not necessarily to their individual parts. We thus have the paradox that the individual events that comprise connective experiences often do not have a connective or unitary quality themselves. The fact is that many different kinds of events are necessary in order to form a full cycle of connective experience. Inherently the individual events are not homogeneous. Since they occur at different points in the cycle, some of them express anxiety, a sense of isolation and despair; yet they are parts of a constructive experience that may eventually bring an initiation to a new sense of truth and an affirmation of life. These individual events are simply the early phases of a broad-ranging cycle. They must be understood as being inseparable and integral parts of a single unit of experience because the connective integration of the cycle could not take place without them.

This has very important implications for the way we carry out our work in this Gatherings sub-section. Let us imagine for a moment that we are an artist and that in that capacity we have achieved recognition because we have a distinctive way of presenting color and form. Now we are trying to explain to friends how we happened to become creative. We recall a particular interior event that took place for us, and we describe it as a visionary breakthrough. We explain that it enabled us to see the outer world of sensory reality in a way we had never been able to see it before. We found that after that event had taken place we could paint differently because now we perceived the outer world in terms of an interior dimension.

That was indeed a connective experience. But if we tried to explain our creativity by referring to it alone, we would be telling only a partial truth. To tell the whole truth we would have to include in our account the fact that our visionary breakthrough was just one event in a cycle. It would not have been possible without the various interior events that preceded it.

To tell the whole truth, therefore, we would have had to move back in our personal history and recall the first intimations we had that life would feel good if we could become an artist. And then we would remember the terrible nightmare dream we had that said, in effect, it was not possible and that we could never be an artist. We would have to describe also the interior event that extended over quite a period of time in which we lived covered by a cloud of anxiety. During that time there was pain as well as fear, and our confusions sometimes became depression. We would have to describe the occurrences of that time as part of the cycle of our connective experience. At the same time, however, that we were describing the darkness of that long period of night through which we lived, we would be reminded of occasional awarenesses that came to us. When these appeared, they seemed to us to be great illuminations, perhaps in contrast to the darkness we were in. They were so fragmentary and transient, however, that we did not give them much importance at the time. And they did not give us anything tangible to use in our lives. We might then recount the painful feelings of emptiness and isolation when those brief moments of light had passed and left us in the darkness again.

All these interior events and more would have to be described as parts of the cycle of connective experience by which artistic creativity came to us. Each had an integral role in the continuity of the process since the cycle could not move through its phases without each of them, or at least their equivalent. This observation is central to the work we do in Gatherings. We want to draw together as many of the interior events as we can recall in order to reconstitute the cycles of connective experience that have been meaningful in our lives. We try to remember and gather here events from all phases of the cycle, whatever their quality, whether pleasant or painful, since all are necessary. We seek to draw memories back to ourselves, but not just fleeting impressions of past happenings. We wish to remember the circumstances of experiences that were of such depth and extent that as we recall them we re-enter them. And these are experiences of such qualitative size that when we are once again inside their atmosphere, we can move around and explore them to see what else they may hold for us. There we may find our way to further perceptions and further understandings that will lead to new interior events in the cycle of our experiences. But first we must recall them so that we can re-enter them.

The question then is how we can re-invoke these memories? How shall we draw them back to ourselves? And how shall we work with them in the Gatherings sub-section?

We sit in quietness, our *Intensive Journal* workbook open before us. We keep a pen handy for the entries we may wish to make. Our eyes are closed, and as the quietness deepens within ourselves our breathing becomes slower.

> Letting the Self become still,
> Letting the breath become slow,
> And slower.
> Feeling the movement of life
> Feeling my own life
> As it moves through its phases
> And changes
> And cycles.
> Feeling the movement of life
> And seeking truth
> Seeking the truth in my life.
> Finding glimpses,
> Glimpses of truth.
> Wondering at the bits of truth
> Knowing and wondering
> And remembering
> In the Silence . . . In the Silence.

As your silence deepens, and as you find yourself going back into the movement of your life, let memories come to you. And record them as they come, giving each its separate place. Leave at least several lines, perhaps as much as half a page, between each memory as you recall and begin to describe it.

Let these memories come to you in your quietness. Do not reach out deliberately to draw them into you, but let them come as you sit waiting for them, holding the atmosphere of the interior events in your life. In that atmosphere, memories will come from many parts of your life, and they will reflect the various phases in the cycles of your experience.

As these recollections come to you, describe them briefly, saying just enough to identify the content of what took place. You may write a few sentences but not more than a moderate-sized paragraph. We have found it helpful to follow the general rule of thumb that when a Gatherings entry reaches half a page in length that is a sign that we have written enough for the present.

Sometimes a memory will return to you with particular strength and energy. It may stimulate you so forcefully that you will have the desire to write about it at great length, even to the exclusion of other memories. If that happens, you should bear in mind the role of this exercise in relation to the larger purpose of our Process Meditation work. We are seeking to give ourselves access as broadly as possible to the full range of our inner experiences. And here in Gatherings we are collecting as many as we can.

In this context, if you find yourself particularly stimulated by the memory of an interior event, the best practice seems to be to write your half-page of description, perhaps adding a few notes for the future, and then turn your attention to receiving other memories. You will not be losing your chance to write at length about that experience. There will be an opportunity to return to it in a little while when we work in the *Re-Openings* segment of the Connections section. You will have ample time to enlarge it there. At that point also you will have an additional perspective with which to return to the experience. The most important reason, however, for setting a limit on our present descriptions is not to distract ourselves from calling up and gathering additional memories of interior events that are related to the cycles of connective experience in our lives.

As we are writing our descriptions of particular memories, we may find that we are drawn up to the surface of our consciousness. To that degree, also, we may be drawn out of the quiet atmosphere of remembering. When that happens we should take the time to sit in quietness once again, letting our breathing become slow again, letting our Self become still. In that stillness additional memories will come to us, and we add them, a half page at a time to our Gatherings. Now we proceed with our inward remembering in the Silence.

*　　*　　*

Since they come from all phases of the cycles of our connective experiences, the range of interior events that we may recall is very broad. These memories may be of the early anxious aspects of our experience, of the high plateau times when we feel permanent and secure, or of the later, ending times when we meet uncertainty again. All of these rememberings have their own integrity, and they are not the same for any two persons. Here are some examples that are indicative and that may remind us of circumstances in our own lives.

I remember the feeling of belonging that I experienced at the close of an Easter service when I was about eleven years old. I felt that everyone there in the church was part of one group. It was a spiritual thing but more a social thing, like a family belonging together. I remember that closeness and I think of it as what religion should be. But it hasn't been.

My grandfather was the cantor in a small orthodox synagogue. On Yom Kippur he wore white robes and only stockinged feet and lay down prostrate before the Ark of the Torah. When I was a small boy I saw him do that and I remember seeing a white light around his whole body as he lay on the floor praying. It was awesome and I felt it was very holy.

I was really afraid through most of the time that I did my first mountain climbing. I thought I'll never do this again. But when we reached a really high place where we could sit and rest and see what was around us, I felt I touched reality for the first time. The vastness overcame me, and draws me back to it.

Singing *The Messiah* for the first time. Singing in a choral group is always a good experience for me, but that time it was more than music. I felt I discovered what religion is about. And I was glad I could sing it.

At certain periods in my life it has been important to feel that I knew God, or that I knew about God. At those times I would wonder about it a lot, and listen to preachers. And then I would forget about it. Those have been each a different time, but they seem to be dealing with just one question.

Football isn't religion, but I have felt very connected when the team was really going right. Certain times in particular the whole team seemed to be like one person, and the spirit was such that everyone knew to do the right thing. It was like being one with the world.

I was in my teens and I thought I wanted to be a monk, so I decided to try to see Thomas Merton. I hitch-hiked to Kentucky and I managed to get to his meditation hut. I didn't see him but I saw some empty beer cans on the floor, and I left in disgust. Later I realized I didn't really want to be a monk and I was ducking the issue. But I still need to understand Thomas Merton. Perhaps I was afraid to meet him.

When I was a little girl I saw my grandmother cover her face with her hands as she said a blessing when she lit the candles on the Sabbath. Everything seemed very safe when she did that. But I could never think of myself doing that. Now I wonder what kind of belief I would have to have. And what kind of woman I would have to be.

When my mother died unexpectedly my first thought was that there is no God and that life is pointless. Later I thought about it further, even considering the possibility of life after death, or reincarnation. I felt the separation very sharply when the death happened, but now I feel a relationship starting again. I seem to be thinking of death in a different way, as a connection perhaps. But to what?

When I joined the Communist Party it was like a conversion experience. There was a great wave of history going to take over the world and make mankind united and happy. And I was now part of it. Then I saw the cruelty within the party towards others. So I left disillusioned. But I still wish there was some way I could feel connected to mankind.

I used to fight and argue about practicing the piano. Then one day I was by myself and it came out just right, more than perfect. It was as though I hadn't played it but something in the world had played that piano just right. I felt it was a mystery. After that I played the piano my same old way, but I didn't argue about it any more. I just wondered if it would ever happen again.

The time when I felt unity in the presence of Swami——. I had never known it before, and although I have known it since then, it has somehow been different. That one experience remains a white light for me.

A variety of memories and awarenesses of such earlier experiences may come to you as you let yourself reflect on the interior movement of your life. Sometimes it will be specific and separated events that you will recall. At other times it will be a whole constellation of happenings or attitudes, an inner situation that extended over a considerable period of time. In either case, they are part of the larger cycles of your connective experiences. Therefore, as you recall them, describe them in your Gatherings. Giving them a place here, they can eventually show whatever their additional message and meaning may be in the larger context of your life.

In recalling our Gatherings, it is not necessary to list them in chronological order. Our purpose in this segment is merely to give ourselves access to as many memories of connective events as possible. Therefore we record them in whatever order they come to us. We may list them very unsystematically, now a recall from a recent period, now one from earlier years, now a memory of a poetic experience of nature, now a political loyalty or concern, now a memory of a religious ritual in childhood, now philosophical thoughts and questions about a mystical experience, now a memory of devastating despair and disillusionment.

We record them as they come to us with no concern for their sequence or their subject matter. We simply describe them briefly, but fully enough to include their main elements, and then we go on to describe the next experience that comes to mind.

For some of us at certain points in our work of Gatherings, it will work better to begin with experiences from early years and then to move forward chronologically. On the other hand and at other times you may find that it is too arduous a task for you to move across long periods of lifetime to identify one by one the particular events that contributed to your sense of meaning in life. You may find that once you have made contact with recent experiences, you are better able to move back in time to the events that preceded them. This may also be influenced by your mood and by the pressures of outer circumstances. Sometimes you may find that it works best for you to begin with experiences that stand out in your memory ·as dramatic events either because they were beacons of light or because of the darkness through which you passed. Describing these standout events, the experiences of intensity that are the first to return to your memory, may be a convenient way to begin because it sets the process into motion with something that readily presents itself.

Once we begin to record our Gatherings, the first memories will be followed by rememberings and awarenesses from all parts of our spiritual history. Each entry that we make tends to stimulate the process, for it gives us reminders of other happenings in the past. We find, therefore, that once we have begun the work of Gatherings, one entry leads to another. While we may have been slow in starting, the associations and reminders soon build a momentum in our stream of consciousness and additional entries suggest themselves to us without our seeking them. For a similar reason we find that when we are working actively in other sections of our *Intensive Journal* workbook, the writing stimulates us to remember events of our spiritual history that were lying dormant within us and which belong in Gatherings.

When we have described all the relevant memories that come to our mind now, we leave the Gatherings segment open-ended, available for continuing entries. We move on to further exercises, but we shall return with additional Gatherings from time to time.

Chapter 11

Spiritual Steppingstones

THE DREAM MODEL OF STEPPINGSTONES

We are each working now in our personal spiritual history, under-standing by the term, "spiritual history," the continuity of all the forms by which individuals reach toward meaning in their lives.

One of the fundamental and very fruitful procedures that has emerged out of the *Intensive Journal* system is the work that we do with *Steppingstones.** The Steppingstones section in the *Intensive Journal* workbook is part of the Life/Time Dimension which in the workbook is marked off by red dividers. In the *Intensive Journal* structure this is where we direct our attention to working with the movement of time in a person's life in order to draw a person's whole life history into perspective. The Steppingstones exercises provide a rapid and effective means of gaining an overview of a person's life as a whole, the cycles of change through which it has passed, and its possibilities for the future.

Working with Steppingstones is especially important when we are beginning to use the *Intensive Journal* workbook because it gives us an operational framework that is objective even while it is private and unique for each person. In the Steppingstones exercises at the basic, beginning level of *Intensive Journal* work, we mark off about a dozen (give or take one or two) of the main reference points in the movement

---

* See *At a Journal Workshop*, pp. 102 ff.

of our life from birth to the present. We record those points, those markings, spontaneously as we think of them in the moment when we are making the list of our Steppingstones. Each list of Steppingstones is brief, unpremeditated, and uninterpreted. We write it as it comes to us.

At a later time, whenever we once again make a spontaneous list of the Steppingstones of our life, we have the interesting experience of discovering that the significant events we are now recording are different from those in our first list. It is the same life that we are describing, but the perception of it is different because, with the passage of time, we are now looking at it and emotionally experiencing it from a different vantage point.

The list of Steppingstones is a large and general outline that provides a context in which we can carry out the further exploration of our lives. By using at an early point in our *Intensive Journal* work the battery of exercises that are based on the Steppingstones concept, we give ourselves a large framework of subjective time as the context for reconstructing our individual life history. It is much like the canvas for a mural on which an artist inserts a figure here, a figure there, as the awareness and the inspiration present themselves in the course of doing the artwork. We establish a broad and open context, and bit by bit we fill in the contents of our whole life history.

As practice with the *Intensive Journal* process has continued, the Steppingstones procedures have been adapted so that they can serve in support of exercises we do in other Journal sections. This is especially true of the Dialogue Dimension where we are engaged in establishing a deep inner relationship with the several phases (or mini-processes) of our life. In taking the step from the Dialogue exercises to Process Meditation we were led to make a further extension of the way we work with Steppingstones. Working as we are here, in that part of our lives where we are reaching toward meaning, the experiences we are dealing with are so delicate and elusive, so easily forgotten or repressed in the midst of our extroverted world, that we find it is too much of a leap to go directly into the Steppingstones work. A preliminary step of preparation is necessary. That is the step that we have taken with the entries in the *Gatherings* sub-section.

The way we collected our spiritual data in Gatherings was deliberately amorphous, but in Spiritual Steppingstones our purpose is to make it possible for our inner life to take form, or to reveal the form that it already has. And we wish to do this without imposing upon it the desires of our conscious mind. We wish to make it possible for our inner life to express its own intention.

The work of Spiritual Steppingstones, we should note, does not involve the collection of historical data. We have collected the data of our spiritual history in Gatherings. In Spiritual Steppingstones we draw the past together qualitatively and cogently by means of its key points and not its details. The Steppingstones list contains the points of emphasis provided by the movement of our life itself as a means by which it can show us its inner goal and direction. In order for the exercise to serve this function for us truly, it is essential that it be carried out at a level that by-passes our conscious thoughts, our wishes and desires. If we manipulate our list of Steppingstones to suit ourselves, it will only be ourselves that we are fooling. Therefore we need a means of carrying out the exercises in such a way that they come by non-conscious means as spontaneously as possible out of the holistic depths of our life. With this in mind, the procedures for working with Spiritual Steppingstones are directly modeled on the nature of dreams. The making of these Steppingstones parallels the process of dreaming.

When the Steppingstones exercises were originally developed in the course of creating the *Intensive Journal* system, the most helpful clue came from an observation regarding a certain type of deep dream. I had noticed that dreams that are brought forth out of a situation of great personal pressure, out of crisis or intense anxiety, carry a clearly visible *time structure* in their symbolism.

Stated briefly, this means that a large percentage of deep dreams are brought forth by the need to find a solution to a pressing and disturbing problem that has arisen in the course of present circumstances. Seeking a source of information and needing a resource on which to draw for solving the present problem, the dream process (which is carrying the *holistic depth* process of the whole developing person) reaches back into the past of the person's life. Out of the large accumulation of memory that is contained in an individual's life history, a small part is relevant and useful for solving the present problem—but no more than a small part. The conscious mind does not know which segment this is; or, at least, it is not able to discern it consciously and to call it to our attention. If it could, it would have been able to solve the problem in the first place and there would be no need for the anxiety dream to come in quest of information.

There is, however, a capacity in our human nature that does enable us to find those contents of our past that we need to recall because they hold clues for solving our present problems. We may refer to this capacity as our "inner wisdom," as a sixth sense of intuition, as "knowing more than we understand." Whichever term we use for it, the fact is that it is an operational quality of our holistic nature. It functions at unconscious levels at the depth of our being, and it is one of the capacities that has enabled the human species to emerge by a selective evolutionary process to the development of an advanced civilization. Since its roots lie in the abilities by which the human species was able to survive in the competition of evolution, it would seem that the faculties related to "inner wisdom" are fundamental to our existence. They enable the human being to cope with the challenges of life, whether it is life lived in the wild or in civilization. There is some evidence, however, that the further the technologies of civilization advance, the more the modern human being comes to depend on external sources of knowledge. The consequence is that, being called upon and used less and less, the capacities of "inner wisdom" tend to fall into atrophy. One of the few remaining places where they are still drawn into use is in our deep, anxiety dreaming. And that can be understood because anxiety dreaming is an atavistic human response to the dangers of living in the world of nature.*

The sensitivities of our "inner wisdom" are still made available to us through dreams, most often in those circumstances where the dangers or pressures of life build a fearful condition of anxiety. There is a movement from anxiety to insight that is one of the basic cycles of inner experience. The messages of "inner wisdom" that come to us through dreams have, however, one serious limitation: our "inner wisdom" cannot convey its information directly to our conscious understanding. It can communicate its information to us only by an indirect, nonconscious process, a symbol-making process; and dreams are historically the most dramatic, and the most widely recognized, vehicle for this process.

In the course of its dreams, the holistic depth process draws up those elements of past experience that are relevant and suggestive for meeting the problems of the present situation. A dream may, for example, take us back to a time in our life which we had quite forgotten but which

* For the conceptual background of these remarks in the context of Holistic Depth Psychology, see *Depth Psychology and Modern Man*, Chapters 6-10.

contained circumstances similar to our present difficulty. We then are brought up against the great handicap under which dreams operate, that they do not speak straightforwardly, but only obscurely in symbols. They therefore only allude by metaphor and give us veiled hints to direct us to the segments of our life history that contain the information we require. Dreams give us *leads* that may be very instructive if we follow them; but we need to have a means of reaching through and beyond their symbolism if we are to know where these leads are taking us.

One of the important functions of the Journal Feedback method is to provide a means of following our dream leads without being caught in the vagaries of symbol interpretation. Since the *Intensive Journal* structure consists of channels, or mini-processes, that carry the inner movement of our life history, it enables our dreams to lead us to the part of our life history that has a message for us. We might compare what takes place then to the experience we have as a tourist when we ask for directions in a strange country. Not sharing a common language, the other person can merely point. As we go in the direction in which the hand is pointing, we find our way to the place we are seeking. Correspondingly, we follow our dream leads like fingers pointing from the depth of us into the particular sections of the *Intensive Journal* workbook. The structure and principles by which the sections are divided do the rest of the work for us and that is how we find our way to the part of our life that we need to recall and reconsider.*

The dream process, then, is our model for devising a means of getting access to the "inner wisdom" of our holistic nature. Judging by historical writings from the Old Testament onwards, dreams have been a primary means of drawing intuitive knowledge to the level of conscious action when people find themselves in a time of personal or social trouble. The dreams reach back into the past and call our attention to those experiences that can give us a clue with which to solve our present problems and move into our future.

Our dreams can give us these clues, however, in the only mode of functioning that is available to them. That is on the unconscious level,

---

* For an earlier (i.e., pre-*Intensive Journal* system) discussion, see *The Symbolic and the Real*. As it has developed in the course of *Intensive Journal* practice, the use of Journal Feedback in working with dreams involves many nuances of application considering the range of dream life. I am planning to publish more of the details of this as part of a larger discussion of Journal Feedback.

by indirection, allusion, imagery and symbolism. Our procedures for working with Steppingstones begin at the unconscious level and move through the twilight range until they are brought to consciousness by means of our Journal Feedback exercises. Since the contents of Steppingstones are in the twilight range rather than on the dream level, they are much more accessible to us. Their messages can much more easily be remembered and more clearly be brought to a conscious level where they can be translated into the circumstances of outer life through the varied procedures of Journal Feedback.

For these reasons we have found that the work we do with our Life Steppingstones in the basic *Intensive Journal* program is a very productive way of drawing upon the inner wisdom that dreams would give us if they could. Working with our Spiritual Steppingstones, however, is an even more valuable method since it draws us into contact not only with our personal inner wisdom but with our intimations of a larger wisdom of life.

THE TWILIGHT WAY TO STEPPINGSTONES

This conceptual background should help us understand the procedures we follow in working with our Spiritual Steppingstones. Our first step is to open a new sub-section here in the Connections sections. Leave a few blank pages in the *Gatherings* sub-section so that there will be room for additional entries as further memories are recalled to you. Now we write the heading, *Spiritual Steppingstones*, and today's date, and we are ready to begin.

Bear in mind that one key to working with Steppingstones in any of their aspects in the *Intensive Journal* process is to stimulate the equivalent of the condition of dreaming and yet to remain on the conscious level. To achieve that, it is necessary first to establish the atmosphere of dreams and to place ourselves within it, but without leaving the waking state. To do that, we try to enter the twilight range in a manner that is direct and simple and as free from thoughts as possible. We move into the twilight range in an altogether neutral mode of consciousness, taking special care to influence neither the content nor the direction of movement of our twilight experiences.

We sit in stillness, our eyes closed, our workbook open to the

Spiritual Steppingstones segment. Relaxing, we breathe slowly, slowly, letting the stillness establish itself within us. We have no special thoughts in our mind, but we let ourselves feel the movement of our life. We feel the passage of time, the changes in our life. We do not think about what they are, but we feel the movement that underlies the contents of our lives. We feel the flow of it, and especially we feel the movement of beliefs and our varied reachings toward meaning through the continuity of our inner life. Sitting in stillness, we feel the flow of our inner life. Nothing more specific than its continuity is in our consciousness, just the flow of it, a moving river at the depth of our being. We feel the flow of it, and we let it reflect itself to us in whatever forms of twilight imagery it chooses.

Now we maintain a quiet receptivity. Being in the stillness of the twilight range, we are open to perceive whatever is presented to us, images that we see, sounds or words that we hear, streams of thought that move through us unbidden, intuitions or insights that come to us as flashes of awareness.

Whatever it is that is presented to us—sensory impressions, emotional feelings, metaphors—we observe it and we record it here in the sub-section we have made for Spiritual Steppingstones. All the entries we make now should be simple and factual, recording and describing without embellishment the perceptions and experiences that come to us in the twilight range. We record in this sub-section what is taking place now so that we can incorporate it as part of the process that draws forth and identifies our Spiritual Steppingstones.

Let the experience continue for some minutes in its own quiet rhythm, and when you are ready to come back up you may begin to describe it. It seems to be a good idea, however, not to come up all the way from the twilight range. Come up just far enough so that you are able to write. Let your eyes be only half open. It often happens that the act of describing your experiences has the effect of drawing you back into the twilight range, taking you inward spontaneously this second time more deeply than before. To keep yourself available for this further possibility, come up only part way, open your eyes only part way, when you first record your experiences. Then you will be able to move back inward more easily.

These are the steps that we take in receiving and recording our twilight experiences as they come to us. But first we must enter the twilight atmosphere. Now we sit in stillness, our eyes closed, breathing slowly—and deeply—slower—and deeper. We let the stillness establish itself. In the quietness we let ourselves feel the inner movement of our life. And we let images of every kind reflect themselves to us in the twilight range. We are open and receptive to observe and perceive them as we sit in stillness now, eyes closed, breathing slowly and deeply, in the silence.

*　　*　　*

The experiences we have at this point are introductory to the main work of drawing together our Spiritual Steppingstones. We are establishing the atmosphere in which they can come to us most fluidly and honestly. The best preparation is to record our twilight perceptions as directly and as unself-consciously as possible. Describe whatever presents itself, describing it in terms that are simple and natural to you. No embellishment, No censoring. No interpreting. No self-judging. Just describe and record what is taking place in your feelings and your interior perceptions as your attention is focused in the stillness at the twilight level of your awareness.

A first descriptive entry leading to the work with Spiritual Steppingstones might cover material like this:

> Doing an entrance meditation as preparation for the Spiritual Steppingstones. Became quiet, but nothing happened. Nothing is there. Stayed quiet but with thoughts wandering and wondering why there is nothing. Thought of my life in general. Thought it is nothing. Then I began to feel my life. Saw the church where the family went when I was small. Various memories, not images, just memories of childhood, one after another. I can write them later if I have to.
>
> The memories have stopped and now I see a high mountain with a light at the top. I am climbing up. It is difficult. Now I seem to be at the top. But nothing is there. Nobody. And there is no light here. Just the top of a sort of mountain.
>
> There was a break in the imaging and I found myself running up and down the mountain. Up and down, up and down. I was just doing it, not knowing any reason, just doing it, and becoming exhausted. Finally I had to stop. I am resting. I become quiet at the foot of the mountain.

Sitting quietly at the foot of the mountain. Yes, sitting quietly, and now I think I can list the Steppingstones of my life, of my inner life. Yes, beginning with going to church as a child.

Another person's entry may be:

I became quiet to enter the atmosphere of my Spiritual Steppingstones. But where are they? It feels like I don't have any Spiritual Steppingstones. But that sounds like my head speaking again. That is my old inferiority feelings and my self-judging. I know that I do have a spiritual history. It's just that it isn't a churchy one. I guess I don't have a religious history, but I do have a spiritual history. At least with respect to the meaning of life, if any.

I think about the times I have asked questions about life and death, and about its meaning. The idea comes to me now that I can put my Spiritual Steppingstones as a series of questions that I have asked, asked various people, or just asked life. And questions I am still asking.

I think back to the first question I asked, that I remember. I was three or four or five, I don't know. I was walking on a country road. Where? When I think of it, that will tell me how old I was. My father was with me and we came to a dead squirrel. I asked him what was wrong with the squirrel. Why didn't it run away? My father said, "He's dead."

Then I asked him what being dead means. I guess that's my first Steppingstone.

THE THREAD OF INNER CONTINUITY

The imagery and the memories that were stimulated in us by our preparatory twilight step now enable us to move at a deep level into our task of drawing together our Spiritual Steppingstones. In doing this we follow the principles of the Life Steppingstones exercise that plays a basic role in the Life Context *Intensive Journal* workshops. Here, however, we extend these procedures to the meditative level.

When we work with our Life Steppingstones, we let the multiple events that comprise our life as a whole be consolidated into just a dozen Steppingstones, thereby reflecting the main line of movement in our total existence. Correspondingly, our Spiritual Steppingstones are the main events of our interior life. They reflect the way we seek, and occasionally find, a larger meaning in our personal and human existence. In saying that they are the "main" events, we mean merely that they are the most striking, the most remembered if not necessarily the most memorable, and that they are the most indicative of our continuing, conscious and unconscious quest for interior significance.

In the lives of many persons the quest for meaning is left implicit and unarticulated. This is true not only of persons living in modern times, but was true of those living in earlier, seemingly "religious" periods of history. While the questions and the wonderings are there, the circumstances of outer life in most societies tend to discourage people from giving outer expression to inward sensitivities and to private intimations of truth. In earlier times these personal feelings and experiences were restrained by the pressures of institutionalized traditions and the powers of authority. In modern times they are repressed by the more informal power of the secular materialism of industrial society. There is a great need to balance the repression of personal spiritual experience in society, and that is one of the roles that the *Intensive Journal* work undertakes to fulfil. Our workbook becomes a place where a person's private intimations of meaning can be articulated, respected and explored. More important even than the basic fact of acknowledging our spiritual feelings and treating them as realities, our method gives us a means of working with them in tangible ways so that their intuitions of truth can be nurtured, can be considered, altered, or brought to further development.

The work we began in Gatherings has this general purpose underlying it. It also has the specific purpose of preparing us for the crystallizing step that we take next in identifying our Spiritual Steppingstones.

In Gatherings we recorded as many memories as came to us of the inner or outer episodes that have been part of our quest for meaning. These Gatherings reflect both pleasant and unpleasant phases in our cycles of connective experience. In collecting this inner data, we were in the first place paying respect to our interior life as individuals by recognizing and recording the facts of its experience. In the second place, we were strengthening its intuitions by feeding it into the integrative process that will carry it toward further understanding.

In listing our Spiritual Steppingstones now we use a procedure that enables these facts to draw themselves together and to wind themselves fine so that they can form and can show to us the thread of inner continuity in our lives.

An important facet of the Steppingstones exercise is that it is both spontaneous and selective. In order to carry it out in an atmosphere that is as free as possible from conscious controls, we take ourselves to the twilight level where imagery and the experience of making the list can take place in a spontaneous way. As we do that, we set a ceiling on the number of Steppingstones that can be included in any single list, limiting it to approximately a dozen, give or take one or two. The reason for this limitation is that the functioning of the Steppingstones exercise requires a list that is neither too short nor too long. It should be long enough to include the relevant phases and variations within the life, thus to convey the quality of movement and the cyclical changes taking place. And it should also be short enough to give a compact impression of the tenor of the life as a whole.

While the number of Steppingstones is fixed, the span of time covered by a list of Steppingstones includes the whole life of the individual. Some individuals may therefore have eight or even nine decades to compress into their dozen Steppingstones. And another person may have only two or three decades of experience from which to draw. Each life thus becomes a unit establishing its own context, regardless of its chronological length. The polarity of these two rules creates a tension within the person, and this often leads to unexpected recognitions regarding the individual's life.

You have written your description of your twilight experiences and returned to the atmosphere of silence. Sit in the stillness again, letting yourself feel the overtones of the imagery and metaphors, the thoughts, emotions, intuitions that have come to you. As these settle and establish for you the context of your inner life history, begin the listing of your Spiritual Steppingstones. Let them come to you not so much by your deliberately choosing them as by their presenting themselves to you. As much as possible, let them be written as though by themselves.

The way we discuss and proceed with our Spiritual Steppingstones is different from the more general exercise of listing our Life Steppingstones as we do at a Life Context workshop. For the purposes of the latter exercise we deliberately confine our basic entry for each Life Steppingstone to a few words or a phrase, no more than a sentence.

That is because our primary purpose there is to form a continuity that we can perceive as a unifying thread moving through the variations of our lives. We have another purpose, however, in drawing together our Spiritual Steppingstones. We are interested here too in identifying the line of continuity in the development of our inner life; but we have the additional goal of stimulating our capacity to perceive and to recall the subjective and elusive events that comprise our inner life. Since these experiences are often so ephemeral that we would not believe they happened if we had not recorded them at the time, we have found that it is a helpful practice to elaborate them a bit after we have made our first brief list. We may use just a few words to identify a particular Spiritual Steppingstone; but then we may return to write a sentence or two, even a short paragraph of description and comment filling in each entry. This additional writing has the effect of freeing the flow of our memory so that it evokes more of our subliminal awarenesses and makes them available to us.

You need not be concerned about the chronological order in which your Spiritual Steppingstones come to you. Write them down as they present themselves. After you have collected the basic material you can sort them out and set them in sequence. Reading them back, then, will give you a sense of the continuity of your inner life. You may start by referring to events that took place early in your life; but often we find that events from more recent years are recalled to us first. Record them in the order that they come to you. The main thing is to catch as many perceptions and rememberings as you can while you are in the twilight atmosphere.

As you proceed you will very likely find that the combination of the act of writing and of recalling to consciousness the memory of events that were intensely felt when they originally took place will have the effect of drawing you out of the twilight range. You realize that your conscious mind has been so stimulated that you are no longer in the twilight atmosphere. The Steppingstones are now increasingly being remembered and described at a mental level that is very close to the surface of consciousness.

On that level, you may feel a strong desire to write extensively about the background and content of the Spiritual Steppingstones you have listed. You may sense that there is a flood of details just over the conscious threshold ready to come in now that you are activating these memories. The urge to describe them may be strong, but do not be tempted by it. It is good practice to write a short paragraph for each Spiritual Steppingstone in your list, but not more than that. Do not be drawn off to write more extensively than that at this point in the work. It is more important that you continue with the project of drawing together the list of your Spiritual Steppingstones covering the whole length of your life, and that you conserve your time and your attention so that you can complete it as a single unit from the vantage point of this moment in time. In that way you can get the benefit of a concentrated and focused perception of the movement of our inner life.

There is an additional consideration that is of great importance. By following the sequence of procedures that we have described, we can maintain the dream model that carries the depth principle underlying our work. Thus we make our list of Spiritual Steppingstones in the atmosphere and by the method of *twilight dreaming*. By means of it we may have the inner perceptiveness that is often a quality of dreams, even while we are recording the information at the waking level of consciousness. This is another reason why it is best to concentrate our attention on completing the list of Spiritual Steppingstones without distraction, leaving the elaboration of details for a later time.

If, after you have listed three or four Steppingstones, you find that you have been drawn out of the twilight range, pause, become quiet, and take the steps that will re-establish the twilight atmosphere. Considering that our purpose is to draw together about a dozen Spiritual Steppingstones, it may be necessary for you to pause to recoup yourself two or three times before you have completed this unit of experience. Each time, as you realize that you have been drawn out of the twilight range and up into mental consciousness, become quiet, deepening the stillness for some minutes. Perhaps you will wish to quiet yourself with an entrance meditation, and then let additional Spiritual Steppingstones be recalled to you until your list has brought you up to the present moment. As much as possible we would like our list of Spiritual Steppingstones to be as spontaneous and as undirected as dreamwork. The more it draws unself-consciously from the twilight range, the more it will reflect the propensities and desires in the seed-depth of our lives.

Now we place ourselves in an atmosphere of stillness, feeling the inner movement of our life. Each in our own timing, we are drawing together our Spiritual Steppingstones . . . in the Silence.

*　　*　　*

It may be helpful for us, in reviewing our own list, to have as part of our perspective the Spiritual Steppingstones that occur in the lives of other persons. With this in mind, I include some indicative lists of Spiritual Steppingstones in the following pages. You can see from these how close the interrelationship is between the inner experiences and the external circumstances of our lives. Each life contains the necessities and problems that set the terms of its individual destiny as well as the possibilities of its integrity. For that reason we may not pass judgment on anyone's list of Steppingstones, not another person's and not our own. But we may draw from them a sense of the range of inner and outer events by which human lives reach toward meaning in the modern world.

The Spiritual Steppingstones of R.A.

1. Birth. I was born into an old-fashioned Christian home, and I believed that everything was true just exactly as I was told.
2. Early farm life. Being on the farm as a little girl, I became very close to the animals. I noticed what was natural in them, and I felt there was something spiritual about it.
3. Teen religion. In my teen years I felt very strong natural urges, and these came up against very rigid prohibitions. I identified religion with rules of moral conduct, mostly with restrictions on things I was not allowed to do. At that point I associated religion with rigidity.
4. Rejection. I reject religion. I don't go as far as being an atheist, but I end my religious affiliation.
5. The time of shopping. I feel that something is missing in my life so I go shopping for another religion. At that time I didn't know that Eastern religions existed, or that they were anything more than paganism, so I just shopped all the Christian religions I could find.
6. Conversion. I decide to become a Catholic because it has a religious quality that appeals to me and I feel deeply at home in it.

7. Disappointment. I become disappointed in Catholicism and become non-practicing.
8. Alcohol. I become involved with alcoholism and various drugs. Somehow this seems to be connected with my religious desires, but it is not satisfying. I realize that it is destructive, and when I become ill I manage to stop.
9. Depression. A terrible period of depression. At this time life seems to be a barren desert. All I can think of is that I want to get out of it.
10. A new discovery. I have an inner experience in which I discover the reality of my life beyond all the suffering I have had and all the joy. I realize that I have had more than my share of both, and that my spiritual life is the reality beyond them.
11. Prayer. I learn to pray as a thankful connection to life. It seems strange not to be asking God for favors all the time. But blessings seem to come when I don't ask. This is a time of peace.
12. Christianity. My various inner experiences of Jesus as the Christ. Sometimes these have been too intimate and intense to bear, but it enables me to know how fundamentally I am a Christian. That seems strange to me as I write it. But it is a very warm as well as a surprising feeling.

    I realize also that these feelings of Jesus give me an especial love toward all the non-Christians in the world. I feel freed from the prejudice I was taught as a child. Perhaps that is the love my whole journey has been for. I feel peace.

The Spiritual Steppingstones of M.T.

1. When I was a young man I wondered about life in my philosophy courses, but I was not concerned in a religious way.
2. The first religious feelings I remember came while listening to music, especially Beethoven and later Bach. At that time I became convinced that the truth of life lies in the beauty that the arts can give us. I especially became religiously devoted to music.
3. With the depression of the nineteen-thirties, I felt the pressures of poverty. That was when I concluded that the arts are not sufficient to meet modern problems. I decided that the arts, like religion, are a means of escaping from the economic realities of life.

4. I became a Marxist. It is not too much to say that I undertook my new belief with religious fervor. I became actively engaged.

5. I became embroiled in doctrinaire disputes and changed my allegiance. I still remained a Marxist, but now I was devoted to a particular group within Marxism. Looking back I can see that in my devotion to this sectarian group I was even more religiously devoted than before.

6. I became embroiled in disputes within the party. Charges are brought against me, and I am thrown out of the party. I think it is very unfair, but I am really glad it happened. I think I felt like a religious heretic, and I realize now that I liked the feeling.

7. I become a business man and am quite successful at it. Making money is a kind of religion in itself, and not a bad·one. I find that I like it.

8. I discover psychoanalysis of the classical Freudian type and become involved in five-day-a-week analysis for several years. My business was doing well enough to pay for it.

9. Although I believed in psychoanalysis, I vaguely felt that it was shallow and inadequate. I remained loyal to my various therapists since I felt that they needed me (as I now am convinced they did) and I was beginning to look for new ideas.

10. I continued to search in the spiritual field even while I remained in psychoanalysis. I explored Buddhism and Yoga, but I rarely told my therapist.

11. I became especially interested in Buddhist philosophy and I studied it as much as I could. I was particularly intrigued by the Eastern conception of opposites in life, and it led me to re-examine the dialectical philosophy of Marxism. I thought I might achieve a union of the two philosophies, but instead I reactivated a great many emotional questions from the Marxist phase of my life.

12. I have recently realized that my philosophical studies of Buddhism and Marxism are only on an intellectual level, and that to that degree they are not adequate. Perhaps as a result of those thoughts, I find myself now thinking a great deal about the vanity of human existence, and this in very fundamental terms. Both Buddhism and the Bible speak of it, but I wonder whether it really has an answer. That is why I am now reconsidering the whole of my life history with an open mind.

The Spiritual Steppingstones of Y.P.

1. My family belonged to a church but they only went on holidays.
2. They sent me to Sunday school, but I decided that nobody really believed in it, so I didn't either.
3. When I found out about sex I decided not to take religion seriously.
4. I got onto drugs and went on experimenting from one thing to another. I think I wanted to believe in something, but I didn't know what it was. So I kept on looking.
5. I had some drug experiences that shook me up. I saw the universe breaking open, and many other visionary things. It convinced me there is a reality I didn't know about.
6. My physical condition became very serious, and for the first time in my life I was close to death. I thought I was too young to die and it frightened me. I decided that if I lived I would change my way of living. I did get better, but changing wasn't easy.
7. I found Swami — and did Yoga. That was a help, but I couldn't stay with it.
8. I tried a lot of different teachings, mostly Eastern, Buddhism, Sufi, whatever. I couldn't really understand what was being said but the vibes of the people were good, for the most part. In most places it was like being high, only it was healthier. I didn't have one place to stay, but going to lots of different places made it a good in-between time.
9. I thought I understood what the single reality is and I was really seeking to experience oneness. Then I joined up with R—— and I really made that my dedication.
10. That was four years ago and I have stayed with it. I feel much stronger as a person, but I don't feel any closer to truth. Sometimes I feel very grateful, and sometimes I feel that I have been used. Lately I sometimes think that I have been had.
11. I have dreams now that seem to encourage me to take a further step toward truth. But right now I don't know what that step is. I may have to clear out some old things before I can take a step forward.

As we consider the various lists of Spiritual Steppingstones, we recognize that each person's life is reaching toward meaning in its own way. Each life has its own roots and background conditions, its particular problems and possibilities. The continuing interplay of these gradually forms the unique destiny of each person.

Parallel with the events of our lives, there comes a sense of the meaning of our existence in its personal and in its larger-than-personal aspects. Sometimes the meaning we perceive is clear and definite; sometimes it is uncertain, problematical and changing so that it places the person in a turmoil of inner confusions. A human life may move through all these phases. In listing our Spiritual Steppingstones, we are retracing the varied, sometimes painful path by which our life has moved toward meaning. Now we are in a position to pick up that movement and carry it forward to new understandings and experiences of the issues that our life has given us.

*   *   *

After we have listed our Spiritual Steppingstones, our first step is to sit in silence long enough so that we can re-establish the condition of inner quietness that enables us to work in a twilight atmosphere. Recalling events and experiences that have been important in our life has the unavoidable effect of stirring the emotions that accompanied those earlier occurrences. It is very likely, therefore, that the waters of our inner life have been muddied during the time that we have been listing our Spiritual Steppingstones. But now, returning to stillness, we let the muddiness settle. The waters at the depth of our being become quiet again. In this quietness we read back to ourselves the Spiritual Steppingstones that we have written.

As you read them back to yourself, try, especially at your first reading, to feel the thread of movement that links these experiences. The continuity that moves through the changes and cycles of your inner life may say more to you than any single experience by itself. As you read, consider the unity of its movement, the direction that discloses itself, and the variations that have taken place in the course of your life. And let these considerings work their effect within you. Let them stir you. Observe whatever response they arouse in you, whatever thoughts or feelings or reactions or ideas. Add this to your Spiritual Steppingstones as a further observation.

In order to make this comment as full as it needs to be, you may wish to read the list back to yourself more than once, in different ways and from different vantage points. You may want to read it through quickly at first in order to get an impressionistic sense not only of its movement and tempo but of its composition as a whole. After that you may wish to read it back to yourself more slowly, consciously considering and responding to the specific Steppingstones that you have listed.

For this purpose, when you are working in your privacy, there is a particular value in reading your list of Spiritual Steppingstones into a cassette recorder and then playing it back to yourself. Hearing yourself read the sequence of your inner experiences can add another dimension to your inner response. This is a practice that can be especially helpful at a number of points when you are working by yourself with the *Intensive Journal* methodology. It is also an excellent means of reviewing and extending your experiences after you have participated in a workshop.

The combination of reading aloud and then hearing your list read back in privacy serves not only to stimulate emotional reactions and thus bring up perceptions that were hidden below consciousness but also provides an opportunity to consider more reflectively the various overtones and implications of earlier experiences. You can hear the tone in your voice as well as the unpremeditated tone in your writing. In some cases you may find that once you have recorded your Spiritual Steppingstones you will return to the cassette again and again, playing them back from time to time in order to reach deeper into your spiritual history. Doing this can be especially valuable as we come to the next steps in our work where our practice seeks to evoke new experiences that take us beyond our spiritual history into our spiritual future.

In whatever way you read your Spiritual Steppingstones back to yourself, let yourself feel their import with the fullness of your being. Sitting in silence, you may sometimes read them back to yourself quickly in order to feel their inner movement or you may sometimes read them slowly in order to recognize and consider the implications of particular aspects. Read them as many times as they continue to be meaningful. And each time take note of the old emotions that stir in you, the new emotions that arise, and describe them following your Spiritual Steppingstones.

These additional entries can be as short or as long as feels right and necessary to you. Let each entry be first a response to the composite of your Steppingstones, their movement and place in your life as a whole. And also take note of specific changes and shorter cycles, as well as particular insights and realizations that come to you now. Especially as you read back your Steppingstones, try to be open to perceive the directions in which your inner experience is taking you, for these may not have been explicit and clear to you before. You may see that you have been reaching toward goals and desires of which you were not aware but which now become apparent to you as you read all your Spiritual Steppingstones together as a unit and can see them as a single life unfoldment. The recognitions that may come to you in this way can be very striking, and often full of emotion. Most important, they can be very suggestive in giving you leads for your continuing work in the other sections of your *Intensive Journal* workbook. Record your spontaneous responses as they come to you, and let them expand of themselves. They will very likely provide valuable clues which, as you proceed, will help you select the material with which to focus the next steps in your meditative work.

As you are writing now, you may be reminded of additional events of your past that are meaningful to you for the role they have played in the cycles of connective experience in your life. You may not have thought of them before, but now they are recalled to you. These may be added to the Gatherings segment, which we left in an open-ended state when we began to list our Spiritual Steppingstones. If additional Gatherings come to your mind, record and describe them. This is part of our intermittent and cumulative work of building the resource of our personal spiritual history.

Chapter 12

Re-Openings:
Spiritual Roads Not Taken

THE UNFOLDING THEMES

When we have written our response to reading back our Spiritual Steppingstones and have added to our Gatherings the further memories that it stimulated, we are ready to work in the third segment of the Connections section. We start a new sub-section, writing the title, *Re-Openings,* at the head of a page. We record today's date, and we are ready to proceed.

The purpose of our work in the *Re-Openings* segment is to draw from the experiences of our past the raw materials for the spiritual experiences of our future. We have given ourselves two resources with which to do this. One is the data we collected in Gatherings, memories of the various phases of our connective experiences. The other is the perspective of our inner life as it presented itself to us in our Spiritual Steppingstones. Those two exercises reflect our interior lives from different angles of vision. The Gatherings focus on particular events of our past while the Spiritual Steppingstones present the continuity of our inner life in its ongoing movement. In this sense they are polarities: on the one hand, the individual occurrence and, on the other hand, the encompassing perspective of lifelong movement. They are, however, opposites that balance and complement one another. Because they come from different directions in time, their effect is to activate earlier experiences that had been forgotten or had seemed to have reached a dead end. Now they can be re-entered and explored anew in a larger perspective of time. That is the key to the way we draw upon Gatherings and our Spiritual Steppingstones in the work we now do in the Re-Openings segment.

We begin by sitting in silence, breathing slowly and deeply. We sit relaxed in the silence, not thinking specific thoughts but feeling the atmosphere of our inner life, its cycles and changes as we have been reviewing it and reconstructing it. In the quietness we recall to ourselves the tone of our feelings as, a little while ago, we were reading back to ourselves our Spiritual Steppingstones. We place ourselves again in that atmosphere, and we feel again the responses and the recognitions that arose in us then. Our attention moves increasingly inward, feeling the continuity of our inner lives.

We are in the twilight range of perception now. At a deeper than conscious level we have the freedom to move about now in a large and open atmosphere of inner space and inner time. In the silence we take ourselves back to the Gatherings we described. We let ourselves feel them, simply remembering particular aspects that return to our minds, not directing our thoughts but letting those memories move through us. We do this until we feel that we are in their general atmosphere again. Then we go back to those Gatherings entries to read them once more. In the beginning we read them lightly. We might better say that we are perusing them than that we are actually reading them. We are touching them to re-establish our contact with them and to remind ourselves of their existence and of their content.

We are moving through our Gatherings now, touching them, and observing, as we pass from one to another memory, the emotions that stir in us and the thoughts that come to us. We find that some of our Gatherings arouse particularly strong emotions within us as we turn our attention to those old events and touch them again. Strong feelings may be stirred in us, and an active train of thoughts, rememberings and associations may be set into motion. New ideas, observations and intuitions may then come to us, as well as imagery and symbolic perceptions that may provide the base for new departures in our next experiences. We record the flow of all of these, as they come to us, whatever their form or their content. That is the first entry we make in the Re-Openings segment.

*   *   *

With our next step we can have a further, a more considered response. We can re-approach our Gatherings in the perspective of inner time that we have established with our Spiritual Steppingstones. That will open another range of understanding and another possibility of experience for us.

When we have made our entry describing our spontaneous response to reading back the memories of our inner experiences, we return to our silence. We let ourselves become still again, our breathing slower and deepening, our eyes closed as we return to the twilight range of perception. We sit in stillness some moments, and gradually we focus our attention on the ongoingness, the continuity of movement that we have noted in our inner life. Listing our Spiritual Steppingstones has enabled us to see the unity of that ongoingness. Without seeking to define it specifically, we let ourselves feel the persistence of the elusive, inner thread that has moved through our lives. It helps us identify to ourselves our own private, interior individuality.

Sitting in silence, we recall the uneven sequence of steps by which we have reached toward meaning, holding various doctrines and beliefs in the course of our life. We have moved through cycles in which there were times of intensity with many contents, and times of emptiness when the main characteristic seemed to be an absence of experience. All of these together in their degrees and their many phases have comprised our inner life; now in our silence we let ourselves feel the wholeness of movement, the thread of continuity within it. This becomes a perspective in the background of our mind, and with it we return to touch our Gatherings once again. We go over them lightly, rereading significant parts, and recalling ourselves to the experiences we had described there. We are turning our attention to them now, not from the point of view of our emotions, but in the perspective of the ongoing movement of our inner lives.

As we consider our Gatherings and Steppingstones from this vantage point, we find that certain of our earlier experiences now appear to us in a new light. There have been striking events that have stood forth in our memory as impressive markers of our inner life. In our view of them they possessed qualities that set them apart as distinct moments in our experience. Now, in the perspective of our whole spiritual history, we see that those events are related to others that came at various times in our life. Each of them was so intense or dramatic an experience that we thought of it as being unique and self-contained at the time. Now we can see the connection of these events to one another, observing how a theme is carried in a particular experience, then dropped, and after some passage of time, resumes its development in another event. In this perspective, we find a continuity of connections moving not only through our past experiences but also extending into the possible experiences that lie in our future.

Now we perceive that there are experiences which we had not thought of previously as belonging to our spiritual history but we can see in our present perspective that they have each played their necessary role, however brief, and have each made their small contribution to the whole. As we reconsider the contents of our life in terms of interior continuity, we recognize many more events that belong in our spiritual history. We add them to our Gatherings, taking note both of the specific events and of their broader meanings in our life. We recall:

> Early experiences of disappointments;
> Feeling connected to the changing colors of the leaves in autumn;
> Feeling connected to the rising of the sun, or the renewal of the spring;
> The time when we were not caught in a lie, but knew we had lied;
> Trying to do good works and realizing how complicated that can become;
> Our political ideals, our activities, enthusiasms, frustrations;
> Perceiving the unity of nature in science, and its disunity;
> Experiencing the unity of nature in sexuality, and its disunity;
> Trying various philosophies, and believing them;
> Being disillusioned in a belief, or in a hope;
> Being alone;
> Following a dream and finding it was not what it seemed to be;
> Following a vision that is partially true;
> Intimations of large truths that come in poetry-type statements;

> Observing the imperfectness of life;
> Degrees of understanding of God;
> Experiencing the reality of other people.

Memories of experiences of this kind in their various individual aspects are recalled to us now as parts of our cycles of connective experience. As we record them we realize that the continuity of the whole of our inner life would not have been possible without events that we barely noticed at the time they took place. We may also consider the implications of the fact that some of the most meaningful of these were events that we would have avoided if we could.

Going back over our Gatherings a second time, we proceed in the perspective and by the light of our Spiritual Steppingstones. We find that the new perceptions coming to us now have broader overtones than our first, essentially emotional responses. They form new configurations of understanding we had not seen before. Of particular importance is our recognition that various experiences that have taken place at widely separated times in our life and that we have perceived as separate events distinct from one another were in fact phases of a continuing process unfolding beneath the surface of our consciousness. They were collectively forming a single theme of meaning in our existence. For that reason they have to be considered in contexts that are different from the circumstances that immediately surround them. They are not limited to any single moment in time but are part of *unfolding contexts* that move through all the periods of our life. Even though the individual occurrences took place at points quite distant from one another in terms of *chronological time,* they have to be perceived in terms of units of meaning that are progressively unfolding across *qualitative time.*

As we go back over the Gatherings that we have recorded, we perceive them now as part of the *unfolding contexts* moving through the inner continuity of our lives. We observe how particular events that outwardly seem to be separate are in fact inwardly connected to one another. With brief entries here in the Re-Openings segment, we describe the essential details of these events, but it is the inner continuity that moves through them that is of the greatest importance. We should describe our perception of this as fully as we desire. By means of these entries we gradually weave together the threads of the various mini-

175

processes that comprise the contents of our inner life. As we proceed and as a number of threads accumulate, we begin to see patterns of meaning being formed of which we were not aware before. As we observe them taking shape, we realize that they have been establishing the direction of our individual destiny. They have been prodding us and drawing us, without our being aware of it at the time, toward the next steps of our inner and outer lives; and they have been drawing us especially toward extensions and further developments of our beliefs. It becomes apparent to us now that, while we are here working with events from our past, it is our spiritual *future* that is being formed.

Considering our spiritual history in this perspective leads to another realization. When those inner experiences originally took place in our lives, they were reaching toward a meaning that we did not know. Since our knowledge of them was incomplete, we could respond only to a part of their possibilities, perhaps a small part. Other possibilities that might have led us to a larger sense of meaning and to a deeper understanding were necessarily passed by. We did not know of their existence, or we were not able to explore them, and thus they have remained unlived and unexperienced.

These are the interior roads not taken in our lives. They contain the possibilities of connective experience that we never followed through to find and develop. And yet these may be the essential opportunities that we missed in the earlier phases of our personal spiritual history. When we read the individual events of our Gatherings against the background of our spiritual history as a whole, we can identify the interior roads that were not taken earlier and the possibilities that may still be available to us. In this Re-Openings segment we can return to those events in order to explore the spiritual roads that were not taken earlier. And as we carry what we find here into the further practices of our Process Meditation work, we may reclaim what might otherwise have been the lost opportunities of our inner life.

We come then to a practical question: How can we know which spiritual roads not taken earlier in our lives will lead to valuable experiences and to a larger sense of meaning if we explore them now? Not every road that was not taken earlier is worth taking now. In most cases the decisions that we originally made, choosing one and rejecting the other, were for good reasons that are still valid in our lives. In some cases, however, circumstances have changed and important understandings that we could not have conceived at the time may now be waiting for us to find in doctrines we rejected long ago.

But how shall we locate them? How shall we find which roads not taken in the past are worthwhile exploring at this point in our life?

When we reconsidered our Gatherings in the light of our Spiritual Steppingstones, we were able to see that many of our memories were part of a larger continuity of events. Certain issues or concerns were present in our experiences and would re-appear from time to time. They contained themes that surfaced again and again in our inner experience. These recurrences indicate that, for whatever combination of reasons, our life intuition perceives that these issues are strongly relevant to the further development of our consciousness. They have an inner importance for our lives, and thus the inner wisdom that is present at the depth of our lives repeatedly calls them to our attention.

The fact of the recurrence of particular themes of experience also leads us to the realization that there is a difference between our more recent experiences and those that came in earlier years. Very often we find that among our earlier experiences there were some that possessed a marked intensity and validity for us. Indeed, it is very often the strength of an early experience that sets us onto a particular path of involvement, as we seek larger meanings within the terms it set. The fact, however, that it was an early experience usually implies as well that we had not attained at that time a sufficient capacity to appreciate the issues that were implicit there. We may therefore have been very much impressed and influenced by the experience, but there were aspects of it, or implications of it, that we were not equipped to absorb, or to understand, or to act upon. We therefore let those aspects of the experience pass us by. Although they possessed great significance, we either did not recognize the significance of those side-aspects of our experience, or we ourselves were not in a spiritual position to act upon them. They therefore became spiritual roads not taken in our life. They may have contained the possibility of taking us to great profundities of spiritual awareness, but we were not able or willing to take or to see those possibilities at that time.

Ordinarily when we have had a moving inner experience at an early point in our development, we remember the event itself, but we are not concerned with the "road not taken" aspect of it. We may not even be aware that that side of it exists. As we become increasingly aware, however, of the spiritual continuities moving through our inner life, we recognize the large concerns for which we have spontaneously been seeking further understanding at a deeper-than-conscious level in the course of our life. Inevitably it becomes clear to us that while our early experiences may have possessed great intensity, they also possessed less understanding of the deeper issues than we have available now. We can appreciate the fact that in those earlier experiences there may well have been aspects that were beyond our ken so that they had to remain spiritual roads not taken. But we might now be in a position to learn a great deal from them if we could take those roads now.

The primary guidance that we can follow, therefore, is to identify, in the perspective given us by our Spiritual Steppingstones, the themes and concerns that recur in a sequence of experiences through the continuity of our inner life. Their persistence calls our attention to the lines of inner process, the various cycles of connective experience, to which we should return in order to find the spiritual roads not taken that might appropriately be taken now. As we go back into those earlier experiences we look to see whether, in addition to the intensity of the events themselves, they contain any implications that were beyond us at that time but which we might be able to understand now. That is one guideline in identifying which spiritual roads may be worthwhile exploring now.

Sometimes the issues that call our attention to the spiritual roads not taken in our life are not first stated in religious or philosophical terms. They are simply events in our life experience, and we do not at first perceive them as having a spiritual significance. Only after we have worked in the broader context of our Spiritual Steppingstones do we realize that they possess large implications, and it is then that we are alerted to look for the factor of meaning in earlier events. When we look, we recognize that something important is there. We also realize that the distance of time has separated us from the reality of the original experience. We are no longer in its atmosphere, and its atmosphere is no longer within us. We do, however, have the intuition that if we could restore our sense of the presence of that experience once again, additional events of connection and awareness would take place for us. If we approach these as spiritual roads not taken, it is not in the sense of opportunities that we have missed but as further experiences that have not yet taken place and which we now can open as new possibilities. It is with this purpose that we carry out the exercises of the Re-Openings segment in order to place ourselves back in the atmosphere of earlier experiences.

MOTHER OF EARTH AND OF LOVE

Let us follow the sequence of T.F.'s experiences to see some of the actualities that may be involved as we take the steps of working in Re-Openings.

One of the important events of T.F.'s personal history was the sudden death of his mother while he was in college. Although it was a shaking event, he had absorbed it in time and had continued to build his life. In his forties he came to a transition point involving both his career and his personal relationships, and it was then that he became engaged in the *Intensive Journal* work.

At the Life Context workshop where he made his basic listing of his Life Steppingstones, he naturally included the unexpected death of his mother as an event that had a major effect on his existence. At the Process Meditation workshop, however, he did not include it in the listing of his Spiritual Steppingstones since he thought of it as a strictly personal occurrence. He placed the material that dealt with his mother and his relation to her in the *Dialogue with Persons* section.*

While listing his Spiritual Steppingstones as part of his Process Med-itation work, however, he made the more general entry, "Questions of death and ongoing life," to describe one of the concerns of his inner life. Reading that back to himself in preparation for the Re-Openings exercise and considering the entries he had made in Gatherings, he realized that the questions he was asking about death and immortality were not limited to a single event in his life. They involved issues that had appeared to him at numerous times over the years, sometimes as a result of outer circumstances, sometimes as part of inner experiences. That recognition now led him to recall and to record additional mem-ories in relation to that Spiritual Steppingstone. After reading back and reconsidering his Spiritual Steppingstones, he added to his Gatherings various memories that he would not previously have considered to be part of his spiritual history:

* See *At a Journal Workshop*, Chapter 12.

The sudden death of my mother when I was in my late teens threw me into shock, but I tried to respond in a "rational" way. I was beginning to read philosophy at the time, and I remember referring to Schopenhauer and talking as a cynic about life and death, as Schopenhauer would. I also remember having feelings of a great extension of life, and thinking there was something profound to be understood about death. I did not quite know what that was, but I had vague feelings that in some way my mother's death would show me. I also remember feeling that I was under too much pressure at the time to deal with such complicated issues, so I just let it go and did not explore it further at that time.

Another Gathering:

About a year after my mother's death, I wandered by accident into the church of a spiritualist religious group. A seance type of reading was taking place as I walked in, and because I was young and a stranger, the lady giving the reading looked up from her Bible and turned her attention to me. I was amazed when, never having seen me before, she told me that my mother had died not long before. And then she assured me that I was being protected by my mother "from the other side." I neither believed it nor disbelieved it; but I did feel some truth in it. I think I acted afterwards as though I believed it.

Another Gathering:

Sitting in a rowboat on a small lake some years later. Sitting alone, just drifting under the shadow of the trees. No one else around. Suddenly a sense of nature comes over me. I feel connected to the world of nature and I have the inexplicable feeling that nature is my mother, my own mother. For some minutes I feel the presence of my mother, very close and very personal. It was a very warm and intimate, a very protected feeling. It was very personal and also much more than personal.

At the time of his mother's death, while he was living through the trauma of the sudden separation, he had also had the feeling that much more could be shown to him if he were able to handle it emotionally and if he were able to assimilate it intellectually and spiritually. But that was not the right time. He felt that he was under too much strain because of the pressure of events to be able at that time to absorb a profound new teaching or understanding about the mysteries of life and death. Therefore some other time; not now, but later sometime.

T.F.'s experience of postponing a deeper meeting with truth is quite common in the spiritual histories of many persons. "The world is too much with us," with its pressures of things that have to be done immediately, so that there are always valid reasons available to explain why we cannot deal with the profounder issues of life at the present time. We are, of course, very interested in dealing with them sometime later, whenever we shall have time. But the world is always too much with us, unless we discipline ourselves specifically to make the time. One of the functions of our Process Meditation work is to end our postponing by giving us a method and an atmosphere that enables us to work at deepening our inner experience while we are in the midst of the outer activities of our lives, Our work in Re-Openings is a means of moving deeper into those truths that we glimpsed in our earlier experiences but that we did not stay to learn of more deeply at the time.

Given the context of his Spiritual Steppingstones and the additional Gatherings that were recalled to him, there were two steps for T.F. to take in his Re-Openings work. The first step involved his re-entering the situation that immediately followed his mother's death, especially since he had the intuitive feeling at the time that there remained more for him to learn about the meaning of the death of his mother. Further understanding was waiting for him, he felt, whenever he would give the subject more time and attention. The second step involved his experience on the lake when nature and his mother became inseparable for him. Each of these events was an intersection in the continuity of his inner experience. The road of his life had taken him to the point of a choice. There were two roads to take. He took one and left the other untaken. If he wishes now at this point in his life, much later in time and circumstance, to learn the knowledge that lay on the road not taken, he must come back to the original road and proceed with it up to the point of the intersection. Then he can continue along the road he did not take before. Those are the steps we follow in the work of Re-Openings.

Let us take these steps with T.F. He is going to return to the time in his life immediately following his mother's death. He is going to re-enter the situation and let it continue to open itself anew.

He begins by sitting in quietness. His eyes closed, he feels himself to be back in the events that followed his mother's death. There were the initial shock and the feelings of disorientation. There were the emotions shared with relatives, but he was too numb then to feel the emotions. At that time he was mechanically saying things to relatives who were trying to comfort one another. But he did not really know what to say.

Re-entering the experience in his silence, T.F. recalls this and he begins to feel again the emotional exhaustion he felt at that time. Eyes closed, he is back again with the mourning relatives. Finally they leave, and he begins to feel alone and quiet. Now he can re-enter the experience in a way that takes him toward the depth of it.

The original event returns. He is there again in the room, in the silence. He has realized and assimilated the event that has taken place. And now he is feeling its implications. What else does it mean? Questions are being asked, and it is as though someone is speaking. That is how it was. Someone is speaking now in the silence. Things are being said about the nature of such experiences in people's lives. He is told that they happen all the time. But there is much more to it than meets the eye. There is more to be said.

Now T.F. has gone all the way down the original road to the intersection, to the point where the new road begins. Moving in the twilight range of perception, he is making it possible for twilight memory to re-open old events in order to move through them and beyond them. Now the original situation is re-established, the atmosphere is there, the experience is being re-opened. T.F. is within it, and now, in the twilight range, it can proceed of itself. It can now bring forth as much as it wishes to provide at this time.

T.F. will record in his Re-Openings segment all that takes place as his experience continues. Later he will turn to other sections of his workbook and describe there the special aspects of the material that has come to him in his Re-Openings experience. In the Process Meditation sections as well as in the other *Intensive Journal* exercises he will feed this information into the context of his life as a whole, and he will work with it in relation to other experiences that have come to him at other times. But more of this as we proceed.

* * *

In his Gatherings T.F. had recorded a second memory which he can now re-enter. He can now return to his experience on the lake in order to re-open the events that were taking place there, to see if they are ready to carry him further along the road that was not taken.

Once again T.F. places himself in a condition of quietness. His eyes are closed, and he is drifting into the twilight range of perception. The memory situation is establishing itself, and it is placing him within it. He is on the lake, in the rowboat in the quiet place under the trees. It is memory, and he is perceiving it on the twilight level. Now the feelings and the tone of the original connective experience return to him. It is memory and more than memory. It is the re-opening of the original event. The original happenings return here on the twilight level. They re-establish themselves as they were, but something additional also becomes present. In re-opening the event, it becomes possible for the experience to move beyond itself and to open the way for further interior events. This is the enlargement of connective experience toward which our exercise of Re-Opening is reaching.

In the silence of *twilight memory,* T.F. lets himself again be drifting in the rowboat. The atmosphere of the situation returns and his sensitivity to the largeness and intimacy of nature becomes present again. There is the feeling of being close to all the natural world, of being supported and sustained by it. It is a feeling of encompassing peace, and of connection to both the animate and the inanimate realms.

Now an additional awareness becomes part of the situation as T.F. feels his mother to be present. She is there in the twilight space as she was at the boatside, hovering in the atmosphere, a presence, but not speaking. There is the increasing feeling that the world of nature and the world of the mother are not separate. In some way they are intimately connected to one another. It is a personal connection, and also more than personal. T.F. has a strong sense now of the personal qualities of his mother. He feels that, as they are being presented to him, they are being somewhat idealized with an emphasis on nurturing love and warmth and bountifulness. But he affirms it all. It is a personal reconnection and a connection with the world. Nature and mother are felt as one, but mother is personal also. She exists and is present. But her existence is now for T.F. a truth that is greater than her personal being. The phrase comes to T.F.: "Mother of earth and of love." He feels the two realms brought together in a unity with a great surging of warmth and emotion within him. He is connected to the world of nature which is impersonal; he is connected to his mother, which is a very personal feeling. And the two are one. He is personally connected to the larger universe.

"Mother of earth and of love." It seems like the first line of a poem, but T.F. also realizes that it is a mantra/crystal. In Part IV of this book—in the exercises that follow this chapter—we shall have the experience of working with mantra/crystals and seeing the active role they play in our Process Meditation work. T.F., however, was already familiar with the use of mantra/crystals. He therefore recognized what it was when the phrase came to him, and he also recognized that, as a mantra/crystal, it would serve as a starting point for him in the further steps he would take in his inner experience.

T.F. could see the several ways in which his work in Re-Openings led beyond itself. By re-entering his earlier experience on the level of twilight memory, he could establish contact both with the past and with the future, enabling his experience to move by its own momentum along interior roads that had not been taken before. He could thus have access to areas of inner experience that had been closed off before. Now they were open, and with them came the possibility of further experiences not only within this phase of the Process Meditation work but in other Journal sections and exercises.

In particular, one part of T.F.'s experience, the phrase, "Mother of earth and of love," would provide a starting point for further practice in the *Mantra/Crystal* section. And beyond that, the experiences that were re-opened here would draw forth material for a progressive enlargement of spiritual contact along various avenues in the *Peaks, Depths and Explorations* section. While we may begin by re-entering a single inner experience that calls to us from our past, we find that the work we do in Re-Openings reconnects us to inner resources which then unfold from experience to experience, providing energies and understandings that emerge unexpectedly out of their own depths. Our Re-Opening experiences often become pivotal points in our personal evolution because they provide the channel by which past experience leads to further experience in building our spiritual history.

PART IV
Mantra/Crystals

Chapter 13

Modalities
for Next Experiences

In working with our individual spiritual histories, we have been recalling to ourselves the experiences in which an awareness of meaning, and/
or a contact with the larger aspect of reality, has entered our lives.
Whatever the form or the degree of these experiences, whatever the
doctrines or the symbols by which they came to us, they have been the
moments when we have been able to recognize our life as belonging in a
more-than-personal context.

The intensity of these interior events was so great that they impressed us as being unique happenings in our life, complete unto themselves. As we consider them, however, we realize that by no means were
they end-points finalizing our beliefs. No matter how convincingly
meaningful they were at the time they took place, more is implicit in
them: a further possibility to which they can lead in time. In this sense,
no matter how profound and complete it has seemed to us in the past,
every connective experience is also a seed experience for further knowings and contactings that can open to us by means of it. Although these
experiences are now part of our spiritual history, their value is in what
they can contribute to our spiritual *future*. We require a means of
working with these past experiences of our inner life so that they are not
left as end-points but can serve as starting-points and can lead to new
experiences.

A major task of every methodology of the creative life, whether in the field of religion or in the arts or sciences, is determining how it can make the bridge between the last experience and the next experience, and how it handles what happens in between. Various persons coming from different directions have developed ways of approaching this issue, and have developed a valuable resource upon which we can draw. There are three that are particularly relevant for our work in Process Meditation. The first is the way of the Russian Pilgrim; the second is the way of the wise, old Lao Tse; the third is a working hypothesis that has emerged from Holistic Depth Psychology with implications not only for religious experience but for the larger range of creativity as well. We shall now consider each of these briefly, observing the modality of process that is at work in each of them. Then we shall proceed to our work with mantra/crystals which serves as the pivot between past and future in the practice of Process Meditation.

THE RUSSIAN PILGRIM AND
THE PRAYER THAT PRAYS ITSELF

One person who tested in his own experience a *process-model* for the inner life is the anonymous Russian Pilgrim. He pursued his quest for spiritual connection in the context of Greek Orthodox Christianity and he recorded his efforts in a book that is becoming a mystical classic, *The Way of a Pilgrim.**

Many modern readers will be familiar with the Russian Pilgrim from J. D. Salinger's popular novel, *Franny and Zooey.*** In that tale of a modern American schoolgirl who is desperately looking for an inner principle that can guide her through her time of confusion, Salinger created a realistic parable of the modern quest for spiritual security. His heroine, Franny, tries to use the Russian Pilgrim's techniques as a means of maintaining her mental stability. She turns to them seeking a source of strength, but her efforts are fruitless if not altogether disastrous.

Working with the Pilgrim's methods, as Salinger pointedly and

* *The Way of a Pilgrim,* translated from the Russian by R. M. French, Harper & Brothers, New York, 1952.
** J.D. Salinger, *Franny and Zooey,* Little, Brown & Co., and Bantam Books, New York, 1961.

accurately describes her, Franny falls into a swoon. But that is readily understandable. The gap between the context of the Pilgrim's experience and the context of her life was very great, and since she had no intermediate experience with which to make the bridge, she collapsed under the internal pressure. The Pilgrim's way of spiritual practice was not related to anything of significance in her life, neither to her cultural nor to her personal existence. Franny's use of the Pilgrim's method therefore made her exceedingly vulnerable. She had used a technique for stimulating the depth of her consciousness without first establishing a place for it in the context of her life as a whole. Since she was attempting her spiritual practice without adequate preparation, there was nothing in which it could take root.

The Russian Pilgrim had a difficult existence, but he fared much better than Franny with respect to his interior life. After a personal misfortune that probably involved the premature death of his wife, this simple anonymous peasant of mid-nineteenth century Russia devoted himself to seeking an ongoing spiritual contact. The manuscript from which we know of his life and his efforts was found in a monastery but with no precise information accompanying it as to who he was or when he lived. All that we know about him we have to surmise from his text. Although he had the substantial attainment for his time and place of being able to read and write he was otherwise an unlettered man. He did possess, however, a very earnest spiritual disposition, so earnest, in fact, that he took seriously and literally the New Testament injunction in Paul's letter to the Thessalonians that a person should "pray without ceasing." When, however, the Russian Pilgrim tried to fulfil that commandment, he found that it was beyond his capacity. He did not know how. He therefore undertook as his special task a pilgrimage of walking across Russia inquiring wherever he could and seeking to discover a method by which he could learn to pray without ceasing.

In his seeking this, we should note, the Pilgrim by no means had a simplistic understanding of prayer. He did not mean by prayer the rote recitation of ritual formulas, nor the repeated request of special favors from God. Prayer rather meant to the Pilgrim a special condition of being, an inner state of unity, freed from the interventions of his conscious ego, in which the ground of his being was connected with and at-one-with the abiding reality of God.

It is apparent from his writing that the Pilgrim had known from time to time the experience of feeling himself to be intimately connected to God. But that state of unity had not lasted. It had been subject to a cyclical movement. He had been in a state of prayer, in a state of intimate relation with God, and then he had lost it. The condition of unity had ceased to be. And the desire of the Pilgrim was to have a method by which the state of unity with God would not be lost to him but would be maintained as a reality of his experience. That was why he wished to learn to "pray without ceasing."

In his chronicle, the Russian Pilgrim tells of his efforts and his experiences as he walked across Russia in humility of spirit seeking an answer to his question. In the course of his search, he met a monk on the road and told him what he was seeking. The monk turned out to be a man of spiritual learning familiar with the *Philokalia*, the Greek Orthodox collection of texts of mystical wisdom and practice. As the Pilgrim interpreted it, that was a providential meeting. He describes how the monk took him into his cell and taught him from the *Philokalia* the doctrine that "The continuous interior Prayer of Jesus is a constant uninterrupted calling upon the divine Name of Jesus with the lips, in the spirit, in the heart." * He told him the words of the prayer. In the Greek, which is undoubtedly the language in which the prayer was recited, it is *Kyrie Eleison*, which is a seven-syllable mantra phrase, as it is in English when it is translated as "Lord Jesus Christ have mercy." Sometimes in English the words, "on me a sinner," are added, but they are not inherent in the Jesus Prayer.

The monk read from the *Philokalia* the instructions given in the passage by St. Simeon the New Theologian. "Sit down alone and in silence. Lower your head, shut your eyes, breathe out gently and imagine yourself looking into your own heart. Carry your mind, i.e., your thoughts, from your head to your heart. As you breathe out, say, 'Lord Jesus Christ have mercy on me.' Say it moving your lips gently, or simply say it in your mind. Try to put all other thoughts aside. Be calm, be patient, and repeat the process very frequently." **

The phrase, "very frequently," was soon made more specific by the monk who now became the Pilgrim's *starets*, his spiritual teacher. "Start to say the prayer three thousand times a day." He was actually to count to three thousand but the discipline of counting the times of saying the

* *The Way of a Pilgrim*, p. 8.
** *The Way of a Pilgrim*, p. 10.

phrase under his breath was not the ultimate goal of the method. The goal was to go beyond counting and to reach a point where the Jesus Prayer would be said continuously and without pause through all the hours of his life.

Once he had mastered that discipline, the prayer would not abate during strenuous physical activities. It would not abate during sleep. It would not abate even when he was talking with another human being. According to the *Philokalia*, as the prayer was said continuously it progressively developed its own power. Increasingly it moved by its own momentum. It became, in the language of another anonymous spiritual, the fourteenth century English monk of *The Cloud of Unknowing*, a "prayer that prays itself."

The Pilgrim's basic and difficult task was learning to repeat the prayer so constantly that it repeated itself without his having to think about it. After that it was present as though it were part of his body, part of the circulation of his blood or the beating of his heart. There were times when he lost that constancy of the prayer, but he was invariably able to re-establish it. And it provided the encompassing atmosphere of his life, undergirding and sustaining whatever actions he was called upon to take.

The fact is that the Pilgrim was not called upon to take many striking actions or to make many strong decisions. A few months after he had mastered his method of meditation, his *starets* died, and the Pilgrim was back on the road again. Now, however, he was not seeking a new teaching as he had been before, for he felt that he had found what he had been seeking. Now he was simply living his life, walking through the Russian wilderness, studying the *Philokalia*, and continuing to use his unceasing prayer as the foundation of his being. From time to time he would have an adventure, as when he was beset by robbers and his copy of the *Philokalia* was stolen, or when he mysteriously lost the use of his legs. But each time something wonderful happened to enable him to overcome his troubles, like having his *Philokalia* returned to him, or finding a peasant who was able to cure his illness. In each case the Pilgrim was certain that his great good fortune came from the fact that he continued to say "that ceaseless spiritual prayer that is self-acting in the heart." *

* *The Way of a Pilgrim*, p. 18.

It is clear that the "self-acting" quality of the Jesus Prayer contributed a great energy and atmosphere of wisdom to the Pilgrim's life. We have also to recognize, however, that the conditions of his daily existence were markedly different from that of persons in the modern world. The events that filled the Russian Pilgrim to rejoicing were exceedingly simple when compared with the requirements and pressures of modern urban existence. Since his experiences took place within a very sparse cultural environment, we may have to concede that the Pilgrim's way may be limited primarily to a monastic type of life or to small communities in which all persons share a single framework of beliefs and traditions. The complexity and diversity of the secular, cosmopolitan society of modern times does not appear to provide congenial grounds for the Pilgrim's lifestyle and practices. Nonetheless there are elements in the Pilgrim's way that form a core of spiritual method and express fundamental principles that may be relevant for the modern world as well.

How shall we state the essence of the Pilgrim's way, considering it as a modality of subjective process and seeing it as contributing to a general methodology for the inner life? Underlying his approach was the recognition that mental consciousness cannot by itself give us a connective experience. The Pilgrim had already tried to achieve his unitary contact by the fervor of his belief, by the intensity of his desire and his will, by the powers of thought and the use of the mind. But none of these had availed, and thus he was forced literally to go on the road for his search.

The essence of his practice of the Jesus Prayer lies in the fact that at the point where the prayer took over within him and became "a prayer that prays itself," the mind of the Pilgrim, his will, and even his beliefs were superseded. The tone and quality of his being, then, was set at a level of his life over which he no longer had conscious control. In terms of the concepts we are using here, it was set at the twilight range of consciousness, and it was carried by an energy that moved at that level. The experience of the Russian Pilgrim makes it clear that the technique of regularly repeating a phrase in a fixed rhythm in conjunction with our breathing is able to establish an inner condition that is governed neither by the ego, nor the will, nor by the analytic intellect. It is centered, rather, in the twilight range of awareness. Thus an atmosphere is established in which a person feels connected to and supported by larger-than-personal powers of life. The combination of this atmosphere with the dedicated repetition of the phrase seems to have additional consequences, including a helpful and sustaining power in the conduct of one's life. That is why the Russian Pilgrim believed that his occasional good fortune in the face of adversity was in some way a result of his continuing to say the Jesus Prayer without ceasing.

One question we must ask is whether the power lies in the prayer itself or in the unremitting repetition of the prayer. The answer seems to lie in a combination of the two, and that takes us to the heart of the Pilgrim's method. Two factors are important. The first is the content of the phrase, or prayer, and the way that it is felt or perceived by the person. The second is the way that the phrase is used repetitiously.

It is apparent that the Jesus Prayer is no ordinary phrase. It carries multiple levels of meaning as well as emotional identifications that connect the individual to centuries of inner experience. It is equally apparent that the Jesus Prayer cannot be a relevant phrase for everyone since its meaning is contained within the culture of Christianity. People who have lived outside of that culture and who have absorbed other traditions into the subliminal levels of their consciousness will require another phrase. It is also true that the Jesus Prayer will not be an effective or appropriate phrase for many persons who have been brought up within the culture of Christianity but for whom the phrase will not have an inner relevance. We can see that there are a number of aspects to the question of what is the right or valid phrase for an individual to use. There needs to be an inner connection between the person and the phrase that is being used. But we need not assume that it has to be a firm or doctrinal belief. It may be that the connection between the person and the phrase is a linkage on the level of emotion; or it may be that the phrase carries a life-intuition, an intimation that a larger meaning is to come by means of the experience of that phrase.

It is clear also that it will not work, that it will not be effective, if chosen for external reasons. It will do no good to choose a phrase because one had learned it by rote during childhood. But if it is deeply felt and experienced by the person, that is another matter. In that case, childhood teachings and traditions have a reinforcing effect which should be honored. Further, it will do no good to accept a meditation phrase simply to comply with the authority of the spiritual teacher who has assigned it. It must come authentically out of the life of the person, not directed by the conscious ego nor by the emotions of will or conscious desire, but as an honest evolution of the individual's own inner experience.

Given a phrase that is appropriate for the individual, as the Jesus Prayer was for the Russian Pilgrim, consistent repetition can prove to be a highly effective practice. It tends to neutralize the factors of ego, wilfulness and mental consciousness. It establishes perception at the twilight level. And it brings about the progressive deepening of the interior atmosphere in which connective experiences can take place.

We can see that the practice of the Russian Pilgrim, derived as it was from the *Philokalia,* contains at its core an effective and subtle modality of subjective process. It will be valuable for us to bear in mind the way the Pilgrim's process operated for him, and also to consider the implications it has for us. It has a significant contribution to make to our modern practice.

THE RHYTHM OF ACTIVE AND PASSIVE

The saying attributed to Lao Tse that "Muddy water, let stand, becomes clear," has played an important role in the *Intensive Journal* work. As a metaphor of life it carries an implicit philosophy; more specifically, it carries a sense of timing in human experience. It refers to the conditions in life and the way they change and move into one another.

Lao Tse's saying suggests a way of positioning oneself in relation to change. It is both passive and active, but a person cannot be both passive and active at the same time. The opposites alternate, but the changes take place at a deeper than conscious level. To be in harmony with the movement of opposites in the cycles of experience requires much more than a conscious decision or a desire to do so. It requires an inner event that happens to us. We cannot just do it but we can act in such a way outwardly and inwardly that it becomes possible for it to happen to us.

"Muddy water, let stand, becomes clear." But how did the water become muddy? And how can it become clear? In the course of the activities of our life, many inner events, the concerns, the thoughts, the projects, the beliefs, the fulfillments, the disillusionments, the emotions of many kinds, all come into the waters of our inner being. These thoughts and feelings are separate from the water, but they are inherent parts of our life. As they accumulate in the course of our life experience, they have the effect of beclouding the waters, both by the simple fact of their being there and by their movements back and forth. The waters become muddied by the many contents and activities of our lives.

We might first think that the solution would lie in removing the contents of the water. Then the water would always be clear. The fact is, however, that without the contents, we would have no life. It would therefore be self-defeating. The waters would be clear, but they would have no purpose.

In the entrance meditation of *The Well and the Cathedral,* the symbol of the muddy water moved to a further phase, fulfilling the larger image. It became quiet and it became clear. When the waters were still, the debris of activity, the results both of the person's activity within the mind and the activity out in the world, could settle to the bottom. The muddiness gradually disappears. The waters become clear, progressively more placid and lucid until they become still as a quiet lake. Now it is peaceful. Nothing is there. At first when we look into the waters, they are transparent. They are clear, but all we can see is the water. As we sit in the stillness, merely gazing into it, the water becomes like a mirror to us. Images appear in it, images of many kinds. Some of the images are reflections of things that are outside of the water; others are reflections of things, and especially of qualities, that are within it, that are within us. They are in the depth of the water; they are in the depth of us. The quietness has brought a strikingly new situation into existence.

In the time of activity, we were engaged in doing things and the waters of our life became increasingly muddied. Now, in the stillness, it is not only that the muddiness settles but that a further source of information is brought to us. Through the clarity of the waters, images are shown to us that are in fact reflections of various aspects of our life. The images that we see in the waters are the symbolic forms by which the contents of our existence are reflected to us. We see images reflecting the external realm of life, images reflecting the inner depths of our being, and we see a large number of images reflecting the intermediary realm in which emotions and twilight perceptions relate our inner and outer worlds to one another. We find that the qualities and contents of our life are reflected to us in the symbolic forms of imagery. As we learn to perceive them, and as we recognize the messages that are being mediated to us by means of their symbolism, we gain access to a varied source of information for use in our life.

Now let us observe the way the rhythm moves with respect to the alternation of opposites in our life. When we were actively engaged in our life, many things accumulated in the waters of our inner being until those waters became muddied. The psychological equivalent of that is simply to say that we became confused. Because of the turmoil in our life, the water became clouded so that we could not see the images reflected in it. That meant that we were deprived of our inner source of information, and without its inner guidance our life came to a condition of stalemate. It is thus that the activities of life bring about a muddiness which forces the movement to come to a stop. A condition of quiet is then established. It may not come about voluntarily, but the net result is an absence of movement.

When our life becomes so muddied that we are brought to a stop, we have a choice before us. We can refuse to acknowledge it and struggle to keep the activity in motion; or we can accept the stoppage as part of the natural rhythm of our life and we can regard it as a message for our life. If we make the latter choice, we place ourselves in a position to follow Lao Tse's way. Since activity has muddied our life, we now become inactive. We take a passive, a waiting stance toward life so that the muddy waters can settle and become clear.

What will happen then? We sit in stillness. We have at our disposal a number of different techniques for quieting the movement of our mind and emotions so that all those thoughts and desires, plans and hopes and anxieties can come to rest. The Mantra/Crystal practices which we shall soon be describing can be helpful in this regard; so also can the entrance meditations of *The Well and the Cathedral*, and especially the meditation from the *Star/Cross*:

> Letting the Self become still,
> Letting the thoughts come to rest,
> Letting the breath become slow.
> Breathing becomes quiet,
> Breathing becomes slow,
> And slower;
> Breathing becomes regular,
> Regular.

195

> The uneveness
> Of nonessential thoughts
> Drops out of the breathing.
> It becomes
> The breathing of the Self.

As we sit, breathing slowly in that stillness, the muddiness of the waters within us begins to settle. The waters become clear as the atmosphere around us deepens in its silence. The waters are quiet and clear, transparent as we look into them. Now the waters become as a still lake, and the lake becomes as a mirror. As we look into it, images appear to us. These images are reflections to us both of the external circumstances of our life and of knowings that are in the depth of us. They are all reflected to us in symbolic forms, and we perceive them in the quiet waters.

These images that we perceive, what do they say to us, what shall we do with them? These images may carry the ideas for our next project. They may carry the emotions for our next friendship. They may carry the energies for our next activity. We were brought to the condition of stillness by a stoppage, a confusion, an apparent failure in the conduct of our life. Our activity came to a standstill, and thus we were forced into the opposite position. Activity stopped, and thus we found ourselves brought to a passive state.

We remain in this state, and we let the silence deepen. The muddy condition within us settles, our inner being becomes clear. We become like the still waters of a quiet lake, as images reflecting the surface and the depth of our life are presented to us. Knowledge we need to know, ideas we have long been seeking, come to us. They come in symbolic form, but in our quiet atmosphere their meaning is apparent to us. Now we have ideas for new projects, guidance for new tasks to fulfil. We are back in motion. The stoppage is over. The time of being in a passive stance is ended; indeed, it is reversed. We are active again. And most significant of all, we are able to be active again just because we were profoundly quiet. In that silence the effects of our last period of activity could settle so that we could inwardly become clear again as a quiet lake. In the mirror of those still waters, the contents, ideas and the energies for new activities were given us. And thus we were propelled from within out of the silence from our passive stance back into our active life again.

We may assume that we shall continue along that path of activity until the muddiness accumulates once again and draws us to a standstill. At that time we shall find our way to stillness and remain in the quiet place until the cycle that has moved from active to passive has provided the resources that return us to an active stance once more. As we move through that cycle again and again, sometimes in spans of short duration, sometimes in cycles of a longer range, we gradually recognize the rhythm that seems to fit best our individual nature. That rhythm is our personal rhythm. It is the rhythm by which the cycle of the opposites of experience, the active and the passive, moves through our individual life. This is the form in which hope and achievement, disappointment and renewal, all find their place in our life. It is the personal rhythm by which the universal cycles of opposites can find a channel in our life.

One of the important functions of *Intensive Journal* practice is the way it enables each person to fill in the details of these cycles. It is a means also for enabling each of us to work out and recognize our own rhythm so that we can be in harmony with the cycles of opposites as they appear and reappear in the course of our life. Lao Tse's sense of having a rhythmic relationship to the cycles of active and passive is a valuable contribution to our methodology of Mantra/Crystal practice.

MTI'S: MOLECULES OF THOUGHT AND IMAGERY

The third modality to which we look for information regarding the movement of subjective process is drawn from the concepts of Holistic Depth Psychology. This is a metaphor that has served as a prime hypothesis in our work, the MTI's, the molecules of thought and imagery. We shall describe it here not in the terms of the depth principles that underlie it, but as a modality that we can consider and apply in the practice of Process Meditation, especially in our Mantra/Crystal work.

Think of a piece of wood. It is solid, opaque, hard to the touch. We can pick it up, hold it, use it as a single solid unit. And yet we know from the science of chemistry that the apparent solidity of the wood is only its outer aspect. Its opaqueness and hardness are only relative. When we approach it from another point of view, we realize that the wood is not solid at all but that, among its other aspects, it is a movement of molecules. In addition to its outer facade, it has an inner dimension that is active and effective. But this fluidity within the wood is not visible to our commonsense perception.

Considering this, we can recognize a number of correspondences between physical reality and our human existence. Two are of particular significance. The first is that physical reality has its outer aspect concealing some subtle and elusive levels beneath it. When we move past the commonsense assumptions of our superficial perception, we come to qualities and energies of physical being that are much greater than we had imagined. That has certainly been the experience of chemists and physicists ever since the discovery that there are molecular structures beneath or within the apparent solidity of what we see on the surface.

In a parallel way, our human existence has its duality of outer appearance and inner reality. We have our social veneers, the various attitudes and behavioral traits that are visible on the surface. And, like the wood, we also have levels of reality within ourselves that cannot be seen. There are very powerful forces working in our depth but, since they are concealed from our view, we are not able to perceive them, much less gain control over them, unless we have a special knowledge and training. In that regard, the hidden level within ourselves, our psychological depths, is comparable to the molecular level of physical reality.

There is a second correspondence between physical reality and human existence that is of even greater significance. In the depths of matter, the molecular level is *in motion*. That was a most surprising realization when it was first discovered. But the same is true of the hidden depths within the human being. A movement of images and subliminal thoughts is actively taking place beneath the surface of our consciousness. Included in it are not only visual images, but ideas, hunches, intuitions, things we feel and hear inwardly, the perceptions and awarenesses that come unguided from within. They all move as molecules move, as images and thoughts coming together to form new combinations.

Both in sleep and in the waking state, imagery moves within us at levels deeper than our mental consciousness. Experiments have repeatedly verified the fact that a movement of imagery and thoughts takes place during sleep. We know that these involve the significant contents of our lives, the situations about which we are concerned, the problems we are seeking to solve, the emotions we are feeling. They continue to move around in our inner space while we are asleep. It may well be, therefore, that the making of dreams during sleep involves essentially the patterning and repatterning that takes place as part of the flux of the molecules of thought and imagery as they move about within us. This possibility opens a number of implications to be explored with respect to the relationship between dreams and the MTI's.

The phenomena that occur during sleep are even more markedly and observably present in the intermediate waking state that we have described as the twilight range of experience. In twilight imagery, as we have seen, the definition of imagery includes all the perceptions that reflect to us in any form the varied aspects of those contents of our life that we experience at levels below our mental consciousness. In addition, an important quality of twilight images is that they are perceptions that come by any of our inner or outer senses, and that they take place without our conscious direction.

In both the sleep and twilight states, patterns of imagery move, change, regroup themselves, and form new patterns again and again. It is very similar to the way that molecules move, interact with other molecules, and repattern themselves into new constellations with new characteristics. When these new qualities appear, they are visible on the surface; but the changes that brought them about occurred at invisible levels. The regrouping of the molecules is the factor that effectively brings about changes which then become visible at the outer level.

The correspondence now is apparent between the molecules that move within the chemistry of a piece of wood and the MTI's, the molecules of thought and imagery, that move at the subliminal levels of our psychological nature. Motion is characteristic of both of them, sometimes a flux, sometimes orderly motion. The coming together into clusters and constellations to form patterns with particular traits and systems of energy is also a characteristic of both types of molecule, the physical and the psychological. And changes in the clustering of both types also lead to changes in the derivative qualities, the outer traits that become visible on the surface. This is particularly true with respect to the *molecules of thought and imagery* because, when the images regroup into new patterns, new qualities of behavior and action soon are reflected at the surface of our lives.

To think of the depth levels of our being in terms of the metaphor of MTI's, the molecules of thought and imagery, may provide one clue to understanding how change takes place in human personality. It may be that when abrupt changes occur in people's attitudes or beliefs, as in the transformation experiences of rebirth that often happen unexpectedly and without explanation, the outer events are reflecting sharp inner changes in the clustering of the MTI's. Most probably it is not relevant to ask the question of which comes first and which is the "cause" of the other. Beyond cause and effect, what we observe is a fact of correlation between the outer and the inner. In some synchronistic way, outer experiences and the inner constellation of the MTI's go together. In their interaction upon one another, they set up new units of outer/inner circumstance which then become the next set of contents and conditions in our life. Considerations like these open the possibility that there are ways of personal practice and spiritual discipline that will be more conducive to the creative self-combining of the MTI's. This hypothesis is in the background of several of our Process Meditation procedures.

Our observations in Holistic Depth Psychology have enabled us to draw several inferences regarding the qualities of the MTI's. They are apparently reflectors of the whole range of our human existence. The personal situations of our lives, our desires and frustrations, are reflected in them; and the more-than-personal symbols of poetry and religion that carry our intimate feelings of meaning in life are also reflected in them.

The molecules of both types of imagery—the personal and the transpersonal—move about together, intermingling in the depth of us. Sometimes the various MTI's fuse freely with others to form new constellations. At those times there is a marked fluidity in a person's thoughts and imagination, usually leading to a period of great productivity both in ideas and actions. At other times the MTI's are restrained and seem to repel one another. They do not intermingle then and it seems that very few new combinations of molecules are being formed. This, of course, is not creativity but its very opposite. It is experienced as a "dry" time. Instead of fluid movement, there is tightness and rigidity. Instead of creative fulfillment, there is frustration. An atmosphere of tension then builds in the depth of the person, and this further hinders the free movement of the MTI's.

This negative aspect suggests the need for a constructive approach that can assist the process by which the molecules of thought and imagery form their larger configurations. It would seem that the MTI's require an atmosphere in which they can be free from constraints upon their movement. They should be as free as possible from pressures that are external to their own nature, whether these are the pressures of social demands or of personal emotions. Then the capacity of intuitive knowing and self-guidance that seems to be a quality of the profound patterns of symbolism can be expressed in the MTI's. As they come together, combining, breaking apart and recombining, they form new groupings and constellations which take expression in new ideas, awarenesses, plans for action, poetic visions and inspirations for belief. That is one reason why we seek a quiet atmosphere. The reason for stillness is not merely to bring about a subjective condition of inner peace and tranquility. It is to establish a profound field of harmony at the depth of our being so that the MTI's within us will be as free as possible to find their way to the most meaningful new combinations. This seems to be the inner ground of creativity and spiritual awareness.

Aspects of the three modalities of process that we have described— the Jesus Prayer that prays itself, the rhythm of active and passive, and the MTI's—are expressed in various forms at several points in the *Intensive Journal* work, and especially in Process Meditation. The principles underlying them come together, however, in making possible the conception and practice of Mantra/Crystals as an instrument for creative spiritual practice. To work with Mantra/Crystals is the next step in our practice of Process Meditation.

Chapter 14

Preparations:
The Elements of Mantra/Crystal Experience

THE MEANING OF MANTRA AND CRYSTAL

We can now take the steps that will enable us to make *Mantra/Crystals* and then progressively to work with them.

What is a Mantra/Crystal? And why is that the term chosen to refer to a procedure that plays a pivotal role in the active experiencing of Process Meditation?

In the course of creating the *Intensive Journal* system and of adding to it over the years, I have had the task of choosing names for the various Journal sections and procedures. In doing this, one criterion that I have followed is to try to find terms that are as descriptive as possible of the operations they embody within the *Intensive Journal* structure. An even more important criterion has been to find terms that reflect the *style of movement* of the procedures they represent; and, if possible, to find terms whose varied nuances and cultural overtones will help carry that movement. This is particularly true with respect to the Mantra/ Crystals.

In this case we utilize a term that has an Oriental derivation, but choose it because it reflects the underlying purpose of the procedures at this point in our work. It expresses our goal of having a means of focusing and deepening the consciousness of individuals in order to assist the process of meditation in its larger aspects. With its many variations, this is the basic role of mantra in the Eastern religions. There are numerous parallels to the function of mantra in various Western religious practices, especially in Contemplative Christianity and the mystical dedications of Jewish Hasidism and Islamic Sufism. Other concepts, however, are not as specific, and I have not found a term other than *mantra* as elemental and as appropriate for our use. We need a broad term whose significance is so general that it is generic to the subject of providing an instrument that assists the work of meditative practice. While there are a number of other terms for this in the various traditions, they tend to refer to practices that depend on doctrines within their own framework of beliefs. Because of the pluralistic nature of religious experience, especially at this point in history, it has seemed to me to be essential to have a term that would not be inherently identified with any particular doctrine.

It is with this thought in mind that the first word in our Mantra/Crystal phrase is taken from its primary Oriental usage. It has a large place in Hindu/Buddhist religious practice, appearing in many forms in that broad tradition. In its most general and fundamental meaning, however, a mantra is anything that serves as an aid to meditation in the general sense of quieting the self.

Mantras may be of many kinds, and they may be used in diverse ways as they serve different purposes. They may call upon a single sense or upon several of the senses. They may use the various modes of perception in different combinations and patterns according to the purpose of the particular discipline and the customs of the time. For example, a mantra may be a single word or a group of words used as an aid in the practice of meditation. Equally, mantras may not be words at all but a sound, a musical note, or a chant. They may be a painting or a sculptured object. Various works of art in the East serve as mantras. Mandalas, for example, which are the symmetrical and symbolic designs presented in the East in many forms, in paintings, in carpets, in woven tapestries, are often used as mantras. They serve in diverse combinations of ritual and religious discipline as aids to meditation in the several Eastern traditions.

Very often the mantra is part of a special initiation ceremony. At those times it is given by the guru as a secret which the disciple is to guard very closely. Its significance may then also be as an object of private knowledge, usually described as an arcane wisdom known only to the master and disclosed to his student. Mantras given in this way are regarded as a special secret key by which the student will be enabled to unlock spiritual mysteries.

Used in such an atmosphere, mantras tend to draw an aura of holiness around themselves. They come to be treated as sacred or numinous objects. Special spiritual powers may then be attributed to them, and psychic phenomena of various kinds may be felt to occur in their presence. Gradually, as the mantras reach the point where they are venerated as holy objects, a subtle shift takes place. The mantra ceases to serve as a means of spiritual enlargement, but it becomes an end in itself. Not infrequently it has become an object of personal pride and cultism. In fact, one of the commonly noted causes of idolatry and superstition within the Eastern religions is the popular misuse of mantras. But none of these misuses negates the basic validity of working with the mantra principle in meditation as a means of stilling the self.

In the exercises which we practice in Process Meditation, we also use mantras as a means of stilling the self. To that degree it is in accord not only with the Oriental use of mantra, but also with comparable practices in non-Eastern spiritual disciplines, like the Jesus Prayer of the Russian Pilgrim, that also seek to achieve an inward quieting. Other religions possess equivalent practices with which to achieve this purpose, but none to my knowledge has a single, simple term as concise and convenient as *mantra*. That is why in Process Meditation we use *mantra* as a generic term, in its basic and universal sense, separated from any doctrinal overtones. We use it simply to refer to the procedures by which we establish an inner quietness in the Process Meditation work as preparation for our further creative experiences.

There is substantial reason for incorporating the term *mantra* into our Process Meditation context, considering the broad spiritual goals of the work we are undertaking. The main disadvantage in using the term lies in the negative connotations that it has acquired through the many abuses in the use of mantra that have occurred in the history of the Eastern religions, and occasionally also in their popular modern adaptations. We thus have two conflicting facts to be set side by side. One is the affirmative fact that mantra represents a concept and a technique that is potentially of great value for modern spiritual experience. The other is the negative fact that mantra has shown itself to be capable of abuse in the past. We are then led to consider the third possibility that it could be very productive to have a modern format for working with mantra *provided* that our method contained ample protections against the cultural tendency toward mantra abuse.

Considering the issues involved in such a development has led to a further observation. The instances of mantra abuse with which I am familiar involve the use of mantra techniques within a context of traditional Eastern concepts, and these were originally devised to meet the needs of pre-modern cultural situations. That observation naturally suggests the hypothesis that if mantra techniques were adapted into a format more congenial to the special psychological circumstances of modern society, the difficulties that arise in mantra work might well be avoided while its spiritual benefits could still be maintained. Exploring that hypothesis led eventually to the Mantra/Crystal concept which has been used increasingly in *Intensive Journal* practice since 1970.

It is significant that this modernized use of mantra helps to fulfil some of the fundamental concepts of depth psychology. One of my goals for many years has been to develop, on the basis of depth psychological knowledge, a methodology that would provide a psychotherapeutic effect while it was engaged in the larger task of providing a way to personal meaning that could meet the special needs of persons living in the modern age. It was that effort that led me to formulate the Holistic Depth Psychology described in *Depth Psychology and Modern Man.*

In the course of that research I was led to certain observations regarding the difference between the quality of life experience in persons who lived in earlier periods of history and those living in modern times. The most basic of these observations eventually became the foundation stone on which the *Intensive Journal* system was built. It was the recognition, first, that the development of individuality (as distinct from individualism) is a characteristic of those periods of history in which civilization reaches a high level; and second, that the modern period of history is unique not only in the *quality* of the individuality that is attained within it but the *quantity* of individuality, the large numbers of persons who are given the hope and the real possibility of achieving a high level of individuality in their lifetimes. The tension between that hope and the many difficulties of fulfilling it is, of course, a primary source of the psychological disturbances in modern times. But these tensions and the forms in which they are resolved provide the main contents of what has become the central fact of modern times: the unique life histories of individual persons.

The special efficacy of the *Intensive Journal* system derives from the fact that it takes the life history of the individual person realistically as its starting point, not only treating it with respect but also objectively as its central subject matter. In my understanding, the reason the *Intensive Journal* method has been able to be of practical value to so many persons is that its processes and techniques provide a means of working actively and in a focused way within the inner space that is created by the fact that modern persons are each engaged in working out their individual life histories. Another way of saying this is that the fact that the *Intensive Journal* method is effective indicates that its workbook structure spreads out the contents and continuity of a human life accurately enough to reflect the circumstances of living in the modern world. Apparently the structure it establishes provides a means of moving around and back and forth within our inner space and inner time in a way that rings true to the modern person's perception of reality. It does this by working out the details and building the energy movements of the central fact of modern times, the life history of the individual person.

The perception of this central fact has provided the guiding criterion whenever decisions or judgments have had to be made in developing the *Intensive Journal* system. It has served in the same way in determining the appropriate use of the mantra principle as a psychological tool for modern persons. Considering the various forms of mantra and the ways they are used, the question we ask is how their form and use fit with the life history of the individual person. It is especially important to bear in mind in this connection the fundamental conception of the holistic development of persons, that growth must be organically related to the depths (the seed) as well as to the ongoing life history of the person if it is to take root and grow in a substantial way.

Now consider the forms and use of mantra as delivered to us out of the traditional religious societies of pre-modern times. Whether it is a word, a phrase, a sound, the mantra is *given to* the person by the spiritual teacher (master or guru). Implicitly a judgment has been made by the teacher as to what is the correct or proper mantra for that person. The teacher as the authority person makes that decision on the basis of information available only to him either through his previous studies, his initiation experience, arcane knowledge that has been opened to him, charismatic energy and power either residing in his own being or transmitted from another guru, heightened intuitive abilities or some other capacity or access to wisdom not otherwise available to the student.

On whatever basis the decision is made and in whatever form it is given to the disciple, the fact is that it is introduced into the individual's life as something from the outside. It may turn out to be pleasant, or helpful, or appropriate for the individual's life. The knowledge or intuition or inspiration on the basis of which the mantra was chosen may even have been divinely guided in some way, as was claimed. But the fact is that it comes from outside the individual life. It is something inserted into that life, directed by a consciousness that does not arise from the inner development of the seed of that life history itself. No matter how correct or valid the mantra may be, the fact that it does not arise organically from within the life history of the individual who is receiving it is of critical importance.

Not being organically connected, there is the possibility that the mantra will prove to be arbitrary and inappropriate for the individual. Whether this is so can be determined after a little while; and if it proves to be an inappropriate mantra that can often be corrected. The more important, irrevocable fact, however, is that the insertion from outside of a factor that is to have great spiritual and psychic importance in the individual's life brings about a break in the continuity of the individual's life history.

The principle involved here is simply what our common observation shows to be the case: factors that are to function at fundamental spiritual and psychological levels must evolve organically out of the fullness of the individual's life history. Only if they are rooted in the total context of the life, with its personal and social contents, can deep spiritual factors be absorbed into the person's life development. In this regard we must note that the response of individuals in modern times may be quite different from that in traditional or pre-modern times. In a traditional culture the uniqueness of the individual person is not nearly as sharply marked as in modern times. Consequently, when the authority of a spiritual teacher assigns a mantra to a person in pre-modern society, there may be hardly any feeling of something alien being intruded into him. In that circumstance, the giving of a mantra by a person in authority is in fact part of the cultural situation. To that degree it is also an integral part of the life history of the person who is receiving the mantra. Giver and receiver are in that context part of a single social unit, since the fact of authority and dependence is organic to that particular time and place.

For the modern person, however, it may not be that way at all. The life history of the individual proceeds out of its own cultural roots and moves toward its own integrity, but in the course of this it may encounter and participate in many events that are not organic to its development. As it experiences these, absorbing some and rejecting others, the life of the person expands beyond its original boundaries, even enabling new roots to be planted in it. The one serious difficulty that may occur is when there is inserted from outside the organic development something that is more than a new experience and is intended to serve as a basic spiritual and/or psychological reorganizing factor in the life. When such fundamental factors, which often are religious beliefs or spiritual disciplines, are not organic to the life history, the result may be a profound personal disharmony and confusion. During the decade of the seventies we have often seen the signs of this in the glazed looks of persons who find themselves participating in religious or ideological movements that are not organically connected to their life history. The popular misconception of this is that such people have been "brainwashed." They have not been brainwashed at all. But they have been severely disoriented at the roots of their being by taking part in activities that contain profound doctrines not organically connected to their personal and social life histories.

As we proceed in our work we shall describe practices within the *Intensive Journal* system that help resolve such spiritual problems by drawing them into a larger context. The form in which mantras are used within Process Meditation, however, gives us a means of anticipating and avoiding the type of confusion that results from spiritual experiences that have no roots in a person's life history.

* * *

In the course of our work in the *Intensive Journal* process up to this point we have each gathered and recorded in our workbook considerable data of our individual life history. The entries we have made while exploring and re-experiencing the past events of our lives now become an important resource for the mantra/crystals we shall make. We ourselves shall create our mantra/crystals, drawing them from the raw materials of our life history as we ourselves have recorded the facts and the memories. In doing this we are following the central principle of the *Intensive Journal* system: to honor the unique life history of each individual person. In effect we are letting our spiritual guidance emerge out of the experiences that have comprised our life, for our mantra/crystals become links between our past and the experiences we can have in the future.

We are here adapting the ancient mantra concept to the circumstances of modern life. In a series of steps which we shall soon describe, we each fashion our own mantras as phrases of seven syllables drawing their content from the context of our life histories. We make mantras that will express significant experiences that have occurred in the course of our inner lives. When we have decided on the aspect of our life history from which we shall draw our mantra phrase, our first step is to condense the whole experience into a single phrase. The mantra that we construct is then a small representative piece of a large and meaningful interior experience of our past. It is because it is so finely compressed and so representative as well that we call it not merely a mantra but a Mantra/Crystal.

Mantra/crystals are crystals in a twofold sense. The first refers to the way that we derive and construct them as very small but representative excerpts of large experiences. We realize that a large experience that may contain many stages and nuances cannot be compressed to such a degree and still convey its meaning. In making the mantra/crystal, however, we are not seeking to give a full description or understanding of the experience in a single phrase. We are seeking merely to put a small, representative piece of it into words in a way that will recall us to the atmosphere of the original experience. The mantra phrase is thus nothing more than an excerpt of the full experience, but it is an indicative excerpt. It serves as a reminder and as a reconnector for us to an experience or a contact with reality that we have had in the past. Our desire is that, by reminding us of the experience that we have had, it will take us back into its atmosphere. It will place us there but not contain us within it.

One purpose of our seven-syllable mantra phrase is that it establish sufficient contact with the past to provide us with a base and a starting point for fresh experiences. And yet, being only a small excerpt, our mantra phrase will not be strong enough to predetermine what our new experiences will be. It will only be a representative crystal carrying in miniature the atmosphere of the larger whole. The seven-syllable mantra phrase that we make is a concise crystal formed from our earlier experience. It is a phrase that expresses the essence of a contact we have known. In the exercises that we shall carry through in a little while it serves us as a vehicle and as an intermediary by which new inner events can be brought into our lives.

In our exercises the mantra phrase serves as a crystal in a second sense. As we learn to use it in conjunction with our rhythmic breathing in the silence, our mantra phrase becomes like a prism of crystal glass. The rays of light, the rays of our consciousness, are refracted through it, being modified in ways that express the quality and the structure of the crystal. Thus the mantra/crystal which expresses a fragmentary essence of an earlier experience in our life history serves as a vehicle by which light in a new form can enter our life. The special function of the mantra/crystal as a *crystal* is that it focuses the light in a way that relates it to what has gone before. By means of it, rays of new awareness may enter our life. In principle these rays of consciousness may be as infinite as the sun; but, because they pass through a mantra/crystal, the light they bring us is neither blinding nor disorienting, but is softened and made relevant for each individual existence.

The way the mantra phrase functions as a crystal of individuality becomes especially important at the practical levels of this work. When we reach the point in our exercises where in disciplined silence we combine the saying of our mantra phrase with the regularity of our rhythmic breathing, the crystal effect becomes clear. Then we see it operating. We all enter the universalizing experience of our meditation by means of an excerpt of our individual life history. Thus we can approach the deep ground of spiritual experience in a personal way. In consequence of this, at the later point when our practice of breathing in the silence with our Mantra/Crystal has begun to bring forth new inner events, we find that they are remarkably relevant in the understanding and guidance that they bring to our individual life. This is the *crystal* effect of our mantra practice that we shall see as we move further into the work.

SEVEN SYLLABLES FOR UNITS OF BALANCE

We may understand by means of a definition the meaning of the word *mantra,* and by definition also the meaning of the word *crystal,* but we can understand the meaning of *mantra/crystal* only by our own experience. Our next step, therefore, is to prepare ourselves to move into our active work with mantra/crystals so that they can become available to us through our own knowledge of what they do within us.

There are a number of concepts that play a role in the mantra/crystal procedures. We shall become familiar with them a little at a time as we work in the actuality of mantra/crystal practice. After we have accumulated some experience with the basic steps and exercises, we shall be in a better position to understand the depth principles that underlie this aspect of Process Meditation. We shall therefore turn our attention to working with mantra/crystals on the experiential level so that, after we are familiar with the primary procedures, we can return to consider more closely the principles that underlie our experience.

The work that we do with mantra/crystals proceeds in two steps. First we construct our own mantra/crystals; then we work with them. We may eventually make several mantra/crystals, even many of them, so that we can have a variable supply of personal mantra/crystals from which to choose as our individual practice proceeds. In order to construct our own mantra/crystals we have to understand the principles on which they are based and the qualities they need to have. Acquiring that information is actually the first step in our mantra/crystal work.

There are several characteristics of mantra/crystals that must be borne in mind. The first is that the mantra/crystals we work with are seven syllables in length.

Setting this length is not an arbitrary or a numerological choice, but has important functional reasons. The mantra/crystals may be any number of words provided that the total syllable count is seven. One necessary quality of mantra/crystals is that they be smooth and rhythmic enough so that we can easily speak and repeat them under our breath. It usually works out more harmoniously if the individual words are no more than three syllables and mostly only one or two syllables each. We try to compose our mantra/crystals of words that fit together smoothly so that each mantra/crystal will establish its own rhythmic flow within its own unity. This rhythm eventually becomes an important factor in conducting our meditations for it enables us to repeat the mantra/crystal without conscious effort or thought. Once the meditation gets under way, the rhythm itself carries it. Especially when it is combined with rhythmic breathing, the continuous repetition of a seven-syllable mantra phrase builds a self-sustaining rhythm that strengthens it and enables it to maintain itself under its own power.

Working with seven syllables enables us to establish the necessary length and rhythm in our mantra/crystals. These two factors, length and rhythm, are of central importance in the making of mantra/crystals because of two primary relationships: the first is the relation between our regularized breathing and the inner rhythm of our mantra/crystal; the second is the relation between a significant inner experience drawn from our life history and a mantra/crystal that reflects in a concise way the atmosphere of that experience. Together these determine the qualities of the mantra/crystal and they provide us with our main criteria in constructing them.

The connection between breath and spirit is a fact that has been widely recognized in religious history. Wherever people have worked seriously with spiritual disciplines, they have noted the close relationship between the movement of the breath and the quality of inner experience. Much of this understanding is stated metaphysically in cosmic conceptions that are largely symbolic or mythological. The concepts are symbolic because the perceptions they express are largely intuitive or poetic and are very difficult to demonstrate in detail. We see a major example of this at the very beginning of the Old Testament where the *Ruach* is the breath and/or Spirit of God. Breathed into human beings, it is also the carrier of life and of intelligence for mankind. There are many correspondences to this with rich variations in the cultures both of pre-literate and advanced civilizations. Especially in the Hindu-Buddhist traditions the symbolic understanding of the relation between breath and spirit is developed in many sophisticated ways. In the forms of Yoga it becomes a fundamental discipline for spiritual development.

We can see from the uses of Yoga that, once it goes beyond social beliefs and symbols, the relation between breath and spirit becomes a matter of personal practice. Without practice, it becomes merely talk and intellectualization; with practice, it expands the possibilities of awareness and action. By means of particular techniques that vary with each religion and culture, breath and spirit are brought together in special ways in each individual's experience. The regulation of the breath plays an important role in balancing the inner and outer aspects of a person's life. In particular, the quieting of the self is related to the stabilizing of the breathing especially in the way that it helps neutralize the hold that habits have on us. It helps us establish at least a degree of freedom from being controlled by our conscious ego. The linkage of breathing and the mantra/crystal is an essential step first in establishing and then in progressively deepening the process of our meditation.

It is important to bear in mind as we construct our mantra/crystal that eventually, when we come to work with it in practice, the mantra/crystal will be specifically coordinated with the movement of our breath. At that point we shall establish a regular rhythm in our breathing, and we shall coordinate that with the saying of the mantra/crystal under our breath.

Because of this coordination, we need a mantra phrase that is not too long and not too short. Seven syllables seem to provide the right length. In order to make sure that the words do not get under our tongue and trip us up, the mantra phrase should also be soft, rhythmic and easy to say. It needs to be long enough to carry a full unit of our breathing, but not so long that it becomes unwieldy or becomes entangled in itself. A clear criterion lies in the fact that a cycle of breathing in and out is a concise unit. It sets its own natural limits. If a phrase is too long or cumbersome, the cycle of the breathing will not fit with it. That is why mantra phrases of nine or more syllables tend not to work in the context of this self-sustaining rhythm. They tend to lag and fall off. Similarly, mantra/crystals of six or fewer syllables tend to be too brief to establish the flow of a rhythm.

The cycle in a unit of breathing gives us a natural criterion and measure. *Breathing in and breathing out.* In fact, that phrase itself with its seven syllables is a good indication of the length and rhythm that a mantra/crystal should have. Breathing in and breathing out. The phrase naturally coordinates with the systole and diastole of our breathing and reflects the underlying cycle. That cycle is a natural unit and it serves as a model for us in making our mantra/crystals.

Practice indicates that a mantra/crystal of seven syllables carries its inherent rhythm so that, as we continue to say the mantra/crystal under our breath in conjunction with our breathing, the rhythm establishes and maintains itself. We can each work out our own balanced rhythm of breathing in and breathing out, fitting it to the seven-syllable phrase. Thus we can breathe in on the first three syllables, hold on the fourth, and exhale on the last three syllables. Or we can breathe in on the first three syllables, breathe out on the next three, and maintain a state of emptied breath on the seventh syllable. There are also alternate rhythms that are possible within the seven-syllable unit. As we proceed in our individual work, we each can devise additional ways to coordinate the breathing with the mantra/crystal. But we can discuss these later in the context of our actual practice. Here we wish merely to set the background and to explain the functional reasons for making our mantra/crystals of seven syllables.

The possible combinations of in-and-out or back-and-forth rhythms that are inherent in the number seven greatly facilitate the process by which we coordinate our breathing with our mantra/crystal. It enables us to establish a mutual balance that is continuous and self-sustaining in that it carries itself along at a depth level without conscious direction. The persistent value of .the number seven in the construction of the mantra/crystals has been one of the surprises to me as the practice of Process Meditation has continued over the years. The role of the mantra/crystals has been considerably reinforced by the experiences that people have reported to me. High among these reports have been descriptions of how the natural rhythm of the seven-syllable phrase sustains the movement of the meditation as though autonomously, even when other aspects of the experience would seem to be causing it to lag.

It may well be that the factors behind this are not to be rationalized, but in my understanding of it the *rightness of size* seems to. be very important. Being not too long and not too short, the seven-syllable phrase corresponds to a full cycle of breath. Thus it is sustained and continued at a physiological level even when it becomes very meager with respect to both its conscious and its non-conscious contents. An important consequence of this is that, at those times when the energy and the motivation of our meditation dip to a low level, the natural rhythm of the mantra/crystal itself can continue the meditation for us. It serves as a riderless horse that knows where to go, continuing through the valley with only the guidance of its inner nature until it comes to the next valid phase of its journey. Many times, when the disciplines of meditation lag in a person, the momentum and rhythm of the seven-syllable mantra/crystal carry the process so that it does not come to a halt before it contacts new energies and can re-sustain itself. In practice this is of tremendous importance.

When we come to the step of making our own mantra/crystals, we shall see that there are some details that may take a little while to learn. We shall have to become accustomed to certain principles and procedures in order to be able to construct mantra/crystals that are appropriate for our individual circumstances. It may therefore take us a little while to learn to do it well. But that is as it should be. Perhaps in a small way, the making of our mantra/crystals is an artwork, and we should be prepared to give it the attention that an artwork requires. As we seek to make our mantra/crystals in a way that will feel right and satisfying to us we shall find that they take at least a little time and effort when we are working at constructing them.

Quite often, however, the mantra/crystal changes by itself in the midst of the meditation. It frequently happens that the original mantra/crystal is replaced by another one, even as the rhythmic breathing and the process of silent meditation are continuing. The observation that has been most interesting to me in this regard is that invariably the new mantra/crystal that is not consciously made but simply emerges in the course of the meditation fits the criteria for making seven-syllable mantra/crystals, and does so without any thought or planning or editing or fixing. Most of the time, in fact, the new form and content of the mantra/crystal is more appropriate to the evolving inner situation of the person than the original one that was consciously made.

There is apparently a factor of inner wisdom that expresses itself at the depth of human beings whenever the circumstances are right for it, and this factor seems to have a direct affinity for the seven-syllable mantra/crystals. I infer that the seven-syllable form and rhythm of mantra/crystals reflects an inherent cycle in the natural world, and therefore it easily comes into harmony with the principle of inner wisdom that is present at the depth levels of the human psyche. One cannot help but feel that the spontaneous making of seven-syllable mantra/crystals in the midst of undirected meditation is a significant reinforcement, if not an actual verification, of the mantra/crystal approach. It indicates that when we meditate in the flexible way that we shall soon describe and practice, the seven-syllable mantra/crystal serves as a means of linkage between our personal human nature and larger principles that are cosmic in scope. How that operates and what it may imply are questions that are well worth exploring; but for now we must continue to prepare ourselves for our direct experience of mantra/crystals.

Sometimes (and especially in some languages other than English which you may prefer to use) there are words that have an additional half-syllable in the way they are pronounced. There are also words containing syllables that can be pronounced either as a single syllable or as two, depending on the local accent or on the style of speech. Sometimes you may have a mantra/crystal that has an extra syllable, or is lacking one, but where you feel that, the way you will speak the mantra/crystal will balance it out so that in practice it will have the desired effect of seven syllables.

You certainly may elect to go ahead with a mantra/crystal that is six, six-and-a-half, seven, seven-and-a-half, or eight syllables, speaking it as though it were seven syllables. If you do decide to do that in individual cases, however, you should bear in mind the several factors in the mantra/crystal work that are the reasons for our choosing the length of seven syllables: the factors of rhythm, balancing, coordination with breathing, and especially the importance of having a mantra phrase that will enable you to neutralize your conscious controls as you are working with your mantra/crystal.

Since we are seeking a rhythm within the mantra/crystal that gives a swinging, back-and-forth effect, it is best to avoid phrases that are based on a list of contents or qualities. For example, we would not want to use a mantra/crystal like:

Wishing, Believing, Loving.

The content of that phrase would be very good, the words are smooth and pleasant to say, and the syllable count is seven. The words themselves have a good rhythm within themselves, and the mantra phrase as a unit has balance. When we think of ourselves, however, as continuously speaking that phrase and repeating it in conjunction with our breathing, we realize that the words being listed in sequence and repeated one after another would build a staccato effect. Inevitably the emphasis would be placed on the individual words, and the feeling for the wholeness of the phrase as a unit would be lost. This rule of thumb may not apply in every case, but in general it is better to have a mantra phrase that is inherently a whole because of its structure. It will then be able to maintain its unity and its identity as a phrase even when we are continuously repeating it together with our breathing.

An example of a mantra/crystal phrase that carries a back-and-forth rhythm inherent in its structure is:

The waters beyond the well.

Let us set to one side for the moment the question of the content of that mantra/crystal, which comes from *The Well and the Cathedral*, and consider merely its structure and its sound. Although it is not your own mantra/crystal, try repeating it at least half a dozen times under your breath just to feel the kind of rhythm it establishes. As you say it, let it set its own balance and tone, with your conscious mind interfering as little as possible.

This is an example of the simplest and the most effective form in which to compose a mantra/crystal. As much as possible let it be a phrase that has a single identity, a phrase that is not broken into separate words that are in sequence or in apposition to one another, but a phrase that can be *spoken and breathed as a unit.* That combination contained within a unity is the most desirable quality to have in a mantra/crystal phrase. It does not break apart into separate words but maintains its wholeness as we repeat it in conjunction with our breathing. It thus supports and builds the rhythm of our breathing in a self-sustaining way. Doing this, it contributes to building the cumulative effect that establishes the deep atmosphere we are seeking.

Some other examples of this unitary balance within the form of mantra/crystals are: *

Feeling the movement of life.
Holding the stillness within.
In the chapel of the self.
The silent work of the monks.

In addition to the inner rhythms of seven and its correspondence to a cycle of breathing, a mantra/crystal is composed of seven syllables in order to serve its function as a crystal of our individual life in the process of meditation. As a crystal it is a concise but representative excerpt drawn from an inner experience in our life history that is meaningful to

* Taken from *The Well and the Cathedral* and *The White Robed Monk.*

us for whatever reason, personal, emotional, social, cosmic, metaphysical. Taking a crystal from that whole experience in our past and making it into a mantra/crystal enables us to use it as an instrument for opening ourselves to new experiences and awarenesses. As a crystal, it needs to be large or full enough so that it can contain or reflect the essentials of that past experience. It must be concise, but not too concise. If we make a mantra phrase that has much fewer than seven syllables, it will be too brief an excerpt to give sufficient expression to the content and quality of the experience we are reinstating. And also if it is too brief, it will not have the requisite quality of rhythm and flow. On the other hand, if we describe the excerpt in much more than seven syllables, it may not be a concise crystal any more. It may then become bulky and even become a hindrance to our rhythmic breathing. Just as if it is too brief, a mantra/crystal that is too long can negate its quality of rhythm and flow. The mantra phrase needs to be able to function as a crystal. But it should not be too long, and it must not be too short.

OPERATIONAL CRITERIA

Since we shall eventually be speaking the mantra/crystal under our breath, repeating it in coordination with our breathing, we require a phrase that is soft and flexible. It should be a phrase that lends itself to being coordinated in a balanced rhythm. It should, whenever possible, be a phrase that carries its own rhythm, preferably dividing naturally into halves to correspond to the rhythm of inhaling and exhaling.

The individual words in our mantra/crystal should be smooth and easy to say. Bear in mind that eventually we shall be repeating the mantra/crystal without having to think about it. We wish to be able to work with it as unself-consciously as possible. For that reason, one of our criteria in constructing our mantra/crystal is that we shall be able to repeat it in an effortless way so that the saying of it can continue by itself without requiring our attention. Our mantra/crystal should be in accord with the old Taoist saying that the virtue of a good shoe is that we can wear it without being aware of it. If the shoe pinches or slides, our attention is called to the fact that we do have a shoe on our foot. But if it fits properly, we do not notice the fact that we are wearing it.

A good mantra/crystal phrase is one that does not call itself to our attention. The words move so effortlessly that, as we continue to repeat our mantra/crystal, it seems to be saying itself. It becomes like the Russian Pilgrim's "prayer that prays itself." At first it requires commitment and discipline, but once rhythm and momentum have been established, it is able to continue by itself. As we proceed it becomes less and less necessary for us to articulate the words. The saying of the mantra/crystal becomes so natural to us that the words roll out by themselves. To that degree we are freed from the need for the self-conscious control of our thought processes. That is one of the primary effects that our mantra/crystal meditation is seeking to achieve. It is seeking to neutralize the controls of consciousness so that the process of our meditation can flow freely without being directed or controlled. As this is brought about, we are also freed from the tensions that accompany self-consciousness.

Toward this general goal we would like to have mantra/crystals that are as natural as the air to us. Then we can work with them without having to be conscious of what we are doing.

The need for self-generated continuous movement is one of the particular reasons why it is so helpful to have mantra/crystals that are just seven syllables and whose unity of form corresponds to a cycle of our breathing. In those cases where the length and form divide the mantra/crystal naturally into two parts, a back-and-forth movement is naturally established to accompany the breathing. This movement first sets up a small rhythm within the mantra/crystal phrase itself. But as the repetitious saying of the mantra/crystal continues, a larger rhythm and ongoing movement is established, carried by the balancing movement of the two parts of the phrase. A rhythmic balance of movement is thus self-contained within the phrase itself, and it becomes the unit of a continuing process. The movement of the mantra/crystal in this larger continuity is smooth and soft, even lulling, and it reaches a point where it can maintain itself without being conscious of its own movement.

Since this is our goal it is apparent that we require words in our mantra/crystals that are easy to say. We find in practice that words of one or two syllables carry an advantage in this regard, since longer words may be difficult to repeat in a rhythmic way that can easily be coordinated with our breathing. While our mantra/crystals should be seven syllables in length, they may contain any number of words. It is the self-balancing rhythm of the whole that is important.

We should take care also to use words in which the consonant sounds do not clash against each other as we articulate the words. Too many hard consonant sounds one after another may have a jarring effect and may work against the smooth, lulling, unself-conscious balance we are seeking. We should especially avoid using hard-sounding words with consonants that would put us in the position of the fabled Peter who picked a peck of pickled mantras; and we should avoid at all costs the sad situation of Sammy who whistled his spirit away through sea shells at the seashore. Like the comfortable old shoes of the Taoist, simple words that are unpretentious and that do not call themselves to our attention are much the best for mantra/crystals. They make it much easier for us eventually to say the mantra/crystals without being aware of what is moving through our lips.

Simplicity of wording is one of the hallmarks of good mantra/crystals. It is true that powerful emotions are often contained in the connective experiences that are the primary source of our mantra/crystals and it is true also that poetry and rhetoric are traditionally the language of powerful emotions. But eloquence is not the purpose of mantra/crystals. Alliteration and onomatopoetic grandeurs may be fine for rhetoric and eloquent poetry, but they should be avoided in the making of our mantra/crystals.

Whatever is soft and smooth, effortless and natural to say will work best with respect to the wording of a mantra/crystal. As much as possible the words should be such that they can flow into one another. In a smooth mantra/crystal, the phrase is said before you are aware of it. The words make the phrase a simple unit that seems to speak itself and can thus repeat itself effortlessly. The words should make the mantra/crystal phrase a natural unit so that we find ourselves saying it as a whole, as for example:

The river flows to the sea.

As we are making our decisions in choosing and forming our mantra/crystals, there is a question that we must carefully consider. At what level of our inner space can we expect our use of that mantra/crystal to place us? Will it take us up to the surface of mental consciousness? Or will it take us into the deeper levels of the twilight range of perception? There are particular kinds of words and structure in mantra/crystals that tend to draw the experience to the surface; and there are others that have a deepening effect. We can learn to identify them.

Let us visualize the basic sequence of steps involved in setting a mantra/crystal experience into motion. When we have formed and chosen a mantra/crystal we use it first to quiet and center ourselves. We do this in coordination with our breathing in order to establish a balanced and self-contained unit of experience. The mantra/crystal contains its own rhythm, a rhythm that derives from its structure. As we speak the mantra/crystal, it establishes itself and becomes coordinated with our breathing. If the mantra/crystal is right for us and if our breathing is smooth this coordination of the two will take place easily and naturally. We will not need to do anything consciously or deliberately in order to bring it about. The mantra/crystal and our breathing will come together as though by themselves while we are maintaining our steady and continuous practice. Presently, imperceptibly, a stillness will be established within us. At the same time our rhythmic breathing together with the saying of the mantra/crystal will continue and each will be assisting the other. In the course of this, the thinking processes that are directed by our conscious egos are progressively neutralized and are gradually brought to a quiet stop. The quality of our inner being is then no longer focused at the surface of our psyche where the conscious mind is, but is focused inward toward the depth of us.

What follows then in our practice of Process Meditation comes not from our surface mind but from depths in us that are beyond our personal or conscious direction. We have noted earlier that between waking consciousness and dream sleep there is a large realm of non-conscious perception that is the twilight range. It is here that we find and incubate the materials that eventually become the products of our creativity and the expressions of our enlarged awareness. One of the important functions of our work with mantra/crystals is that it puts us into touch with the depths of the twilight range in a manner that enables new contents of consciousness to become accessible to us. Even more important, our mantra/crystal work draws up this material from our twilight depths in a way that is beyond the intervention of our conscious mind. It is neither guided nor manipulated by the purposes or desires of our personal egos. At least that is the principle and the goal that underlies the mantra/crystal work. We seek to draw new experiences and awarenesses from the depth of the twilight range within us beyond the limitations and inhibitions of our personal habits, beyond our egos and our emotions.

For this reason the qualities of our mantra/crystals must be such that they take us into the twilight range of our inner space with a minimum of hindrance. One way of focusing the question is to ask ourselves regarding a mantra/crystal: Will it draw me toward the deeper levels of the twilight range where the silence can deepen? Or will it draw me up toward the surface where my emotions and my analytical thoughts will continue to go around in their circular movement? Answering that question to ourselves will give us a good operational criterion as we proceed.

There are many kinds of experiences that can serve as sources of mantra/crystals. Whether they are events that serve on the outer or the interior level of our life, they are events that activate strong emotions and energies within us, and they also carry intimations of larger meanings in our life. It is this latter quality that transforms an ordinary life event into a *source experience* for mantra/crystals. It evokes a sense of meaning within us that is more than merely personal.

This is also the point at which we can ask the question of an experience that we are considering as a source for a mantra/crystal: Where will it place me in my inner space? If the meaning we perceive in the experience comes to us in the form of intellectual thoughts or interpretations, it is drawing us to the surface of our consciousness. If it arouses an emotion in us, it is drawing us toward twilight levels. With respect to the inward pull of emotions, however, we should note that it may be taking us only toward the surface of the twilight range. In a manner of speaking, it is drawing us to the upper levels in the depth of us.

The third possibility, however, is when the meaning comes to us by means of twilight imagery. Whether the imagery is visual or comes by any other mode of perception, that is a sign that it is drawing us into the deeper levels of the twilight range. It is taking us into the dimension of inner experience where symbols have larger than personal connotations, and that is an especially fertile resource for mantra/crystal work.

The meaningfulness of a deep inner experience comes to us in symbolic forms. That is one way we can recognize a source experience. Its meaning is not contained in an intellectual statement of it, but it is *inwardly experienced.* Another way to say this is that the event is being assimilated into our life with the energies of emotion and symbolic perception that have the quality of the twilight range. We experience it at the level of emotion, but it is more than personal emotion that we feel. The symbolic perceptions we have in the twilight range give us intuitive indications that there are further meanings contained in the inner or outer event that has taken place. There is something in it beyond what we have recognized so far. The practical question which we need to answer, then, is: How can we traverse the distance from the experience we have already had to the next larger experience that lies beyond it but is also contained within it as the future seed lies within its flower?

Our mantra/crystal practice offers a direct answer to this question. We construct a mantra/crystal from the original experience, then work with it as a seed from which new awarenesses will grow in the course of our meditations. The conception that underlies the mantra/crystal work is expressed in the goal of having a vehicle that will enable us to make the journey between a previous experience that took us deep into the twilight range and the next experience that lies beyond it. That next experience may be a modest one, or it may be opening new inner territory to us and taking us to new depths. Whatever it is, we proceed, making no judgment. All the steps in the practice of mantra/crystal meditation are directed toward our next experience. We draw a seed/crystal from a previous experience of depth, and we use it as a point of entry into the future, moving as deeply as we can within the twilight range of experience.

When we construct our mantra/crystal, we are not seeking to re-enter or to repeat our original experience. Nor are we going back to it as our specific starting point. We are returning to it only to touch it, only to make contact with it, and then we keep the possibilities of our next experience altogether open and unconditioned. This is a very important point in our mantra/crystal work, for it expresses a basic principle. We are proceeding on the double hypothesis, firstly, that there is a further experience lying beyond each experience that we have had; and secondly, that the seed of our next experience lies contained in the previous one. On this basis we draw a seed/crystal from our past experience and we plant it as a seed in the form of a mantra/crystal at the twilight depths of our being. There, in the silence of our meditation, we let it incubate and regenerate itself, reshaping itself into its own integral form, until it is ready to emerge in its own timing in a new context of symbolism that we could not have predicted.

As an illustration of how a previous experience serves, let me refer to one of the experiences described in my book of entrance meditations, *The Star/Cross.*

In the experience I described in that book, I was walking in the woods. It is worth remarking that, from the point of view of our inner work, it does not matter whether it is a physical forest or whether it is a symbolic forest perceived in the twilight depths. The experience itself, with its attendant awareness, is the reality.

In the forest the trees were tall and full of leaves. They overlapped one another so that it was dark and quiet in the forest. It had a cathedral effect. I was walking deep into the forest when suddenly I saw a small bush in a place where such a bush could not grow. As I looked closely at it, I noticed that it had no trunk and that it did not seem to be growing from the ground. It seemed to begin about a foot or two above the surface of the soil. And the bush itself was aglow. It was covered with white flowers and they were luminous with a glow that came not from their color but from within the bush itself.

As I stood before it, the bush became more than a bush. Another reality became present, present in the atmosphere as a whole, and present in the bush itself. It remained a bush, and it also became other than a bush. I found that I could speak with it as with a person. I could meet it in dialogue. Later, when I let the dialogue be written, I discovered that many things were said that I would not consciously have thought to say. I truly felt, "I have met a friend in the forest," a friend that could be with me thereafter wherever I would go. And I also felt that there were many more things that could be said and known if that friendship in the forest could deepen.

It could be deepened, we must note, in two ways. It could retain its present form of forest and bush and dialogue, and continue itself within those terms. Or it could transform itself so that its outer content would no longer be recognizable—it would no longer be forest and bush and dialogue—but the underlying theme of the experience would be extended and carried to a further point of understanding. If the next experience did not use the symbols and images of the original experience, it could be that the next step in awareness required other vehicles, other symbols, more appropriate to its message. We must bear this point in mind as we work in our mantra/crystal meditations, for it is fundamental to the open-ended process of our work. We recognize that the unfolding of meaning is not embodied nor contained by our experiences but is only carried by them. We therefore let our experiences be channels for the themes that are unfolding through them, and we let each experience be free to take the form and symbols that it requires for its next development.

As we consider now the forest experience itself, we see that it carried a strong contact with reality, subjective and more than subjective. The experience took place within the twilight range of my being, but several things that were said in the dialogue and that were shown to me in the inner experience of the meeting expressed truths and understandings that were valid in their own right. Although they transpired within the twilight range of my consciousness, as I personally knew it, the awarenesses they carried knew no such boundaries. When the experience was over, I was no longer in the atmosphere of that forest. Its reality was no longer present, and yet I was convinced that, if the contact could be re-established in any degree or form, further awarenesses would be open for me.

That feeling on my part leads to a general question that applies to all of us. By what means, when we have had an inner experience that is of great depth and private importance to us, can we re-establish contact with the atmosphere of the experience and with the creative process that was working in us by means of it?

The tone and style of inner experiences vary with each individual, but those experiences that have a profound effect upon the person tend to be large and to contain many aspects. My observation of persons who have had strong inner experiences is that they find upon close reflection that their experiences were much more complicated with respect to the contents of the experience and its overtones than their enthusiasm or emotionality at the time of the experience had led them to believe. It would certainly not be simple to recreate the experience, and it would not be possible, any more than it would necessarily be desirable, to go back into the experience as it originally took place.

The fact is that we would not want to go back into an earlier experience, no matter how powerful and valid it seemed to us at the time it happened. To do that would simply be reading an old script over again, replaying an old tune, whereas the reason the experience in the forest seemed so important was precisely because of the feeling that it contained greater possibilities than it yet had shown. It could lead to more. It could go further. But in order to go beyond the original experience, it is necessary to re-establish contact with at least an element in the experience itself. By re-establishing that point of contact we can reach through to the underlying process that is moving through the experience. And then we can go further into the open future without any preconception and without any restrictions as to the symbols or contents of our next experience. That is a key to the principle and method of our mantra/crystal practice.

The small excerpt that I chose to represent the large experience with its many aspects was expressed in the seven-syllable phrase, "The glowing bush in the woods." That was indeed so small an excerpt that a person who had not actually been within that experience when it happened could not possibly know the many small events and aspects of the full experience to which the phrase referred. In that sense it was not at all a "representative excerpt." But to the one person who had experienced it, that small phrase, "The glowing bush in the woods," was indeed representative of the experience as a whole. And that one person, in each case the person whose experience it was, is the only person who is to be drawn back into the experience.

That is how each of us is able to carry out our own work. We take that brief phrase, which is also the mantra/crystal we use in our meditation, and we make of it our point of contact. Brief though it is, it is a truly representative phrase for the one person, ourself, who knows the content of the original experience because that person was in the midst of it. It is a representative excerpt because it calls back to mind the total reality of the experience as a whole for the one who knew it from within. It renews the contact and makes re-entering the atmosphere and the process possible once more.

Are there any special characteristics of which we should be aware as we choose the excerpts from our experience that we put into the form of mantra/crystals?

In addition to the qualities we have been describing, we must remember to invoke our basic criterion and ask the question: Where does it place me in my inner space? Does it cause me to use my analytical mind and thereby draw me up to the surface of my consciousness? Or does it enable me to be in the twilight range of awareness? And if so, does it allow me to move into the deeper levels of the twilight range? Or does it draw me up to the thinner levels of personal emotion?

As a general rule it seems that if the representative excerpt we choose is a feeling of anger or of joy or even of love, it tends to place us in the more superficial levels of the twilight range. Mantra/crystals of this type may function well enough to get the meditative process into motion, but they tend to be short-lived. They need soon to be replaced.

If the excerpt we choose is the statement of an idea, a thought, a concept, a doctrine or a conscious belief, it will draw us up out of the twilight range toward the surface of mental consciousness. In that case the possibilities of our basic meditative process are cut short. On the other hand, the possibilities of our being brought into the twilight range, remaining there, and moving deeper into it, are greatly increased if we choose the kind of content that is native to the twilight level.

Choose an image, therefore, a symbol, a metaphor, since these can move about naturally in the twilight range like fish in the oceanic waters. Symbols and images take us to deeper levels of our inner space. They can move freely in the twilight range since that is their natural habitat. Bearing this in mind can be very helpful to us as we are making decisions about the content of our mantra/crystals. It should draw our attention to the type of material in our source experiences that will function best in the process of our mantra/crystal meditation.

We have already discussed some of the factors that determine where and how a particular mantra/crystal will position us within our inner space. This may involve the form of the mantra/crystal, its content, its relation to the source experience from which it has been drawn as an excerpt; and it may especially involve the question of whether the mantra/crystal is symbolic and composed of imagery or whether it is analytic and intellectual. We find, perhaps unexpectedly, as a consequence of this, that there are aspects of grammatical structure that affect the position of mantra/crystals in inner space, their capacity to enter the twilight range, and their ability to move about within it. We have to bear all these factors in mind as we proceed with the making of our mantra/crystals.

One of the grammatical factors concerns the relation between a sentence and a mantra/crystal. By definition, a sentence is a complete thought. We have to note, however, that a thought is a product of the mind, and that it belongs especially to the territory of the analytic intellect. The effect, therefore, of working with a mantra/crystal that is grammatically a complete sentence is that it takes us to the level of intellectual thought. But that is not the level of the twilight range of consciousness where our main work is to be done. A mantra/crystal in the form of a grammatical sentence tends to draw our attention up toward the surface of consciousness and into the realm of the analytical mind. Like a cork in the water, then, it bobs up out of the twilight range and comes to the surface of our experience. To have that happen in the midst of a mantra/crystal meditation can frustrate our whole effort by drawing us out of the depth where non-conscious experiences take place.

Since the beginning of our *Intensive Journal* work we have used a metaphor to help us understand the dynamic of what is involved here so that we can relate it to our inner experience and our practice. It is the metaphor of the well in relation to the Underground Stream, a metaphor that is expressed in the entrance meditation of *The Well and the Cathedral.*

In the terms of the metaphor, we consider each human being to be a well which must be entered privately and separately, level after level. Progressively inward, we move through all the layers of psychic deposit, memory and habit and desire: all that comprises an individual existence. As we continue moving deeper into the well, we come to depths that are beyond the individuality of our personal life. Moving through the well, we ultimately go beyond the well itself, as we come to its source in the underground stream that unites all the wells. In this symbolic process, we reach beyond the personal to the source of individuality in what is greater than personal. It is both a personal and a self-transcending process.

The procedures by which we do this follow the principle of progressive deepening which operates all through our *Intensive Journal* work and especially in our Process Meditation. Systematically we follow procedures that enable us to move from "depth unto depth" in our effort to make contact with the ultimate source from which our lives draw their sustenance. The underground stream carries in its flow the contents and the energies for life, and it supplies the well of our personal existence with waters of every kind. It is the metaphor for the deepest level of content and experience in the twilight range. In the language of Holistic Psychology, it is the Holistic Depths. Operationally it is the source to which we must go to find the contents that will bring spiritual creativity into our lives.

The metaphor of the well and the underground stream is only one of the symbolic forms by which we can inwardly conceive the essentially incomprehensible reality to which it refers, and the dynamic of the process by which we can experience aspects of it. It is an operational metaphor. It has things to do, new experiences to bring about. The ultimate test of the value of the metaphor is its capacity to help us make the connection in the tangible terms of actual experience. There is no value, after all, in possessing a deep well within us if it does not reach to the underground stream. But connecting the two in the actuality of our lives is the work in which we are now engaged. And that is the point where metaphors must be operational.

In carrying out this work we are brought again and again to the realization that, while the tasks of spiritual development are subjective and delicate, their success depends upon solid facts which we must acknowledge and to which we must respond in a tough-minded way. Among these is the fact that when, by any factor, such as the thought-structure of a mantra/crystal, we are drawn out of the twilight range, the effect is to separate us from the source of our inner experiences. When we have been moved from the twilight range to the level of analytic intellect we become capable of a quite different kind of activity. The analytic intellect, we know, is the part of us that is able to comment on the products of creativity after the creative act has taken place. It is the part of us that complains or criticizes if the creative act has not happened, or if it has happened inadequately or if it has produced something that we are not predisposed to approve. But, by its nature, the analytic intellect is not able to cause a creative act to happen, for it is not a source of new experience and it can never be. When, therefore, we are drawn out of the twilight range we are being separated from our inner source of creativity.

The grammatical form of the mantra/crystal, therefore, can play a significant role in making possible the type of experience that places us within the twilight range. Or it can prevent it, as often occurs when a mantra/crystal is given the grammatical form of a sentence with a proper subject and predicate. A sentence by definition, as we have seen, contains a unit of thought, and a unit of thought belongs not in the twilight range but in the realm of the analytic intellect.

The reason for my describing this at length here is that when they begin the Process Meditation work, many people seem to have a predilection for mantra/crystals that express a unit of thought, whether in the form of a sentence or not. And the result is to block the effectiveness of their mantra/crystal meditation. It is a problem that we can avoid, however, if we are aware of it.

One factor that causes people to make their mantra/crystal into a sentence is that their interior ear hears it stated to them that way. They hear it within themselves as a statement of a truth in which they believe. In their mind they hear a seven-syllable phrase, and to them it is a natural expression of a truth, the consciousness of which they wish to strengthen. The making of a seven-syllable phrase that states that truth in a form which they can easily and continuously repeat seems to them to be an opportunity to establish that truth more strongly within themselves. Therefore they put their belief into the form of a statement.

As they repeat it they feel that they are pressing it more securely into the depths of their being. But of course even the greatest outward pressure cannot hold the underground stream in place. It will go where it listeth. And it is just as well that it does. For if, by the resolute statements and affirmations of our particular beliefs, we did succeed in holding them in place, we would simply be anchoring ourselves to the fixed spot of our beliefs. In the underground stream we have fluidity, and because of that we also have the possibility of creative new inspiration being given to us again and again. But when we anchor ourselves by the resolute affirmations of our beliefs, as may happen when we put our mantra/crystals in the form of definite statements or units of thought, we limit the possibility that new experiences can be given to us.

As a practical matter of working with our depth procedures, then, it is better to make our mantra/crystals in the form of phrases rather than of whole sentences. In that way they do not express a whole thought, but are merely an excerpt of a thought. Thus they do not draw us as easily up into the realm of the analytic intellect.

Most of the time we can achieve the desired result without changing the meaning or framework of belief that is contained in the mantra/crystal. What we do change, however, is its grammatical structure. And that makes the difference as to whether our mantra/crystal is expressed on the level of intellect or whether it is within the twilight range and gives us access to the underground stream.

Let us consider some examples for the sake of practice.

You may wish to state in mantra/crystal form your belief about

God. And you may wish to express your positiveness by stating your belief in a direct declarative form. "The Lord is good in all ways."

The problem is, however, that setting your statement of belief in the form of a declarative sentence with a noun and a verb, a subject and a predicate, makes it a unit of thought and thereby lifts it from the twilight range to the level of the analytic intellect. At that point it becomes more a statement of theological doctrine than of the actuality of your inner experience.

The mantra/crystal, "The Lord is good in all ways," can be altered so that its essential content and especially its interior spirit remain integral, but so that it also enables us to move about actively within the twilight range.

Once we understand the principle involved, we can each make many variations on our theme; and we shall be able to do so with little difficulty. Some possibilities of an equivalent alternative to "The Lord is good in all ways" are:

> Knowing the goodness of God.
> Holding the Lord in my Heart.
> Feeling the Love of the Lord.

Each of these expresses the essence of the original statement of belief, but does not present it as a statement. It does not make of it a unit of thought. Thus it does not take us out of the twilight range. It enables us to remain in the flow of our inner experience.

An incidental observation that will be valuable to us in other connections is to take note of the fact that each of the three alternative mantra/crystals begins with a participle. Each is grammatically a gerundive. A very interesting observation has emerged for me in the course of the mantra/crystal work: that mantra/crystals in the gerundive mode are particularly good vehicles for extending our inner experience. This is apparently because their grammatical form by its very nature maintains them as moving excerpts that are part of the flow of an ongoing experience.

In all of this work it is clear that fluidity is the key. A primary goal of any mantra/crystal that we individually construct is that it enable us to move about freely in the twilight range, and give us continuous access to the underground stream. Those who are familiar with the philosopher Henri Bergson's classic work, *The Two Sources of Morality and Religion,* know his distinction between "static religion" and "dynamic religion." The difference between the two lies in a person's ability to reach into the underground stream, to be carried by it, and to draw from its resources. In making and choosing our mantra/crystals we must be especially aware of their capacity to do this for us. It depends to a great extent on whether a particular mantra/crystal helps place our experience in the twilight range. When they meet this criterion, mantra/crystals are instruments that help fulfil Bergson's description and vision of dynamic religion. In fact, we can now see that the underlying thrust and goal of our Process Meditation work is to provide a methodology for dynamic religion in the life of the modern person.

Chapter 15

Making Mantra/Crystals

SOURCE EXPERIENCES

We have enough basic information now to enable us to make our first mantra/crystals.

In the structure of our *Intensive Journal* workbook we have a full section for our mantra/crystal work. Our first step, however, involves the other Journal sections. The entries we have made at various times describing the interior events of our lives now become the raw material from which we construct our mantra/crystals. The goal of building such a resource has been an important factor in the exercises we have carried out in both the *Meditation Log* and *Connections* sections. As we begin, you may find that some particular inner experience comes strongly to your mind so that you feel that you already know the subject matter of the mantra/crystal you wish to make. You are undoubtedly correct in that feeling. There is, however, an additional fact to bear in mind.

While we work with one mantra/crystal at a time, we find it valuable to have a number of mantra/crystals available to us so that we can use different ones at different times. In this way the various facets of our inner lives are reflected in our mantra/crystal work. Since we each have more than one area of concern or belief in which we wish to deepen the scope of our understanding, having a number of mantra/crystals available to us enables us to explore the various pathways of our spiritual interests. By means of the several mantra/crystals that we shall eventually construct, we shall be able to pursue each path from time to time, sometimes going just a short distance and sometimes making great headway whenever our brief earlier experiences come together and crystallize into a new awareness. For this reason we not only seek to collect a resource of several mantra/crystals but over a period of time we work with each one in continuity. In this way we progressively build the multi-faceted contents of the experiences of our inner lives.

Now we can begin the actual work. The first Journal entry that we make with respect to mantra/crystals is not in the Mantra/Crystal section but in the Meditation Log. Let us turn back to the third segment of the Meditation Log, Inner Process Entries. We have already made some entries there, and now we prepare to add another which may, in fact, become quite extended as our mantra/crystal work proceeds. We use this segment of the Meditation Log as the place where we do the background work for our mantra/crystals as distinct from our mantra/crystal practice.

To begin this phase of our work in Inner Process Entries, we record today's date and write an introductory factual statement. The gist of this statement should be that we have now come to the point of undertaking to work with mantra/crystals and that we now find such-and-such thoughts, feelings, intuitions stirring inside of us. This is the place also for us to make note of any striking ideas we may have had regarding the possible subjects for mantra/crystals we may construct. If we describe these briefly here, we will have them on record so that we can refer back to them at a later point when we come to the actual work of making our mantra/crystals. In the meanwhile, by placing them on record, our minds are freed to explore in other areas of our *Intensive Journal* workbook to uncover *source experiences* that will provide us with additional mantra/crystal themes.

When we have completed the entry, we can begin our exploration, traveling through the various sections of our workbook in search of source experiences for future mantra/crystals. Our immediate purpose in doing that is to identify the interior events that can contribute to our mantra/crystal practice, but the quest for source experiences can have additional benefits for our spiritual history as a whole. It often has the effect of renewing our contact with parts of our spiritual history that we had overlooked before.

The work we have done in Process Meditation so far has two main purposes: first, to give us a perspective of our personal spiritual history, and second, to give us a resource of facts and experiences with respect to the actualities of our inner lives. We now come to draw upon this resource for making our mantra/crystals.

Some of us have more data to draw upon than others. This may be because some of us have lived more years and therefore have had more time to accumulate experiences. Others of us have lived with greater intensity and involvement in the years that have so far been given to us. And some of us now have more data available to us simply because we have been working longer in the *Intensive Journal* system and have had the opportunity to use the full range of sections in the *Intensive Journal* workbook. Those of us, on the other hand, who are beginning our use of the *Intensive Journal* system with our present work in Process Meditation have much less material to draw upon at this point. We have just the exercises that we have carried out so far. But that is sufficient to enable us to take our next steps.

No matter at what point we have entered the *Intensive Journal* work, we now possess our individual life data with which to proceed in Process Meditation. At the least, we now have the varied entries and elaborations that we wrote in the Connections section, our Gatherings, Spiritual Steppingstones and Re-Openings experiences as well as the Spiritual Positioning entries and the entrance meditations that we recorded in the Meditation Log. What we have done so far is ample for beginning our active work with mantra/crystals.

Looking for past interior events that can be a productive source of mantra/crystals, we have some clear critieria to guide us. One prime identifying characteristic of source experiences is that they carry with them a strong and deep emotionality. Their feeling tone is very high. The context of life events in which these source experiences occur invariably carries an atmosphere of great intensity. This intensity of emotion, it should be said, is not necessarily the emotionality of personal disturbance. It may sometimes be connected with personal difficulty and upset; but it may also express the profound emotionality that accompanies an experience of great calm, such as a feeling of unity with the natural world, or a moment of timeless knowing that seems to have the qualities of Cosmic Consciousness.

The intensity of emotion indicates two other basic qualities of source experiences. One is a sensing that the strong emotions being felt are not merely personal in nature, but that they have a larger, transpersonal significance. The second is an intimation that whatever meaning or understanding has been gained from the basic experience or has been learned from it so far, there is still much more that lies implicit and is waiting to be given when the proper time and circumstances arrive.

The experiences that serve for making our mantra/crystals can have many different kinds of content. They may be personal in the sense that they involve relationships with other individuals or particular projects or artworks in which we are engaged. The emotionality then may seem to be a merely personal type of emotion. We find very often, however, that the personal factors are primarily the point at which the emotions of the experiences become visible and are felt intimately. There is usually some larger-than-personal concern, some fundamental principle of human existence, underlying the emotion. An important characteristic of a source experience is the image of intimation that accompanies it. We sense that, whatever we have already learned from the experience, it has additional understanding still to give us at some later time. Therefore, the emotionality that we feel with it is not only deep and intense, but also profound in the sense that it reflects levels of life or of wisdom that are more encompassing of reality than our merely individual existence.

As we turn now to draw together the source experiences from which we shall fashion our mantra/crystals, it is especially important for us to recall the *cyclic quality* that we observed when we discussed our connective experiences. The same applies here. The experiences that serve as sources for our mantra/crystals include a continuity that moves from one polarity to another. It is necessarily a movement of opposites and, as we have seen earlier, that is essentially what is comprised in a cycle of experience. The cycle moves from pole to pole and back again with many degrees and variations in between. When we consider any particular point in an event or an emotion within the larger cycle of the experience, we have to bear in mind that it is not the entire process, but that it is an expression of merely one transition point between the polarities. Since it is only partial it can be very misleading if we attribute to it the significance of the whole. We know that a passing aspect of any interior process can be felt with very dramatic intensity, especially in emotional areas of the inner life, and yet not contain at all the essence or the eventual meaning and direction of the experience. Not only in choosing valid source experiences but throughout our Process Meditation work it is essential that we keep in mind this perspective of the full cycle of experiences.

Let us now go through our various Journal entries in search of source experiences for our mantra/crystal work. The three segments of the Connections section are undoubtedly the best place to start, but after that each of the Journal sections may be fruitful ground for us. Our memory of what we have written and our intuition regarding its present significance may be the best guides for us to follow. Depending on how great a volume of Journal material we have, we may read each of the entries back to ourselves slowly and carefully, or we may begin by skimming, seeking to find more quickly and intuitively the source experiences that will be most relevant to us at this point in our life.

As we read back a past interior event, we may recognize the possibility of a mantra/crystal being made from it. Then we may have some counter-thoughts. Following that, we may think of some other possibilities, and then some variations, and then some reconsiderations, and then we may arrive at some alternative possibilities of mantra/crystals. Making mantra/crystals tends to become interesting and stimulating work, and it evokes awarenesses of many kinds, especially while we are engaged in forming and refining our mantra/crystals. As much as we can, we record the continuity of our thoughts, our observations and the creative process of constructing our mantra/crystals in the segment for Inner Process Entries in the Meditation Log.

We describe whatever we find, the thoughts that come to us, the ideas for mantra/crystals. We record the embryonic, partial ideas for mantra/crystals, the flaws as we notice them, the changes and variations and refinements that occur to us. We notice, also, that while we are engaged in making mantra/crystals, the source experiences that we uncover evoke many memories and insights with respect to our spiritual life as a whole. It leads us to reflect further on experiences that we have had in the past, and it also causes us to recall events that have a place in our spiritual history but which we had not remembered before. As such memories are brought to us, we describe them in the appropriate Journal section, in the Life History Log, in Connections, in one of the Dialogue sections, as the case may be. But wherever we describe them in detail, we also make a note of them in the segment for Inner

Process Entries so that we keep a running record of the continuity of our inner experience as it is taking place.

When, as we go through our Journal sections, we come upon an experience that seems to be a suitable source for a mantra/crystal, a creative process is set into motion. We find that many additional awarenesses are stirred in us as we consider the implications and the possibilities of its providing us with an appropriate and well-functioning mantra/crystal. We become actively engaged in finding the right words, the rhythm, the unity of structure of the mantra/crystal, and especially in making it a representative excerpt of a source experience that will also be a seed-experience for our future. We should record the full flow of all that is taking place in the Inner Process Entries segment of our Meditation Log. It is also the place where we record the reflections that come to us after a mantra/crystal experience has come to a close, and when we are spiritually in-between times, considering what our next experience may be. Over a period of time as we record the varied aspects of our mantra/crystal practice, we find that our Inner Process Entries become a significant part of our growing spiritual history.

THE SHINING STAR ON THE TREE

Since its basis lies in source experiences that are unique to each individual life, the making of mantra/crystals is a very personal process. Nonetheless we can learn from one another's experience. We learn not by copying one another's mantra/crystals nor by modeling ours on someone else's but by understanding the principles involved in the work. Considering how each individual life reaches toward meaning amidst both hopes and obstacles, we can appreciate how mantra/crystal work assists the quest by deepening it so that it moves toward a level beyond ego. After we have observed some aspects of the mantra/crystal process in other persons' experience we can return to focus our attention on our own lives.

We find that the whole mantra/crystal process, making them and working with them, has a greater effect when the data with which we begin are not general or abstract or intellectualized but are drawn from the specific contents of our inner and/or outer life experience. We see an instance of this in the entry made by R. N. in her Meditation Log, as we noted it earlier,* and as she then used it as a basis for a mantra/ crystal. After describing an emotion and a realization that arose in the course of her *Intensive Journal* work, she wrote, referring to the cause of her unexpected tears, "I opened something that I had hidden in a box."

That phrase could provide the basis for her mantra/crystal. It might be:

Looking in a locked-up box.

That would be an appropriate mantra/crystal phrase. It has seven sylla- bles, a relatively easy rhythm, and it could take her into an atmosphere reflective of her life situation but without directing or shaping the tenor of her meditative experience. A question might, however, be raised about this mantra/crystal because of the consonants that come so close together in the words, "locked-up box." Those sounds might become jarring or difficult to say in the continuous repetition of the mantra/ crystal under her breath. But the judgment on that score would depend altogether on how it feels to R.N. when she is engaged in her mantra/ crystal meditation. It might very well be that while that mantra/crystal would have its limitations, it would last long enough in her use of it to open the way to new experiences. It might very well enable her to explore the contents of that box and eventually to move beyond it.

Another type of entry that leads more directly to the making of mantra/crystals on the twilight level is that of D.F.** After referring to the general qualities of this spiritual and intellectual period in her life, she described the images that had come to her up to that point in her workshop experience. The parallels between her life and her twilight imagery led her to a symbolic interpretation of her experience, consid- ering that it was carrying a message for her life, She had seen a tree reflected in a lake. Its leaves were golden but they came off the tree as though it were autumn. Eventually there remained at the top of the tree only a cluster of leaves in the shape of a luminous star. The trans- formations that took place in the tree in the course of her imaging suggested to her that a movement of change was taking place, or was about to take place, in her life. "Perhaps my intellect is changing."

* See page 123.
** See page 123.

That last thought was itself a thought of an analytical nature. To that degree the perception and understanding that it involved took place at the level of mental consciousness, closer to the surface of awareness rather than in the twilight range. If a mantra/crystal were made directly in the intellectual terms of the thought, that would take it to the surface and keep it out of the twilight depths. Since her experience came in the form of an image which seemed very much to be a metaphor for her life situation, some aspect of the image could serve for the mantra/crystal. One possibility would be:

From golden leaves to a star.

That phrase would meet the main criteria for a mantra/crystal in that it would set the experience at the twilight level. It would also have the advantage of carrying in its atmosphere the context and the changes of the individual's life. That same factor, however, might become a disadvantage insofar as the phrase, "From golden leaves to a star," expresses a movement of change. Because the awareness of change comes via an intellectual perception by being thought about, it would tend to draw the individual's attention up from the twilight level to a mental level of thinking. If that would happen, the mantra/crystal meditation would again not fulfil its goal of deepening the quality of consciousness.

Considering that possibility, D.F. might prefer an alternative mantra/crystal that would express more directly a simple excerpt of her twilight experience. Perhaps the mantra/crystal:

The shining star on the tree.

That phrase would introduce no factors of movement or thought that might draw the quality of awareness out of the twilight depths to surface levels of personal thinking. It would tend, rather, to maintain a quiet atmosphere with an even rhythm of smoothness in its seven syllables. "The shining star on the tree" is an example of a mantra/ crystal that can open very intimate inner contacts for a person at a particular time, and can also continue as an effective mantra/crystal that opens contact with transpersonal dimensions. It has a quality that reaches into the universals of life as well as religious history, even while its immediate point of contact is with a personal experience. Mantra/

crystals that combine the personal and the more-than-personal levels of life in their rhythm of seven syllables tend to be especially productive and evocative in mantra/crystal meditation. They often continue to be used over a long period of time in a person's life as they become a valued possession.

THE WATERS IN THE HARBOR

L. H. is a man who was struggling through the problems of an active life utilizing the *Intensive Journal* program as a whole. He came therefore to Process Meditation with a variety of personal experiences and problems already having been fed into his *Intensive Journal* work. I am citing this particular entry at some length at this point in our discussions because of the numerous phases of life experience in the midst of the world that are reflected in it.

The entries quoted here enable us to see how specific personal sections in the *Intensive Journal* workbook feed into the deepening process of the work as a whole. Some of the references are to sections in the *Intensive Journal* workbook other than Process Meditation, and these may not be familiar to persons who are beginning their *Intensive Journal* work with this volume. These references are meant to be indicative, however, so that you can infer from them the general way that we draw the full range of our life experience into the quest for meaning in the *Intensive Journal* program, and see how spiritual perceptions tend to crystallize in the course of our Process Meditation.

The following extended entry by L.H. was written in the Meditation Log in the segment for Inner Process Entries, which is to say that it was written not in a workshop situation but as part of his private continuous use of the *Intensive Journal* method in dealing with the personal problems of his life. It is interesting to observe the inner movement that takes place as though directed by itself as it brings about experiences that lead to the mantra/crystal work:

I began earlier to write in the Daily Log to describe the downward movement of my thoughts and feelings. Considering what took place, I think I should recapitulate it in the Meditation Log.

In the Daily Log I was describing the anxieties I have been feeling

241

lately, and I felt that I was just going around in circles talking about my fears of one kind or another. My depression was deepening as I wrote.

Then it occurred to me that this is not the way to do it, but that I should go directly to the section where my problem is. I thought that would get me out of my rut. But in my anxiety I became confused as to which section of the workbook I should go to, and in my depressed state I couldn't make a decision. I thought, the reason for my worries is R.W. I feel that he isn't trustworthy, and yet I am in a position where I have to rely on him in the organization. What should I do? Should I go to the Dialogue with Persons section to see if I can establish a dialogue relation with him? I started to do that, but I didn't get any further than turning the pages of the Journal. I felt a real antagonism, a real revulsion against having a dialogue with R.W. Then I thought, well, if I have such intense negative feelings about it, that proves that I really need to work at having a dialogue with him. So I forced myself to go to Dialogue with Persons and I started a sub-section for working out my relation with R.W.

I began by following directions and writing a focusing statement to start with. I know that this is supposed to be a brief statement, but I couldn't keep it brief. First I mentioned the dilemma I feel in the fact that I don't trust him but the situation I am in forces me to rely on him. Then I found that I couldn't just describe it and stop. It kept going on and on, going in circles. I thought, this isn't going anywhere. So I stopped.

I was feeling more and more depressed so I decided to read back what I had written. Maybe it'll make me laugh, I thought. Well it didn't make me laugh at all. As I read it back I noticed that the things I was saying in the section for R.W. didn't really apply to him. What I was writing about wasn't R.W. but the work he and I are doing. I saw that what I am really anxious about is not R.W. but our project, and with that maybe the situation in the whole organization as well. Then I really became depressed.

But I had another idea at this point. I thought it was progress for me to see that R.W. wasn't personally important to me but that it was the whole work project that I was anxious about. I saw that what really matters to me is what I am doing with my life right now. Then

I thought that the reason I am depressed is that I should be depressed. And the reason I am so anxious right now is that I am a realist. At that point I laughed at myself, and felt really miserable. What great progress!

I let the Journal work drop then for a while because I felt tired, really, really tired. In fact not just tired, not even very, very fatigued. It was something else, something I still feel now. Just a little less. It's a feeling of heaviness inside me. It's a heaviness I feel inside my bones, a very unpleasant feeling. One way to say it is that it is like little knots tied all over my body. Little knots tied over my body, but inside me. It's as though they are tied around my bones and rubbing there. Very unpleasant. I still feel it now; but as I write about it, it seems to change. It's as though the knots are loosening. Or relaxing. When I write about it I seem to feel a distance from it. It's as though I know something that I don't really know yet.

After a while I decided that since the anxiety is connected to what I am doing in my life, I should write about it there. So I set up a sub-section in Dialogue with Works for [the project]. Then I went to write a focusing statement and it started well. But it also wouldn't stay short. I couldn't keep it brief. It was expanding, bringing in more subjects, but it was also going in circles. I found myself writing about R.W. again, but when I read it back I realized that it was not really appropriate. Then I saw that I was more than anxious and depressed. I was angry as well, and it was showing in the way I wrote. I realized that I must be very frustrated in a way that is larger than I know.

Then I was more than anxious; I was frightened. I wanted to pray but where and how? At that point I felt even more frustrated than before. And that was when I turned here to this section. I thought that if I describe everything up to now, that will position me, that will say where I am, and that will be like the first part of my prayer.

And one thing more. When I was writing in Dialogue with Works and I saw my anger and my frustration, it occurred to me that part of my anxiety comes from the fact that I am up on the surface of things. Then I thought, and I wrote there, that it might make a great deal of difference if I could get off the surface, if I could get myself into a different place, into a deep place. I have all these problems that I don't see any answer to. So here they are. What shall I do with them?

Then I thought, suppose I do what he says, let them float on the surface while I go down deep. If I go down the well to the underground stream, what will it be like?

At this point there was a break in the Journal entry. L.H. had been writing in the Meditation Log, simply recording the flow of his thoughts and emotions. Now he apparently made a conscious decision to try to take another step inward. Perhaps it would be like the prayer he desired. He would try to go into the twilight range of experience and see what happened there. He sat in a quiet place so that he could recline, half lying back. He had the blank sheets of his *Intensive Journal* paper nearby in an accessible place so that he could record his thoughts and images—whatever would come to him. He closed his eyes and waited, making brief entries from time to time, entries that he rewrote and enlarged afterwards.

I have let go of everything. I am drifting inward. There is nothing here—just a blankness. Now the image comes to me of mountains, mist-covered mountains. They are high, snow-capped, jagged mountains. I am looking as hard as I can. I am straining to see, but I am looking inward. I am concentrating on seeing the imagery and I realize that my neck feels more relaxed now than before. My whole body feels more relaxed now as I am concentrating on my imaging.

I am quiet but now I hear a plane flying nearby. It takes me back into the outer world and my mind starts going in circles again. Thoughts of business, politics, competitions, anxieties, angers. All at once I feel tense as I had felt before. I feel exhausted by these spinning thoughts, these anxieties and angers. I lie still.

All at once I hear the words, "Where is God?" I think they are my own words. Why don't I feel Him present? And yet I do. Why don't I feel Him connected to me? Yet I do feel a connection of some kind.

I feel a quietness coming over me. It seems to be related to my thought of God. I think it is a feeling of God, in a way. I feel quiet now, much quieter than before.

I think I have been lying here for some time aware of nothing, feeling nothing, seeing nothing. It is possible that I dropped off to sleep for a little while. But I still feel calm and rather warm inside. That feeling of God I had before is still here, but somewhat stronger than before. I am not quite sure what it is. But now I see an image and it seems to me to be expressing my feeling of God. I see an ocean. A vast ocean, endless. It seems to have no boundaries on any side. It has no limits, and yet there are waves within it, and tides and movements and changes within it. But it is endless and boundless. I have a feeling inside me that says, "This is God."

I continue to see the ocean with no boundaries on any side. It is limitless. I feel this boundlessness and it feels good. But it is also frightening somehow. Can it come to me? Or is it simply out there?

I am continuing to look and the image is becoming more focused, more specific. The ocean is becoming a bay and it is a harbor. Now the bay is continuing to move upward and inward into land. It is becoming rivers and they are moving up into the mountains. I have a sense that the rivers are individuals and now the image seems to have a message for me. It is telling me that individuals are provided and filled with their content by a great cosmic force, a universal ocean.

Now the image changes. I see snow-capped mountains again. The sun is shining on them and the snows are melting. Now the waters are running down the sides of the mountains forming streams. And the streams are forming rivers. And the rivers are moving down into the harbor where they meet the bay and move out into the ocean.

I have another realization now. The rivers were not formed by the ocean. The rivers were formed by the snows melting high in the mountains and coming down the streams into the rivers. And all the rivers flow to the sea. Here they all meet. The rivers flow to the sea. And the ocean coming into the harbor moves into the bays and then up into the rivers. Does the ocean supply the river or does the river supply the ocean? It is hard to say. They each seem to flow into the other.

I am silent with the image. Is my individual life a river being supplied by the ocean of God? Or is my life an individual river flowing into the ocean of God? I do not know. I wonder. I know I do not know. Now a warm feeling sweeps over me. It is a warm feeling within me. I seem to know something. The rivers and the oceans are flowing toward each other. They meet in the harbor and supply each other. The rivers and the ocean together. They seem to need each other. I feel very quiet and content.

An inner event of this scope carries messages on many levels. It provides a number of leads into the Journal process, leads for following the various aspects of this experience into the separate channels of our life via the sections of our workbook. Most important, however, is the underlying quality that unfolded in the experience. It deepened the atmosphere in which L.H. could *perceive and continue to think symbolically* not only about the specifics of his life but about the larger realities of the universe, issues of human existence which he felt as ultimate concerns of his life. Thus the tone of cognition, the inner atmosphere in which he could perceive and consider the conditions of his life, was changed by the experience. The anxiety that was deepening into panic was brought to a stop and was transformed by a deepening of another kind. This was a settling, a quieting, a coming together and a becoming whole in feeling the larger context of his life.

We can see in this inner event and its first consequences an indication of how it is that entering the meditative dimension has an integrative effect upon the whole of our lives, personal and transpersonal. We are not referring here to the temporary sedative effect that some meditative practices may produce in quieting our fears and lulling us into feeling better. Rather, there is an integrative effect that comes from deepening the level of cognition so that we are perceiving reality in a larger-than-personal context. It gives a perspective of the wholeness of life and time. One way to understand its effect is that the experience of it neutralizes our anxieties by extending the vistas in which we can perceive the significations of our life.

It is in this context that we can read L.H.'s closing sentence, "I feel very quiet and content." We cannot help noting the marked contrast between that state of being and the condition of confusion and anxiety with which he began to write in the Meditation Log. But now, his experience having taken him this far and having brought him to a level. that many people would consider to be the place of prayer, the important question is what next steps are to be taken. There are, in the context of the Journal procedures, a number of leads that suggest themselves and that can be followed one by one into the personal sections of our *Intensive Journal* workbook. These will take us back into the outer involvements of our life where they meet the issues of our old anxieties, but now they can do so in a new perspective.

Another possible path of movement that is available to us within the *Intensive Journal* framework is to continue in the twilight mode and to seek a further deepening of experience. Having come to the depth in his twilight imaging, L.H. can now go further by means of mantra/crystal meditation. The deepening in the twilight range established an integrative atmosphere in which the turmoils of anxiety about work and personal relationships could come to rest. To that degree it provided a resolution of the problem. At least with respect to his state of anxiety, it provided an ending. It was also, however, a beginning because it became itself a source experience which could serve as a starting point for a new exploration, moving in a broader perspective and carrying the issue to a greater depth. This is the step from twilight imaging to mantra/crystal meditation.

L.H.'s experience provided him with numerous options for the making of a mantra/crystal. The eventual choice becomes largely a matter of personal preference depending upon how one feels subjectively about the particular words and phrases that have to be repeated in working with the mantra/crystal. It is good to remember, however, that the mantra/crystal that is constructed and chosen at the beginning does not have to remain permanently the one that represents and carries the experience. It can be readjusted and altered in the course of the actual meditation.

The mantra/crystal that L.H. first made from this source experience was a matter of his own choice and was personal to him. He found that he had created it inadvertently in the course of his writing in his Meditation Log:

The rivers flow to the sea.

An excerpt of his twilight experience was expressed in that phrase. That there were many additional aspects to the image, including its opposite, the ocean meeting the rivers in the bay and seeming to supply them, was additional information that needed to be known only by L. H. himself. It is necessary for a mantra/crystal to express only a small part of a large experience, since the person knows the rest and can fill in the details required. Only the meditator needs to know what the mantra/crystal is pointing toward. Nothing needs to be stated explicitly, for the meaning is implicit and is carried at the level of twilight consciousness.

When we proceed to construct our own mantra/crystals, we should bear in mind that L. H. formed his inadvertently. When he created it, he was only engaged in recording the movement of his inner experience as directly and as honestly as he could. He was then writing spontaneously, and he was not engaged in so conscious an act as creating a mantra/crystal. But his unself-conscious involvement in describing the unvarnished facts of what was taking place at the twilight level proved to be the best way to compose a mantra/crystal.

The inner process did it. That is a frequent experience in mantra/crystal meditation, and the reason is not hard to find. A main principle of mantra/crystal practice is expressed in the effort to provide a vehicle for the process that moves at the depth of our lives, to reflect it and to assist in its movement. Since our mantra/crystals are inherently excerpts of our inner process, we may well expect to find them in the midst of the flow of our lives. In that sense, the task of making a mantra/crystal may be compared to drawing a representative bucketful of water from the river. What we are seeking is not isolated in one particular place, but is present all along the flow of our experience. It is merely that a mantra/crystal requires, in addition to its content, a smoothness of language and rhythm that can fit with our balanced breathing. But that also seems to come about naturally as though by itself when a person is recording spontaneously and with commitment the movement of an inner experience.

Since this is often the case, you will very likely find that your mantra/crystals do not need to be carefully and consciously written like the rhymed lines of a sonnet. For the most part they will be waiting for you to find them, contained, but sometimes hidden, in the descriptions you have spontaneously written. A good first rule to follow, therefore, in making mantra/crystals, is to read your own Journal entries with sufficient care and appreciation. You may find your mantra/crystals "ready-made" and waiting for you there.

WATCHING THE BIRD BUILD HER NEST

Sometimes a very brief event that happens unexpectedly in the midst of the day's chores becomes a valuable source experience. But we can easily pass it by unless we have the practice and the sensitivity with which to perceive it. Once we have recognized it, we can record it, and then we can use the procedures we have learned to draw out the possibilities it contains. An example of such a spiritual seed event happening unannounced in the midst of everyday chores is contained in the following Journal entry recorded by H.B., a suburban housewife:

> I was standing at the window in the kitchen feeling bored as usual. I was just looking out, sort of daydreaming, or thinking a little. Not much. I became aware of this bird in the back yard. It was flying back and forth, very active. I couldn't help noticing that it seemed to be very active. Suddenly I realized that wherever it went, it always came back to the same tree. And it always came back to the same place in that tree. And something was accumulating there.
>
> Now I began to watch the bird closely. I noticed that wherever it went, it would pick up a twig, or a bit of grass, or some soil and bring that back to its place in the tree. It was building a nest. The realization of this hit me with great force, and I thought: Wow! Then I became very quiet—even reverent. I felt as though I were watching something sacred, watching the bird build her nest. I stayed there quite a while, and then through the day whatever I did I always managed to come back to that window so I could keep an eye on what she was doing.
>
> Many emotions have been going through me. I feel close to nature, much closer than usual, even at one with nature as I watch the bird at work. I feel identified with her as she is building her nest. Saying that fills me with emotion. I may cry. After all the mixed feelings I have had about being a housewife, I think I see something, and know something, that I don't understand yet. I think I am understanding it, though, a little at a time as I stand at the window and watch her, just watching her build her nest.

A log entry like this can appropriately be made in the Daily Log section as a simple kind of diary recording. But it can also be written in the Meditation Log as the description of an event that we feel is reaching toward and is pointing toward a larger meaning in our life. The fact is that when we begin to record such an event we have little reason to think that it will become an experience with spiritual significance for us. It is taking place merely as part of our daily life. We may then continue to describe it in our Daily Log as a diary-type entry, until it becomes clear to us that this is an event that pertains to our meditative life. At that point we make a cross-reference and resume our writting in the Inner Process Entries segment of the Meditation Log, or another appropriate section.

H. B.'s experience carried implications for several sections of the *Intensive Journal* workbook. Later in this book (Chapter 17) we shall discuss the way that individual experiences feed into the whole-life structure of the *Intensive Journal* system, and in that connection note the two types of Journal Feedback leads, the personal and transpersonal leads. H. B.'s experience contains both of these. Among the personal leads are the memories that stir in her of her own nest-building. These take her to the *Life History Log*. As questions arise of her relationships with the other individuals in her "nest," the leads go to the *Dialogue with Persons* section. And if she finds herself thinking of the building of a home as an artwork, the Journal section in which to pursue its implications is *Dialogue with Works*.

There was an additional aspect to H.B.'s experience beyond the personal leads. Watching the bird build its nest carried overtones of the sacred for her. This opened the possibilities of a deeper relation not only to nature but to the spiritual meaning of the universe as a whole. It was this intimation of a larger truth being shown to her in a simple natural event that led H. B. to see it as a source experience for her mantra/crystal work.

Seeking to construct a mantra/crystal that would be a representative excerpt of her source experience, H. B. found hers in the same way that L. H. found his: by rereading the Journal entry in which she had spontaneously described the event as it was taking place. There, writing without artifice, she had used a simple phrase that expressed the very essence of what was happening. It was a natural phrase that described what she was doing, "watching the bird build her nest." But that simple, uncontrived phrase is a perfect example of the qualities a mantra/crystal needs to have. It is composed of seven smooth syllables, easy to say and put together as a unit in a rhythmic form. It expresses the essence of a large experience that has transpersonal overtones, carrying its atmosphere and drawing us into the twilight range of perception.

H.B.'s was another example of a "ready-made" mantra/crystal produced by life experience itself and opening the way for the next steps in her mantra/crystal practice.

MANTRA/CRYSTALS FROM THE WORKSHOP FLOOR

The source material from which mantra/crystals can be drawn comes not only from the depths of our individual experience but from the cultural and spiritual resources of civilization as well. We may draw our mantra/crystals from the events of our own lives and from texts and traditions created centuries before we were born but which speak to us in the immediacy of our present existence. The range of mantra/crystals that may be appropriate for us at one or another time in our life is therefore exceedingly broad.

I have collected in the following pages a number of mantra/crystals, including a diversity of types arising from a broad range of subject matter. These mantra/crystals are not classified or systematized but are given here as they have been articulated by participants in *Intensive Journal* workshops.

As you read the mantra/crystals given below you should bear in mind that they are actually spoken out by participants at workshops. It will be good if you can envision the situation and the atmosphere in which this exercise takes place. Consider that we have been engaged in constructing our mantra/crystals and that we are now preparing to work with them in a silent meditation exercise. Before we do so, however, we want an opportunity to test out how they will sound to us and how they will feel to us when we actually use them. We do that by speaking them out into the air of the workshop. Participants who wish to do so speak out their mantra/crystal one at a time without explanation or elaboration, unless they wish to add some further description of its source or how it was formed. The speaking out is therefore essentially an anonymous act that supports the private inner process.

It is a means of testing by one's own ear and feelings. It is also a means of comparing the mantra/crystal with others that we may be thinking of using at this time. Persons who are working with three or four alternative mantra/crystals, trying to choose among them, often find it helpful to articulate the mantra/crystals aloud at the workshop. The decision then makes itself. Many participants find that they work out the form of their mantra/crystal and recognize the changes that need to be made in its content as they hear themselves speaking the mantra/crystal aloud.

When individuals speak their mantra/crystal from the workshop floor they often add a brief statement regarding its source, telling whether they have derived it from a dream, from a twilight imagery experience, a waking life event, from a scripture that is sacred to them, from a poem, a prayer, a literary text, from another mantra/crystal used previously, or from some other source. The private and subjective nature of the material that we are using makes it difficult to communicate in detail, even if we want to do so. We can say a few indicative words about our inner sources, but what we are doing is essentially too intimate to be described. We therefore simply speak out our mantra/crystal and we mention, if it is relevant for us to do so, the source from which it was derived. But we do not attempt the details. We are not seeking to communicate our mantra/crystal to anyone else. We are only taking the opportunity to test and refine it so that we can acknowledge to ourselves, and thus pay respect to, the interior sources upon which we are drawing.

The mantra/crystals listed below are taken from these *speak-out* sessions. They are given as they were spoken from the workshop floor.

A tree of many flowers
> *(An excerpt from a twilight image.)*

The secret place in the house
> *(A dream image carrying a sense of something in the past to be discovered.)*

Feeling the pain of my life
In the hollow of a tree
> *(From a twilight image.)*

Circle of friends and lovers
Doors close and others open
> *(Formed during a time of personal disappointment and life transition.)*

Deep swimming with my brother
> *(An image of spiritual friendship in the context of the metaphor of the underground stream.)*

The sea gulls floating at rest
> *(An image of nature in tranquility. It could be an actual physical perception or a twilight image, equally valid in either case.)*

My life for the love of God
> *(Suggested by reading the text of Brother Lawrence and considering his life.)*

Kingdom of God receive me
> *(A spontaneous outcry in the course of an inner experience.)*

Out of the silence it comes
> *(An experience of finding renewal when there seemed to be no further possibilities.)*

Dark smoke in the chimney
> *(A dream experience that reflected a time of great personal difficulty.)*

I'm flowing into the tree
> *(A twilight image that carried a connective experience.)*

All the treasures in the trunk
> *(An indicative excerpt from a dream experience.)*

The waves roll in and roll out
Watching the waves rolling in
> *(A waking experience of closeness to nature. The difference in style and tone between this and the mantra/crystal preceding indicates how each mantra/crystal reflects its own experience in its characteristic way.)*

A rose on purple velvet
> *(An excerpt from a twilight imagery experience.)*

The old and the new both go
> *(This mantra/crystal is an observation of a phase of process. It came at the close of a twilight imagery experience.)*

Sweet love of the universe
> *(The mantra/crystal helps re-establish the atmosphere of this private inner experience and move further into it.)*

The morning song of the birds
Hearing the rain on the trees
> *(These are mantra/crystals that may recall particular life-situations, and then enable us to go beyond their personal aspects.)*

In stillness on the mountain
> *(Essentially a Biblical theme, this may, however, be*

recalling an outer physical environment establishing an image as the basis for an inner environment.)

The Yom Kippur glow of light

(A mantra/crystal arising from an experience in the synagogue on the Jewish High Holy Days.)

Saul of Tarsus marching through

(A mantra/crystal of a theological student placing himself in the atmosphere of New Testament days. It is an excerpt from his own experience.)

Doing my Father's business

Doing the work of the Lord

Being at one with the Lord

(Adaptations from the Scriptural texts.)

In the place of Unity

I am like an olive tree

(Drawn from the larger phrase and image: "I am like an olive tree in the house of the Lord." After a year of general personal use, this mantra/crystal served as an anchor to reality in the crisis of a severe, disorienting illness.)

Soul of Christ sanctify me

(A Christian text mantra/crystal.)

Corpus Christi salve me

(A Christian mantra/crystal in Latin.)

Passion of Christ strengthen me

(A Christian prayer mantra/crystal. Note that the three preceding mantra/crystals have sometimes been used in special situations as a mantra/crystal series to serve as a means of religious dedication within a particular framework of symbolism and understanding.)

A faceless girl in the field

(Andrew Wyeth's famous painting becomes the equivalent of a twilight image and thus a profound representation of life to this person.)

Clean clothes hanging on the line

(A twilight image that carried great meaning for a person at a turning point in life.)

Being silent to listen

(Derived from the Mosaic injunction.)

Singing new songs to the Lord
> *(Based on the psalm that says, "Sing a new song to the Lord." Note that the mantra/crystal does not retain the commandment style in which the statement was originally given.)*

The ground of naked being
> *(Drawn from the text of The Cloud of Unknowing.)*

Who are you, Lord, who am I?
> *(A prayer phrase attributed to St. Francis.)*

A straight road going uphill
> *(Reflecting the present situation in a life.)*

Feeling the presence of God

Nothing is here but the Lord

Holding the finger circle
> *(A statue of the Buddha appeared in an image in which the fingers were held in a particular way. The finger circle became of symbolic importance to the person and is the subject of the mantra/crystal.)*

The third eye of the Buddha
> *(In a dream, the Buddha appeared with a third eye that was felt to be a special source of wisdom.)*

Crying in the wilderness
> *(An image from the Old Testament prophet applied to one's own life.)*

Charged with the grandeur of God
> *(Drawn from a poem by Gerard Manley Hopkins.)*

The point of hollow water
> *(A paradoxical teaching that came in a twilight image.)*

Taking the path to the depth

Rocking gently on the sea

In the running stream of time

A tree planted near water

I and my Father are One

Footprints in the sands of time
> *(From the poem by Longfellow.)*

Returning to my center

Father, Son, Holy Spirit

My life is now becoming

Walking toward the midnight sun

Gardening in the holy place
Seeking wholeness on the Cross
Relinquishing to the Lord

> *(An interior decision and spiritual commitment is carried
> by this mantra/crystal. The four-syllable word at the
> beginning has a marked effect on the breathing rhythm. In
> this case the effect is salutary because it fits well with the
> atmosphere and content of the mantra/crystal.)*

Lying down in green pastures

> *(Adapted from the psalm and retaining its famous image.
> For some persons, meditating with a mantra/crystal of this
> type can provide an equivalent to reading psalms.)*

A jade teardrop on my cheek
In my house are many rooms
A red sunset on the beach
At the center of myself
Breathing the movement of time
In the very soul of night
Chanting on the way to faith
Rocking the baby within
River flowing into sea
In the forest of my life
The undertow of the sea
A flower opens to me
Seeing the rock from the hill
Taking the hand of a child
With an everlasting love
Having no resource but God
Sun shining down from above
The flux of life around me
Now the Christ from darkness comes
Standing on the mountain top
Quiet stillness in the night
The serpent nurtures the soul
The beads of life in the grass
The sound in the cathedral

When spoken from the workshop floor, the range of mantra/crystals seems to be infinite. Since we each can work with several, choosing one mantra/crystal does not mean rejecting another. It is most important, however, that we each find our own, make our own, choose our own, use our own in our mantra/crystal practice. The test of what is truly *our own* is the atmosphere of our life, especially our inner life, and the way it feels when we work with the mantra/crystal. With the diversity listed above as an indication of what the possibilities are and how flexibly we can work with them, we may now each proceed to make some mantra/crystals of our own to prepare ourselves for the practice of mantra/crystal meditation.

Chapter 16

Working with Mantra/Crystals

When you have constructed a mantra/crystal that feels right to you so that you are ready to proceed with the active use of it, there is one final test to make. Speak it aloud. Even though it is only in your own presence, speak it aloud so that you can have the experience both of saying it and of hearing it. And let yourself respond with your whole being to the way it sounds to you and the way it feels to you.

Eventually, when you work with it, you will speak the mantra/crystal under your breath. Speaking it aloud, however, is a way that you can verify for yourself that it is a mantra/crystal that feels comfortable to you. By speaking it aloud you can also double-check the fact that its words and sounds will move smoothly through your lips, and that there are no harsh sounds to get caught between your teeth and break your rhythm in meditation. But that is not the most important test. It is essential that it feel right to you, for a mantra/crystal is a very private thing.

Once you are satisfied with your mantra/crystal, you can turn to the Mantra/Crystal section in your workbook. Our first step will be to give our mantra/crystal a definite, recorded place, and then we can proceed to work with it actively.

The Mantra/Crystal section is divided operationally into two segments, the *Mantra/Crystal Index* and *Workings*.

The *Mantra/Crystal Index* is at the front of the section where we use it to keep track of those mantra/crystals that we have used more than once, and especially those that we feel we shall use from time to time in the future.

People who find mantra/crystal meditation to be a congenial way of spiritual practice tend to accumulate a number of mantra/crystals over a period of time. They therefore have various mantra/crystals available to them, and they work with different ones according to the circumstances and the inner promptings that come to them. Sometimes, however, when you are in the midst of a tense or troubling situation, you may wish to practice a mantra/crystal meditation in order to quiet yourself in a meaningful way, but just because you are tense you cannot decide on a mantra/crystal with which to work. Having the Mantra/Crystal Index before you can be very helpful at such a time.

We often find that certain experiences in mantra/crystal meditation are particularly memorable and meaningful to us. After some time has passed we may recall the experience in general but not remember it specifically, and not remember which mantra/crystal we used. It is helpful then to have a quick means of identifying our experiences and the mantra/crystals which helped bring them about. When we make our Index, therefore, we do not simply list our mantra/crystals one after another, but we leave ample space between them. Depending on your individual taste and on how much time you spend working in your inner experience, you will probably not want to have more than two to a page. In the lines between the mantra/crystals we record concisely such information as when we first developed this mantra/crystal and the dates of using it. If anything of particular significance took place during the experience of that date, we add a word or a phrase to remind us of it. We may also add a note to indicate cross-references to other mantra/crystals or to other Journal sections that are related to the mantra/crystal; for example, when it is related to a particular memory in Gatherings or to an experience in Re-Openings, as in the case of the mantra/crystal, "Mother of earth and of love." Or when the mantra/crystal is drawn from a dream or a twilight image.

As they accumulate over a period of time, these small bits of data can say a great deal to us as they remind us of inner events that were intense when they happened but that have since dropped from consciousness. It is important to note in this regard that since deep inner experiences take place on the twilight level, they are as easily forgotten as dreams if they are not recorded soon after they occur. Once they are recalled, however, they can be remembered in vivid detail. The small bits of information we record in our Mantra/Crystal Index are intended to provide the cues we need.

The composite of information that will gradually fill the Index will be a concise way of making us aware of the extent and breadth of our inner lives as our Process Meditation proceeds. During those inevitable times when we feel separated from the depths in us, that awareness is an important factor in our being reconnected.

The *Workings* segment of the Mantra/Crystal section is the place where we carry out our mantra/crystal exercises, and where we record our experiences as best we can while they are taking place. As the name suggests, Workings is where the core of the mantra/crystal practice takes place. Or, better said, mantra/crystal practice takes place in the depth of ourselves, but Workings is the segment of our *Intensive Journal* workbook where we give our interior experiences a definite form so that they can continue on the outer level of our life.

Our mantra/crystal work becomes a process of transforming intangible inner experience into tangible new awarenesses and actions and we have a core of procedures for doing that. Whenever we are engaged in a mantra/crystal meditation, we write the mantra/crystal phrase at the head of a page together with the date. We then record all that transpires in our experience on that page and on the pages that follow. If at any later time we use that mantra/crystal again, we continue in that same part of the Workings segment. When we begin another time of practice with that mantra/crystal, we write the date of the new experience following the first one and we then record the occurrences that take place.

Sometimes a particular mantra/crystal is intensely felt in relation to an outer circumstance or an inner experience, and its use may then be concentrated into a short period of time. More generally, however, the use of a mantra/crystal tends to be intermittent and to stretch over a longer range of time. It will be intermingled with the use of other mantra/crystals, and there may also be times when no mantra/crystal meditation takes place at all. The fact that there is irregularity in a person's practice does not mean that there is not a continuity of process within the person corresponding to that mantra/crystal. That continuity of process may indeed be present, but since it is within the person it is taking place by inner time; and that may appear to be very irregular and inconsistent when judged in the light of external or chronological time.

One principle that underlies the structuring of the *Intensive Journal* system as a whole is the effort to provide an instrument for recording the intangible and irregular movement of inner time, and for drawing it into such a form that its data can be worked with. This is especially important where the practice of Process Meditation is concerned, since the primary means that we have for maintaining the continuity of our inner process is the way we make our Journal entries.

In the Workings segment, each mantra/crystal that we use retains its own continuous sub-section so that whenever we work with that mantra/crystal our experience is recorded there. For example, we may work with a particular mantra/crystal on two consecutive days, then a week later, than a month later, then not for four months, then six months later, then on three days in the following week when something in the content or the atmosphere of the mantra/crystal has become inwardly important again. Each of these times of practice with that mantra/crystal will be recorded in the same sub-section, one following the other. The dates will be irregular, but as the person whose experiences they are, we can easily recognize the continuity of the process that moves among them and that is working in the depths of ourselves.

As we continue in our meditation practice, those mantra/crystals that we use again and again soon accumulate substantial sub-sections containing the sequence of the various times that we have worked with them. Over a period of time these mantra/crystals, being well and productively used, seem to develop their own life history with their characteristic style and atmosphere. They also seem to acquire—or you will tend to associate with them—a particular quality of energy and an emotional attachment. The relationship with a mantra/crystal can become very intimate and profound, with many overtones, as the actualities of inner experience accumulate. It is all part of the process by which we deepen and extend our experience of mantra/crystals here in *Workings.*

* * *

Now let us proceed with our active practice of mantra/crystal meditation. Having formed and decided upon a mantra/crystal with which we can at least begin, our first step is to write the mantra/crystal at the head of a fresh page. We add today's date, and we keep our workbook open, holding a pen handy as we move into the quiet of the twilight atmosphere.

Preparing for a mantra/crystal experience, we sit in stillness, our eyes closed. The first thing we do is nothing. Just sitting in stillness. Not thinking. Not planning. Not actively preparing. Just sitting in stillness, letting the muddy waters of our spirit settle and become quiet. Starting in stillness, these inner waters can become quieter than they were. But perhaps not yet quiet enough to become clear.

We sit in stillness doing nothing, letting our whole being just be. As we remain that way, in whatever position we are sitting, we find that our breathing becomes slower and softer. We try not to be conscious of our breathing, just sitting in stillness and observing our breathing as though we were outsiders to it, looking at it furtively as though we were peeking in at our breathing through the window. We want our breathing to continue by its own inner principle so that it can balance itself and establish its own rhythm without our interference. We let it be. Our breathing proceeds by itself while we are doing nothing. The longer that the muddying movements of our inner waters are still, the more those waters become clear, and the freer our breathing is to find its own rhythm. We notice that this takes place of itself. As we remain quiet, doing nothing, our breathing gradually settles into a slower rhythm. This is not a rhythm that we give it, but a rhythem that our breathing finds and establishes for itself. It is a relaxed and steady rhythm, breathing in and breathing out, breathing in and breathing out at a gentle and regular pace. We let that rhythm continue to establish itself, as we sit in stillness, giving it as much time as it desires.

When our breathing has settled into a regular rhythm that feels comfortable to us, and when we feel that the pattern our breathing has established is strong enough to continue of itself, we are ready for our next step.

Now we say our mantra/crystal under our breath. We repeat it and repeat it, again and again, continuously. As we are saying it under our breath, we link our mantra/crystal with the movement of our breathing, connecting it with the rhythm that our breathing has established. It may require three or four times or even more of saying our mantra/crystal together with our breathing to draw the two into an interconnected linkage. Gradually they fit together, until their rhythms become intertwined and balance each other. At that point we find that our mantra/crystal and our breathing are actually carrying and supporting each other. Once they fit together, our mantra/crystal and our breathing bolster each other and carry each other along.

> The mantra carries the breath:
> The breath carries the mantra.

That is a rhythm that establishes itself as the two move back and forth. The regular breathing and the rhythm of the seven syllables of the mantra/crystal become a self-sustaining movement that draws itself inward. The two together sustain each other, each drawing the other forward into its next movement. The mantra carries the breath through its next cycle of breathing in and breathing out. The breath carries the mantra/crystal through the cycles of its own seven syllables. And each supports the other. Each draws the other forward.

> The mantra carries the breath:
> The breath carries the mantra.

As it continues we realize that this self-balancing movement is building its own momentum. Its continuity is derived from itself. The mantra/crystal and the breathing have formed a unit that is self-contained. Each supplies the other so that the energy for the continuous back-and-forth movement of the whole is provided by the mutual movement itself. Nothing else is required. Just the mantra and the breathing fitted together into each other. Together they are self-contained, as they draw each other along. Our breathing, fitted together with saying our seven-syllable mantra/crystal under our breath, creates a pendulum movement, continuously swinging back and forth, each cycle of movement leading to the next one.

The pendulum movement established by our mantra and our breathing recalls to us the method by which the Russian Pilgrim learned to pray without ceasing. Once it has been set into motion, the pendulum movement proceeds by itself, carried by its own energies and the alternating rhythm of the two factors within it, the mantra and the breathing. It becomes in a special sense a "prayer that prays itself." Like the prayer of the Russian Pilgrim, it continues without conscious or deliberate thought, having no predetermined purpose except to continue its movement. There is one important difference, however, between the self-propelling prayer of the Russian Pilgrim and our mantra/crystal meditation. While both proceed with no predetermined purpose, the Russian Pilgrim believes that his practice of repeating his prayer is a permanent good-in-itself. He perceives his practice of prayer as not only unceasing but also unchanging.

Mantra/crystal meditation, on the other hand, sees itself as part of a process that contains cycles of changing experience within its continuity. Our mantra/crystal phrase sets itself into motion as a prayer that prays itself and it continues in repetition by its own power. Since we know that it is part of a cycle of experience that is contained within a larger process we do not regard our mantra/crystal meditation as a final or unchanging event. We expect it to change, even though we do not know what to expect—and do not try to predetermine—what will come when it changes. We do, however, have some indication of the general sequence of cycle and process that will take place if we are able to continue as diligently with our mantra/crystal meditations as the Russian Pilgrim continued with his Jesus Prayer.

What will take place if we are able to continue the pendulum movement without interruption and without the intrusion of our mental consciousness? As our mantra/crystal and our breathing carry each other in their self-balancing continuity, our ego and our consciousness of what is taking place become superfluous. The event is happening without them. Therefore they can drop away. As we continue the pendulum movement of our mantra/crystal and our breathing, our ego-consciousness does drop away. Only the back and forth movement remains.

We continue the pendulum movement or, better said, the pendulum movement continues itself. The regular rhythm of our mantra/crystal in balance with the continued repetition of our mantra/crystal, now without the presence of our ego-consciousness, creates an atmosphere of its own. It is a twilight atmosphere, deep and still. The pendulum movement with its repetitious sound adds to the stillness. As it continues, it becomes like the soft sound of lake waters lapping at the shore while the waters at the center of the lake become progressively still and clear. The pendulum movement establishes the equivalent of the cycle that Lao Tse described, "Muddy water, let stand, becomes clear." Without our seeking it, for our attention has been directed only toward maintaining our mantra-breathing pendulum, a core of quiet has formed itself and has become present to us. It is like the clear waters of the lake, except that it has no specific symbol or image. It is simply a core of stillness, a quiet center, an absolute openness in which images and thoughts of every kind can take shape and show themselves to us.

The repetitive practice of our mantra-breathing pendulum leads to silence beyond ego-consciousness. And that, in turn, enables the deepest parts of the twilight range of our being to open themselves to us. Molecules of thought and imagery take shape in that twilight range. Freely forming, without our conscious intervention, they reflect them-selves to us in the clear waters of our silence. At first we do not realize that something is being shown to us. The repetitious inner sound of our mantra-breathing pendulum has placed us in a glazed state of empty-mindedness, separated from our ego-consciousness. It is similar to the experience of being in a heavy sleep when we suddenly become aware that a deep dream is unfolding before us. In the first stages of surprise, we miss the early parts of the dream. They have slipped past us before we could realize what was happening. Gradually our consciousness returns and we may have the presence of mind to realize that, if we do not now record what is being shown to us, we will probably forget it forever. If it is a deep dream that is taking place, we have to draw ourselves out of sleep in order to record it. If it is a mantra/crystal meditation, however, we can learn to record it while we are perceiving it and while the experience is still happening. We can even learn to record it without leaving the deep atmosphere of twilight space in which the interior event is taking place.

The key lies in the difference between recording the essentials while they are happening and describing an inner experience in full detail. As you become aware in the midst of your mantra/crystal meditation that something is being presented to you at the twilight level, you will experience a tugging at your capacities of attention, as though some-thing is pulling at you. It is similar to being drawn to a waking state by the impact of a strong dream. Having been in a deep sleep, suddenly your interior cognition is activated. You realize that you are being called to pay attention to something that is taking place within your-self. The dream awakens you from your sleep, and the effect is similar in your mantra/crystal meditation.

It is not necessary, however, for you to be drawn out of the deep twilight level as you recognize your inner experience and as you proceed to record it. The act of Journal recording may actually help you remain in the deep place so that the inner experience can be extended.

With paper and pen available, you may have to open your eyes only very slightly in order to record what is taking place. A few words, a phrase or two, will suffice at the start to record what you have just perceived. The first written words establish a point of contact for you so that you can now function in both realms. You can remain quietly placed in the twilight range where new perceptions and awarenesses, new combinations of MTI's, continue to be presented to you. And you can record them as they are happening, letting the brief entries that you make serve as tangible embodiments of the inner exercises while they are taking place. In this way, your Journal recording does not diminish the inner process. It strengthens it because it gives those ephemeral experiences a permanent form. The fact that the experience actually occurred is now incontrovertibly established no matter how it may eventually be judged or regarded. Its existence is proved by its contents as they are being recorded.

You find yourself now in the position of being an intermediary between the inner and outer realms. The side of you that faces inward, your interior cognition, is engaged in observing a self-moving process that continuously brings new material to your attention. The side of you that faces outward is engaged in recording it. After you have become accustomed to it, you will find that playing the role of intermediary between the two realms has the effect not of separating but of connecting them so that your outer recording stimulates and assists the flow of inner experience.

When you are first made aware that an interior event is taking place, begin by writing just a word or a phrase with your eyes barely open, and with the paper just visible enough for your pen to find it. As you are coming up from the twilight range, that first writing will establish your contact with the physical fact of the Journal paper and the act of recording. When you start, write only what is essential to be written. The rest can be filled in later since you will have written clues to remind you. As you proceed you will find that you are able to record with increasing fluidity while still maintaining your inner contact.

After a few tries at it, you will very likely be able to record your experiences even while your mantra-breathing pendulum continues to be in effect, just as the Russian Pilgrim continued to say his Jesus Prayer while he went about his chores. Even if you have to stop the saying of your mantra/crystal in order to record your experience you can nonetheless remain in the midst of the atmosphere. In whatever forms they come, whether as visual experiences, as words that you hear, as intuitions or as body feelings, let the MTI's that present themselves move through you directly to the words you write. Make of yourself merely an instrument for your experience, and nothing more. Do not interpret it, nor explain it, nor elaborate it; merely be an instrument for it so that your experience can be transformed into words and can be recorded for your later use. If you remain only an instrument and do not become an interpreter, the atmosphere can retain its hold on you and keep you within it. In that way it becomes possible to record your experience even while you are in the midst of it and while the movement of interior events is continuing.

As you proceed with it, you will find that working with mantra/crystals has many aspects and varied applications. Sometimes it leads to large and extended experiences, rich with symbolism, carrying messages of profundity and inspiration. Sometimes it deals with current situations of our lives as dreams do, although it tends to do this more directly with less obscure symbolism than dreams. Sometimes it brings creative new ideas, solutions or suggestions for problems that we did not realize we were thinking about. These new awarenesses may come in visionary forms, as simple thoughts directly stated; they may come as phrases or lines of poetry, as a feeling or as an intuition that has no words. They may carry messages that have great meaning for us, but we should not approach our mantra/crystal practice with the expectation or desire that it achieve any preconceived goal for us. To do that tightens and restricts the work by making it self-conscious. We should rather approach our mantra/crystal experience as a self-quieting process that sometimes evokes the depth of us, opening limitlessly from within.

The primary role of mantra/crystal practice is to give us a means of stilling and centering ourselves in relation to the continuity of our lives. Once we have constructed a mantra/crystal or two, we have a means of pausing in our life and quieting ourselves at any time. It is always available to us as a method for centering ourselves in the midst of the activity, and in relation to the unfolding contents, of our life. We may adapt a mantra/crystal to particular circumstances and uses. Most practice with mantra/crystals is done in a sitting position, but there is no reason to limit it to that. For example, "Walking at one with the world," is a mantra/crystal that I have used considerably in walking meditations. I suppose it could have a jogging or a running version for those who are more energetic. Naturally, the pendulum aspect of the meditation has to be greatly modified when it is used in this physical form.

Various adaptations will occur to you after you have built up sufficient experience in your personal work with mantra/crystals. You will find that there are certain mantra/crystals with which you work again and again. Over a period of time these tend to establish a particular quality, an atmosphere or an aura around themselves, expressing your cumulative experiences with them. They become like old friends available to you as you need them. You may find, for example, that on a number of occasions a particular mantra/crystal serves as the means by which you become deeply centered and aware. You grow accustomed to working with it when you are sitting in stillness, but a crisis carrying great tension arises one day in the course of your life and you find that you spontaneously call upon that mantra/crystal. By means of it you establish your own "atom of silence" in the midst of the pressures of your world.

The core of each mantra/crystal experience is established at the point where our rhythmic breathing combines with the mantra/crystal to establish the pendulum effect. This is when we are taken into the twilight range, a restful and a freeing place to be. To be there is good and valuable and renewing in and of itself. That is why, when we have worked in mantra/crystal meditation to a degree sufficient to establish the pendulum effect, even if "nothing" additional transpires in the form of a definite twilight experience, we must recognize that a great deal has already happened. The deepening of silence, the neutralizing of mental consciousness, the movement of the mantra/crystal, are all substantial interior phenomena. They establish their atmosphere and they place us in the twilight depth. That is why the practice of working with a mantra/crystal until we experience the mantra-breathing pendulum moving within us is valuable for us to do whenever we feel called to it. In addition to the atmosphere it establishes within us, it opens the way for new awarenesses to come to us.

There is a great range and flexibility in the times and forms of working with mantra/crystals. Some individuals prefer to establish a definite discipline and fixed times for their practice. Others prefer to follow their spontaneous promptings and to work with their mantra/crystals when an inner stirring calls them. Either way, or a combination of both, is valid. After your first several times of working with mantra/crystals, as you are building a resource to draw upon in your Mantra/Crystal Index, you find that this area of your inner life seems to generate its own energy. Certain mantra/crystals not only sustain themselves by reappearing in our experiences but they seem to be moving toward a further awareness in the course of each time of practice. While we may set regular times for our disciplined mantra/crystal meditation, we should also be responsive to the irregular times when these mantra/crystals call to us spontaneously.

As your resource of mantra/crystals grows, you may soon feel that you are suffering from an over-abundance of riches. You find that you possess several mantra/crystals in your Index, each of which has good potentialities. Which shall you choose?

Since your life has many facets, it is appropriate for you to have many mantra/crystals available for your use. Each suggests its own directions of emphasis and experience. Thus you will work with different mantra/crystals according to the varied circumstances of your life. In choosing a mantra/crystal for a given time of practice, there are two main criteria to consider: the first is your feeling that this is a mantra/crystal that will enable you to reach a condition of centeredness in which the mantra-breathing pendulum can take effect; the second rests more on your intuition that the subject matter or the area of your life from which a particular mantra/crystal is drawn contains something to be unfolded further and to be disclosed to you at a deeper inner level. It is your intimation that something more is contained here and that it will express a message for your life when you give it the opportunity.

In considering these two criteria, we recognize that the first is concerned with establishing a stillness within yourself while the other concerns the evoking and creativity that can be a by-product of mantra/crystal work. Let the first consideration be your primary one. Choose a mantra/crystal that feels especially congenial to you as a vehicle for achieving a quietness of being. The rest will come of itself, if not this time in your meditation, then in the course of your further practice. When you work with your mantra/crystal, let it not be in the hope of achieving some predetermined purpose but rather to establish the continued movement of the mantra-breathing pendulum within yourself. When that has taken place, you will have set a process into motion that has its own autonomy. It brings about first an inward stillness, and then a quiet activity that opens from within. The second stage in your mantra/crystal experience corresponds to the second half of the cycle of active and passive, the phase in which new movement stirs in the depths of that which lies passively at rest. That is when images take shape and disclose themselves on the quiet lake of our consciousness, in accordance with the modality we have adapted from Lao Tse regarding the rhythms working at the depth of life. Our mantra/crystal meditation draws us into harmony with the timeless principle that underlies that rhythm so that we can experience it in the particular terms of our individual existence. That is how new molecules of thought and imagery, new MTI's relevant to the conditions of our lives, take form and emerge as though by themselves out of the depths of us. They are expressions of the creative principle of life reaching toward meaning and disclosing its intimations of truth to us in the midst of our stillness.

Our mantra/crystal meditation may bring forth new ideas and understandings as products of creativity, but we do not regard that as its purpose. Stillness in the midst of our active and committed life is the purpose of the total practice of Process Meditation of which our mantra/crystal work is a part. Creativity is merely one of its occasional by-products, an extra gift that is sometimes given to us to encourage us in the continuity of our life.

PART V

Process-Plus-One

Chapter 17

From Resource to Continuity: Personal and Transpersonal Leads

Each of us who has carried out the practices described so far in this book has done a great deal of work. Many pages have been filled by now in our *Intensive Journal* workbooks. We use the word *work* with a number of different connotations in the course of our practice of Process Meditation, but here we can speak of work in its ordinary, everyday sense. Much of what we have done has involved arduous and difficult effort, and we know that more of the same will be required as we continue. It has been *work*, and it will be again.

Having come this far, however, we may have reached a point where our work will become less arduous as we proceed. This is for various reasons. One is that, as the pieces of our inner lives come together, we begin to see not only patterns forming but purposes and new directions disclosing themselves. Now we have indications of where the movement is heading, and that makes it easier to go ahead. One of the special capacities that we develop in the course of our Process Meditation practices is the ability to proceed toward goals that have not yet been announced to us. We do not know what they are, but we can press on toward them because we have already had the experience of having new meanings disclosed to us in the course of our work although we had not envisioned them before. That has undoubtedly happened to a number of us in our work until now, especially in the mantra/crystal meditations.

Another reason that our Process Meditation work may be less arduous in the future is that we have had to pass through a preliminary time of laying the foundations for our ongoing work; and that is mainly completed by now. The practice of Process Meditation divides into two general phases. The first is the time of gathering the data of our personal spiritual history and also of learning to work comfortably with the various Journal sections and procedures that comprise the Process Meditation methodology. This is the resource phase of the work and it provides the basis on which we can proceed to our ongoing and deepening practice of Process Meditation.

As we have carried out the exercises of Process Meditation until now, working in the Meditation Log, in Connections, and in the Mantra/Crystals section, we have seen that each procedure generates new experiences. Consequently it increases the inner data available to us. It gives us a spiritual resource that we did not have before. It also raises the question of how we shall utilize this new material in extending and deepening the contents of our inner lives. This is the essence of Process Meditation as a method of continuity in spiritual experience.

In speaking of a *continuity phase* in Process Meditation we do not mean simply that it keeps on going. Continuity has a much larger significance in the context of Process Meditation. It means that, after we have established as our foundation a resource of information drawn from our spiritual history, and after we have established a framework of structure and practices in our *Intensive Journal* workbook, we have a means of working continuously at our own pace and tempo whenever and for as long as the quest for deeper meaning personally involves us. The quest for meaning in life in which we are engaged is, after all, not like a task that we can expect to complete in a definite time, or an illness that we shall cure and then be finished with. Process Meditation is as infinite as the meaning of life is infinite. It is as open in possibilities as our personal potential for wisdom and sensitivity is open, and it increases with our capacity for finding the poetry of human existence.

In this perspective we can see that what we are engaged in here is a process of lifelong meditation reaching toward what is qualitative in human existence. Many of us have already had the experience of discovering that this process of lifelong meditation draws us into mysteries as profound as they are obscure; but from time to time they may open for us and they become like a bud that has iridescent jewels in its flower. As we work in it, we gradually recognize that the quest for meaning which is at the heart of the meditative life is not a quest for a fixed object. It is not like seeking a new land nor a gold mine nor an oil field; nor is it even like seeking a truth that objectively exists and is waiting for us to find it. It is a quest, rather, that builds and grows as our capacity to experience grows. The meditative life is a cumulative reaching toward meaning that is its own goal. Ends and means are a unity in it. The apparent paradox which becomes clear to us as we experience it is that meaning grows in and by the process of what we do as we are actively engaged in seeking it. Another way of saying this is that meaning is being created and is being added both to our lives and to the universe as we proceed in deepening and in extending our individual inner experiences.

This recognition, stated in varied contexts and symbolic forms, that a qualitative evolution beyond the physical is taking place in the universe by means of the inner experience of human beings, has been the crowning understanding of such modern thinkers as Teilhard de Chardin, Jan Christian Smuts, Henri Bergson, Jacob Bronowski, Sri Aurobindo, L. L. Whyte. In my own life, it was this personal recognition of spiritual evolution in the cosmos while I was writing *Depth Psychology and Modern Man* in 1958 that opened the sources and the commitment within me for my subsequent work.*

This is the large context in which we should think of the continuity aspect of Process Meditation. It involves our individual experience in a way that makes it a process of lifelong meditation. It is a personal quest, but it reaches beyond itself since its essence is more than personal. There is, in fact, a very significant parallel that can serve as a metaphor for continuing inner work. Just as a process of qualitative evolution takes place across the millennia in the life of the cosmos, so it may also take place across the decades in the lives of those persons who are actively engaged in the quest for meaning. The evolution of the individual parallels that of the cosmos, and occasionally the two may intersect and reinforce one another as well.

*   *   *

We want now to take our first step in the continuity phase of Process Meditation. Up to this point in our work, our attention has

---

* *Depth Psychology and Modern Man*, Chapters 6-10.

been concentrated on the Process Meditation sections in the *Intensive Journal* workbook, but now we move out into the full range of the *Intensive Journal* system. This will enable us to experience in actuality the implications of conducting our spiritual practices in a framework that includes the history and contents of our life as a whole.

We began our Process Meditation work by making a brief statement of our spiritual position, describing spontaneously what we felt to be our interior situation. That was our starting point. Since that time we have had many additional experiences, stirred memories and emotions, opened the way for new awarenesses. What is our interior situation now? What have we learned? What do we now believe? And what further steps have been indicated to us?

Having collected considerable information in the course of our Process Meditation work, it is not necessary for us to make another spontaneous statement of position. We are, in fact, engaged now in repositioning ourselves in the movement of our inner process, but we can do that now more empirically. We have already gathered a resource of our life-facts so that, as we draw these facts together in the next steps of our Journal work, they will indicate to us what our present spiritual position is, and they can direct us toward our further experiences.

To do this, let us now turn to the Meditation Log section, and particularly to the segment for *Inner Process Entries*. This is where we draw together the facts that pertain to the present situation of our inner life.

The first entry we made here had the purpose of describing the movement of inner process that we observed within ourselves as we took the first steps in getting Process Meditation under way. The last time we wrote in Inner Process Entries was when we were engaged in working out our mantra/crystals. Since then we have proceeded with our mantra/crystal meditation and any additional inner experiences that have come to us. This is the time, then, that we return to this segment of the Meditation Log to fill in our account of the continuing movement of our inner process.

We begin by sitting in stillness. We write today's date to start our entry in the Meditation Log. We begin by describing directly and simply the facts of our present situation. We report on the fact that we have carried through at least one mantra/crystal meditation since we last wrote here. We may take note of the mantra/crystal that we eventually used, perhaps adding some brief comments at this point on our mantra/crystal experience. We wish to reach back beyond our mantra/crystal work, however. We want to recapitulate the main movement of our Process Meditation work as a whole up to now, so that we can consider our present spiritual position and determine what our next moves shall be.

Sitting in stillness, we go back in our minds over the way we felt when we began to record our Gatherings, the specific memories of our inner life. Time has passed since we wrote them, and that distance gives us some perspective. We are not interested now in recalling the contents of those Gatherings but the emotions we felt when we wrote them. In particular, we note that some of the memories we described in Gatherings have a greater emotional intensity than others. There may be some also that we now feel more strongly about than when we first recorded them. In making our Inner Process Entries, we especially take note of our emotions and the changes in our emotions.

As we proceed we recall also the feelings that came to us as we were listing our Spiritual Steppingstones. It may be that additional thoughts or considerations come into our mind now, and that we find ourselves reflecting further about particular aspects of our spiritual history. We include these reconsiderations in our Inner Process Entries.

We take ourselves back also to recall the experiences we had in Re-Openings. It may be of interest to us now to note which event we chose to re-enter and to re-open. We recall the emotions that stirred in us then as we were engaged in that exercise. As we think of that, other events may suggest themselves to us as containing unexplored aspects that would make it worthwhile re-opening them at some later time.

Having gone back over the varied exercises that we did in the Connections section, we may now take note especially of the feelings that stir in us with respect to our spiritual history as a whole. Writing now, we may find that there are new perspectives taking shape in us, that our standards of evaluation and our responses are changing. We should record these observations and reflections now as expressions of our inner process in motion.

We come now to make the Inner Process Entry that records our feelings with respect to our mantra/crystal meditation. We have recorded the details in the Workings segment of the Mantra/Crystal section, but now we want to write a spontaneous overview. The spontaneous quality of the summary description that you write now is an important aspect of it. Do not analyze what took place. Just describe your emotions and especially refer to the thoughts and images that stirred within you and that came to your attention in the course of your experience. Perhaps a metaphor now occurs to you to describe the movement as a whole as it was taking place in the course of your mantra/crystal meditation.

In reviewing the experiences of the resource phase of our Process Meditation work, there are a number of entries to make. Most of them should be brief entries, but some may stimulate us to greater elaborations. Let those entries move as freely as they wish. At this point in the work, entries that seek to extend themselves by their own power are very likely bringing us information that will contribute to our next experiences. We let them say all that they have to say.

The important question to which we come next involves the possibility that these entries, with the symbolism and the imagery of the events they are describing, may be opening paths for us to a deeper awareness. They may contain hidden messages and clues to our next experiences. The practical question then becomes: do we have a means of discovering what these clues and this information actually are so that we can make use of them? To do this we draw upon a procedure that plays an important role in the *Intensive Journal* method. We look for the Journal Feedback leads.

The Process Meditation exercises with which we have been working up to this point have primarily been directed toward the possibilities of evoking meaning in our lives. They have involved experiences of connection, the development of our beliefs, and the varied practices by which we have sought a larger understanding of the mysteries of our life. Our Process Meditation work has been focused toward experiences that are related to the fundamental meanings of life, and yet we know that such experiences come about as part of our life history as a whole. They are reaching toward what is more-than-personal, but they take place within the context of our personal existence.

More than that, we have already recognized that our perceptions of meaning do not involve merely the surface of mental consciousness, but that they draw upon the depths of us. The imagery and intuitions that lead to perceptions of meaning have their source primarily in the twilight range of our awareness. We have seen that some of their qualities parallel those of dreams. We thus have reason to believe that experiences that come to us in the course of our Process Meditation work may be significant carriers of the *inner wisdom* lying at the twilight depths of our consciousness. Our task lies in finding and deciphering the messages our inner wisdom may be trying to give us.

We have made the entries that review the movement of our inner process when we were working in the Connections sections and when we were engaged in our mantra/crystal meditations. These are now available to us as a resource from which we can draw our Journal Feedback leads.

The operative principle that underlies Journal Feedback has provided the dynamic for much of the therapeutic and growth effects that have resulted from the use of the *Intensive Journal* system. Its procedures are based upon the structured concept of feeding the data of our life experiences into the *Intensive Journal* process, using the sections of the workbook as channels for the many mini-processes that comprise the whole of a person's life. As the contents of the various Journal sections combine among themselves, cross-fertilizing one another in the course of the sequence of exercises, new integrations are formed. And these become the base points for our next experiences. The core of the *Intensive Journal* process lies in this systematic rhythm which the Journal structure makes possible. In individual practice it opens out with many ramifications as we progressively learn how to move from our life experiences to the appropriate Journal sections and back to life experiences in a constructive way.

The process of feeding in and feeding back is a cumulative one. Our use of the term, *feedback*, in *Intensive Journal* work of course differs from the use of the term, *feedback*, in the computer model because the process at work in the Journal is human and not mechanical. Two of its most important differences derive from the fact that Journal Feedback draws upon the intuitive capacities that lie in the twilight depths of persons; and also that it stimulates the organic process of growth that is inherent in human beings as part of the living world of nature. The feedback procedures that move through the *Intensive Journal* structure are thus able to generate energy as they proceed. These energies are drawn both from the emotions of individual experience and from the dormant potentials latent in the seed-depths of persons. One of the consequences of this combination in Journal Feedback work is that intuition and energy progressively come together to give a creative quality to the material that has been fed into our Journal sections.

In setting the Journal Feedback principle into operation, the step of primary importance is the move we make in taking a life experience to the Journal section that is most appropriate for it. This is not a question of finding the proper category as might be expected. It is a question not of classification but of process. We want to feed experiences into a Journal section where the exercises will draw them into a larger life movement while evoking additional energies and awarenesses from the depths of ourselves.

The best way to proceed in setting up the Journal Feedback movement seems to be not to try to figure out the answers ourselves. In fact, a good rule of thumb to observe is that if you feel definitely convinced that you are sure of where the contents of this particular life experience should go, pause. The chances are very great in that case that your judgment has been made at the level of mental consciousness and that it has in its background some analytical concept drawn from the habits of psychologism in past times. Therefore pause and do not rush to judgment. If we move more slowly, we can proceed in the empirical way of letting our experience itself tell us which area of *Intensive Journal* practice it desires for its next step. It will show us the Journal Feedback lead to the next exercise that its own nature requires. But we must first clear a path for it, and keep the way open without intruding our premature opinions.

To find our next Journal Feedback lead, we begin by sitting in silence. With our eyes closed, we inwardly consider the movement of the Process Meditation work we have done so far, the reconstruction of our spiritual history, our mantra/crystal meditations. We do not interpret them nor analytically think about them, but we let ourselves feel the whole of our life in the atmosphere of our Process Meditation. In this atmosphere we find that, without trying to understand the contents of our various experiences, some aspects of them fit together with especial harmony. Others do not seem to fit together at all. Where they do fit together, forming pairs or clusters, we are given an indication that something is trying to form a new integration of various factors within us.

We have noted in another connection that there appears to be a holistic principle in the world of nature that moves toward the formation of ever more focused integrative units. It is a phenomenon that takes place irregularly and unpredictably, but the holistic principle is nonetheless an understandable factor as it occurs in the physical world. When it is expressed, however, in the subjective contents of our individual lives, we tend to think of it less naturalistically. We attribute it then to the inner wisdom that is in the depth of the human person. So be it. The term we use is not important; but it is important that we place ourselves in a quiet, an essentially passive, interior attitude, with the contents of our varied meditation experiences moving around inside of us. It then becomes possible for our *inner wisdom* or the *holistic principle*—whichever you prefer—to draw together clusters of contents from our experiences and to form them into new integrative units within us.

These new integrative units are *wholes* in a special meaning of that term. They do not include all the parts of our previous experiences, and thus they are not *wholes* in the sense of including the whole of everything. But they are whole in the sense of being integral. They are whole in relation to the total movement and intention of our varied experiences. They express the essence of their direction, and they reflect their integrity. The varied contents of our experiences come together to form these new wholes. They are the emergents brought forth by the movement of our experiences.

As we have had many experiences, we let their varied contents move around inside of us. Sitting in stillness, we let these contents come together. Some of them fit together and join one another as though they are finding each other. Others do not fit together and drop away. Of those that do naturally come together, new clusters are formed. As you remain with them in quietness, they refine themselves further and new integrative units are formed. It comes about, then, that the multiple contents of your sequence of experiences have now been reconstructed by a natural, integrative principle. They are available to you now in a concise form. You may very well be able to find in them the essence of your experiences, their direction and their implicit meaning, while the extraneous contents have eliminated themselves. The tone as well as the contents of these new integrative units that have formed within you give you a means of recognizing the intention and larger purpose that lies in the background of your life experiences. It also provides the materials with which that purpose can unfold as the work proceeds.

One way to think of these new units that have formed at the twilight level is as MTI's, new molecules of thought and imagery. We consider them, therefore, not only from the point of view of their role and meaning in the inner development of our life, but also in terms of their own intrinsic content. In addition to their significance for our life, new MTI's may also be carriers of a new hypothesis for our scientific work, a new image to use in our painting or poetry, a new idea for a project we would pursue in the world. As we become conscious of their formation within us, and as we describe them in our Meditation Log entry as part of our interior and subjective life, we should not overlook the objective contribution they may contain for our creative work.

Sitting in silence with the contents of our experiences moving around inside of us, we let the stillness deepen within us. Let it remain still, quiet, empty, passive, long enough so that new integrations can form of themselves. Do not rush the process. Do not place yourself in the position of cleverly figuring out an answer and knowing just what to do next. Do not take your cake out of the oven too soon. Let the stillness last long enough so that the essentials will have time to come together, and so that whatever is extra can drop away. Make sure that the stillness is sufficient so that the new integrations can take place as though of themselves.

When a new awareness, a new MTI, is presented to you in word or thought or image, record it without judgment in the Inner Process Entries segment of your Meditation Log. It may be brief or extended. There may be a single one, or there may be several. Record it as it comes to you, and remain in your silence.

Out of your varied and extended experiences there has now come a crystallization; one or two or three new integral units have been formed. They contain the essence of your experiences, as the message of their movement has been brought together by the holistic principle working in your life, which is your inner wisdom. This will become the starting point for your next cycle of experience. Now that they have been formed and recorded, we can look to these new crystallizations for guidance. As they become Journal Feedback leads, they will show us how to proceed.

There are two general directions in which our Journal Feedback leads can guide us. As personal leads, they can take us to the Journal sections that deal with the private issues of our individual life. As transpersonal leads, they can direct our attention to those areas of

281

human existence that have a significance beyond the needs and the desires of our individual life. These are more than personal, but they may be the primary concerns of our life as we are reaching toward meaning.

In the context of our *Intensive Journal* work, the distinction between personal and transpersonal leads is primarily functional. It points in the direction of two different kinds of emphasis in our life, but the two are not separate. They are the contents of our single life, looked at from different angles of vision.

In the structure of our *Intensive Journal* workbook, certain sections and their accompanying exercises are set up to enable us to perceive and respond to the events of our lives from a personal point of view; others give us a transpersonal vantage point. These are two different approaches, and each is appropriate at times in our lives and in particular situations. Eventually our lives require both, and that is why both are present in the *Intensive Journal* structure.

In the personal sections, we work in more pragmatic terms. We deal there with the pressures and the problems of our lives in terms of the immediacy of the issues. When, for example, we have to make decisions relating to our body—to deal with an illness, to participate in athletics, choose a diet regime—the frame of reference is altogether in terms of the particulars of our individual life. It is *personal* in that sense. At such a time the Journal Feedback lead that would come to us would very likely be a personal lead directing us to the various procedures we follow in the *Dialogue with the Body* section.

In comparable terms, there are several other Journal sections to which personal leads might direct us for particularized work. They are *personal* in the special sense that they involve issues and decisions that are unique to us as individuals in that they can only be decided within the context of our own life. There may be questions, for example, of how we should seek to earn our livelihood, of the kind of role we shall play in society, of marrying and raising a family, of friendships and relationships with other individuals, of the tasks and responsibilities we will undertake in our work and in our life. All these are issues that arise and can be decided only within the context of an individual's own existence.

The personal leads that will be calling our attention to these areas of our life experience may be directing us to several sections in the *Intensive*

Journal workbook. In addition to *Dialogue with the Body*, they may be pointing us toward *Dialogue with Works*, or *Dialogue with Persons* or *Dialogue with Events*. Especially, if you are at a crossroad of decision in your life, they may be directing you to the procedures in a very important personal section, *Intersections: Roads Taken and Not Taken*. These sections and the varied exercises for using them are described as part of the basic *Intensive Journal* work in *At a Journal Workshop*.*

In general, when personal leads emerge from our Process Meditation work, it is because our life intuition is calling our attention to specific situations that need care. It is setting our priorities for us. On the other hand, our life intuition may also give an opposite type of guidance. People often feel convinced that if some particular situation in their lives were changed, all their difficulties would be solved. They see their lives in terms of personal-type problems. They are surprised, then, when a *transpersonal* lead comes to them and directs their attention to another area of their life. That is only an indication, however, that their inner wisdom knows better. It is indicating that in their present life situation, the sequence of concerns should be reversed. For them the priority is to work first with the questions that involve their sense of meaning in the transpersonal contexts of life. After that, their specific circumstances can fit into place and the problems can be worked out in the personal sections.

We might assume that the strongest emotions occur in the personal areas of life where individuals are moved by love and anger and jealousy. We find, however, that emotions of the very strongest power arise in the transpersonal area of experience. It is merely that these emotions are felt in a range of reality that reaches beyond the individual life. The emotions are felt personally and with great intensity, but insofar as their subject is God or immortality or truth or science or nature, the framework of the emotions is more than individual and therefore more than personal. Even in our secular and highly rationalized modern society, it is not uncommon for individuals to express a tremendous intensity of energy and emotion in relation to a transpersonal dedication. They feel it very personally, but its object is transpersonal.

We should bear in mind the additional implications of transperso-

---

* You will find a convenient, brief guide to the sections to which personal Journal Feedback leads may take you in the Checklist on pp. 126 ff. in *At a Journal Workshop*.

nal experience. Its spiritual significance is only one aspect of it. Because of the great power of the emotions and the tremendous energies that may be generated by transpersonal experiences and dedications, they have a major social and historical importance. Since experiences and beliefs with regard to meaning in life seem to be essential for human beings, we know that they will inevitably arise. The only question is whether they will be thrust up in history as over-arching passions that take over large groups of people and lead to violent events, or whether they can have an orderly and constructive development person by person. And whether in the individual life they can lead to a deepening of meaning as we seek in our Process Meditation work.

The personal and the transpersonal are the two complementary areas of our life experience. We live in both realms and each is essential to the other. One effect of our practice of Process Meditation is that it deepens the atmosphere in which we perceive our life. This does not necessarily mean that work in Process Meditation will always lead to transpersonal experience. It is a question of what is appropriate at the time, and in the circumstances of the life of the person. By establishing a deep and quiet atmosphere, the practice of Process Meditation places us in a position where we can recognize what our life intuition is saying to us. And with our *Intensive Journal* method as an instrument that we can use, we are then in the further position of being able to follow up in specific ways the things our inner wisdom is telling us. We can explore what is shown to us, testing it, applying it, modifying or enlarging it as need be.

If the leads that are given to us are personal leads, we can follow them to several different sections of our workbook, depending on their special content. If they are transpersonal leads, however, we have one main section to which we take them. We go to *PDE,* the section for *Peaks, Depths and Explorations,* where we draw upon whatever leads and hints and clues are given to us and whatever resources our basic *Intensive Journal* work makes available. This is the Journal section where all our interior efforts are consolidated, all our inner experiences and our most intimate intimations of truth brought together, so that we can see what larger understanding they can bring. PDE is the section for the continuity and progressive deepening of our spiritual work, whatever its contents of doctrine and symbol.

*   *   *

With these varied considerations in the background, aware of the multiple possibilities of interior knowledge that are open to us, we sit in stillness. Our eyes close and we let our breathing become slower, relaxed and deeper and slower. We sit in stillness, considering. We review within ourselves the new units of experience that have shown themselves to us. Certain aspects of those interior events speak to us more strongly now. They have more to say to us in words. They have more to show us in images and symbols. We let them be free to continue to add to what they have been, to continue their development within our experience.

Sitting in the stillness, we are asking them what their desire is. In the silence we are not seeking answers from them, only indications as to where their interest lies. What is the direction of their next development? We are not seeking answers, only leads. We are prepared to do the rest of the work ourselves in the continuity of our interior life.

Through our pen they can speak and tell us. Which are the areas of our life, what are the issues and concerns, that we wish to consider more deeply? That have more to say to us and to show us? We are willing to receive even those guidances and directions that we do not desire to hear. And we will explore whatever is shown to us.

We let the leads of every kind come to us in the silence. And we prepare to follow them on both the personal and the transpersonal paths of our *Intensive Journal* work as we proceed.

Chapter 18

PDE:
Peaks, Depths and Explorations

THE ONGOING USE OF THE MEDITATION LOG

Our transpersonal leads take us to the *Peaks, Depths and Explorations* section. Whether we perceive our life in religious or in secular terms, this is the section where we each work with the questions which we feel as fundamental concerns in our life. Here we develop the themes that have the greatest personal importance to us, paradoxically, because their meaning to us is beyond our individuality. But that paradox lies at the heart of the definition of transpersonal themes. Such themes are issues that arise in areas like philosophy, religion, ideology, human destiny. They are larger-than-personal in their scope, and yet we feel them, think about them, worry over them, and eventually commit our lives to them—*personally*. In his neo-theological language, Paul Tillich spoke of them as *ultimate concerns*. We work with them actively, in detail, and especially in continuity in *Peaks, Depths and Explorations*.

This section is different in basic ways from the other Journal sections with which we have worked so far. The difference lies primarily in the fact that *Peaks, Depths and Explorations* is solely devoted to extending and deepening our inner process. The other sections have been preparing us for this. Exercise by exercise, they have been providing the materials and teaching us the methods that would eventually enable us to continue our personal, self-directed spiritual development using Process Meditation as our vehicle. Now we have arrived at the point

286

where we can take that further step. The *Peaks, Depths and Explorations* section is the place where we coordinate our use of the data and procedures that we have gained from all the other sections in our *Intensive Journal* workbook. We inter-relate them, drawing them together in an ongoing format as we seek to evoke and experience more of their meaning.

We find that a large part of the work we have already done in other sections calls our attention to the transpersonal areas of our life. When we reread our earlier Journal entries, we see that we have been seeking to establish a larger contact with our transpersonal concerns both for emotional and spiritual reasons. Something within us has felt the need to know them and to experience them more fully. The transpersonal leads steer our deepening Journal work to these themes. They are able to indicate which areas of further Journal experience will be productive for us and will respond to our profound inner needs because, as original entries, they reflect the unpremeditated concerns of our life.

Now we take them as leads, as starting points, and enable them to unfold with the self-expanding format of *Peaks, Depths and Explorations*. The exercises we carry out here essentially apply procedures with which we are familiar from our work in other Journal sections. It is the combining, the coordinating, and especially the continuity of these that is important here. Since each theme unfolds in obedience to its own principle, the sequence of procedures that we follow in *Peaks, Depths and Explorations* is unique for each exercise. It is probably true that the work we do in this section is the most individualized and the most open to improvisation of all the sections in the *Intensive Journal* system.

While our work in *Peaks, Depths and Explorations* draws upon the other Journal sections, using their customary procedures, there are special adaptations that have to be made in some cases. This is particularly true with respect to the *Meditation Log* since it has an expanded role as the supplier of transpersonal leads. At the beginning of our work in *Peaks, Depths and Explorations*, our transpersonal leads tend to come directly from the other sections of our workbook. They involve our primary concerns and usually occupy a more obvious position in a person's life. As our practice of Process Meditation is continued and extended, however, we find that more of the transpersonal leads come to *Peaks, Depths and Explorations* from the entries that we have made in the *Meditation Log*. Segments of the *Meditation Log*, such as Spiritual

Positioning and Inner Process Entries, increasingly act as intermediaries between the contents of the events of our lives and the larger awarenesses that give us a sense of ultimate meaning.

In the preceding chapter we carried through an exercise that plays an important role in gathering resources for our work in *Peaks, Depths and Explorations*. In the Inner Process Entries segment of the *Meditation Log* we recapitulated our work in *Connections* where we had begun the large task of reconstructing our spiritual history. In addition to the perspective which we drew from our work in the three segments—Gatherings, Spiritual Steppingstones and Re-Openings—we also built a resource for *Peaks, Depths and Explorations*. Recapitulating the outlines of our spiritual history enabled us to recall the themes that spontaneously recur in the depth of our thoughts and feelings. That helps us identify the transpersonal concerns that are working in us beneath the surface of consciousness.

The segment for Spiritual Positioning in the *Meditation Log* also serves as a source of transpersonal leads, especially after we have had occasion to make several entries there over a period of time. When we began our work of Process Meditation, we set a base for ourselves by writing a first statement of our spiritual position. That statement was written as spontaneously as possible so that it would provide an honest and unpremeditated expression of our inner life. It was also deliberately made as a concise statement, since at that point our need was not for completeness but for a brief and focused statement that would enable us to dip at least one toe into the underground stream and thus get started on our inner work. We took for granted at that point the fact that, as our Process Meditation proceeded, there would be opportunity for further statements of Spiritual Positioning.

We do make such additional statements from time to time. We write them usually at pauses or at points of reconsideration in our interior process. We find that they are helpful in enabling us to see our situation from within. It is a convenient way to take stock of ourselves spiritually, to see where we are, and to consider where our inner life is moving.

Our speaking of Spiritual Positioning as a recurrent exercise may lead you to feel that now is the time for you to do it once again. Perhaps it is already time for you to write a new statement of your spiritual position; but perhaps not yet. There are criteria to consider.

If you have begun your Process Meditation work with the exercises in this book, you should consider that it may still be a bit early for you to write a new statement. It is best to allow ample time between statements of Spiritual Positioning so that a sufficient number of new events and experiences can take place. It is also important to allow enough time for our new awarenesses and for changes in our beliefs to be absorbed into our inner life as a whole. We should bear in mind that absorbing our spiritual experiences into the tissue of our emotional life can be a slow process, much slower than having the experience itself or merely thinking about it. We should guard against making new statements too frequently or too close together. To do that can mislead us by giving importance to beliefs and attitudes that are only transiently passing through us.

Even though it is a matter of subjective judgment, there are objective considerations in determining what is the proper length of time to wait before you write a fresh statement of Spiritual Positioning. It depends upon your evaluation at each step of the movement of your inner life. One way to state it is that the right time to write a new statement of your present spiritual position is whenever you feel that so much has taken place within you that you need an opportunity to sort it out and make it clear to yourself.

Take notice in this regard that the criterion is not at all whether a dramatic new breakthrough has taken place in your experience, changing your beliefs and filling you with new enthusiasm. If you write a fresh statement of your spiritual position at such a time, the effect will most likely be to reinforce your new opinions. And the purpose of Spiritual Positioning is not at all to confirm you in your most recent experiences but rather to set them in perspective. The best criterion to follow, therefore, is the *muddy water* principle. When new inner events have multiplied in your experience, to the extent that you feel the need for clarification, that is a good time to write a fresh statement of your present spiritual position.

We thus have two balancing criteria to follow with respect to writing new statements of Spiritual Positioning. On the one hand, we wait long enough between statements to allow a sufficient number of inner events, experiences, changes in belief and awareness to accumulate. On the other hand, we proceed to write a new statement whenever the flux of interior life leads us to feel that it would be helpful to stabilize our viewpoint. At such times, you may pause in your Process Meditation work and turn to the Spiritual Positioning segment of the *Meditation Log*. Sit in quietness and make sure to allow sufficient time for a twilight experience to come to you. In that atmosphere the metaphors and symbols that come as twilight experiences can tell you a great deal in very cogent terms regarding your true spiritual position. Record what comes to you on the twilight level, and then proceed to describe your inner situation as you presently perceive it. The correlation between those two can be very instructive to you.

Whether you write new statements of spiritual position frequently or sparingly, from the point of view of *Peaks, Depths and Explorations* it is valuable to have a number of them collected in the *Meditation Log*. After we have written a few such statements spread over a period of time, reading them back to ourselves in sequence gives us a sense of the movement of our inner life. Reading back enables us to recognize the themes, concerns, questions of belief that recur in various aspects in the course of our statements of Spiritual Positioning. Their reappearance indicates to us that these are the *leitmotifs* of our inner life. By the fact that they arise again and again as our deep concerns we are led to acknowledge them as requiring our further attention. Over a period of time these Spiritual Positionings in the *Meditation Log* become a valuable source from which we obtain transpersonal leads to *Peaks, Depths and Explorations*.

A further important and ongoing source of transpersonal leads in the *Meditation Log* is the record that we keep in the segment for Inner Process Entries. After we have recapitulated the experiences we have had in carrying out the exercises of Process Meditation, we continue to record in Inner Process Entries the interior events of our lives on a current basis. This is the active recording of our experiences, our concerns and our searchings, as we are engaged in them and as they are taking place within us.

The material that we record in the continuity phase of Inner Process Entries covers a broad range of experience. Some entries seem unimportant to us when we consider them by themselves. Succeeding entries, however, pick up and discuss varied aspects of the same concern. After a period of time, when we read back to ourselves a series of Inner Process Entries, we can perceive that a single theme has been building as it moved in and out of the other subjects we were describing. It is thus by their interweaving continuity among our Inner Process Entries that we can identify the transpersonal themes which, by their persistent recurrence in our spontaneous Journal entries, are telling us that they will have a still larger message for us when we transfer them to *Peaks, Depths and Explorations* and work with them there.

We can also infer from this a valuable rule to follow as we make our ongoing entries in this segment of the *Meditation Log*. As much as possible we should try not to prejudge any of our inner experiences as being "unimportant," for that may cause us to eliminate them without knowing their full meaning or their possibilities. It is better to record them, even if only briefly and with no comment beyond our basic description of them. In that way we have them on record. If subsequent experiences carry them further we can extend them and build upon them. If not, we can let them rest where they are.

The primary criterion of the materials that we record as Inner Process Entries in our *Meditation Log* is that in some aspect or degree they pertain to our personal quest and concern for deeper meaning in our life. The subjects of these entries may be of many kinds, reaching into diverse areas of our life experience. The following are examples of how such entries may begin, indicating all the subject matter that they may proceed to explore.

Sitting in silence waiting for the meeting to begin, unexpected thoughts and feelings stirred in me . . .

Listening to the music and thinking of nothing, images and awarenesses began to form before my mind . . .

Gathering the statistics for the research, I found myself wondering about the principles behind what I was doing. I began to think about the relation between God and science, and I was considering whether . . .

Reading the poetry of ——, I found myself sharing the imagery and having the feeling that I was in the same place as that in which the poetry was formed. Then my experience moved on, and I had the feeling that . . .

Sitting at the lake alone under a tree, I felt the quietness of nature all around me. Thoughts of life and a work that would be valuable began to move around in me. I found myself thinking that . . .

The text of the sermon was. . . . Reading it by myself later on I was especially struck by the passage that said . . .

The death of —— raises questions in me that reach much beyond the personal aspect of my feelings. I should not continue to postpone the question of what I believe about death and what my attitude is toward the event of dying. And also aging and serious illness as part of a human existence. I think of the situation of ——. The feelings and images that come to me are . . .

These are instances of Inner Process Entries that we may make in our *Meditation Log* to express the various experiences that come to us in the course of our lives. Not infrequently, as we write them we find ourselves in a position where it seems that we have just taken the cork out of a geyser. That is an incongruous metaphor. But the point is that, as we do something simple like making a *Meditation Log* entry, we suddenly realize that a tremendous energy has been set free. We realize further that this energy is carrying many unknown contents, some of which will become resources for understanding and new experiences at a later point in our life.

Thoughts and feelings, intuitions and images as well as fundamental life concerns begin to articulate themselves as we write in the Meditation Log. It becomes apparent that we each carry within ourselves a quality of caring that reaches beyond our individual existence and contains intimations of truth beyond our personal knowledge. After we have started our *Meditation Log* entries and the process of our writing them has begun to build its own momentum, we begin to sense the possibilities.

THE STEPS OF DEEPENING EXPERIENCE

It is apparent that the *Meditation Log* serves as a great deal more than a spiritual diary. As our work of Process Meditation continues and as we enlarge the scope of our experience, the function of the *Meditation Log* grows with it. It expands its role so that it can eventually screen and select the transpersonal themes that we follow in *Peaks, Depths and Explorations*. This progressive development of the *Meditation Log* makes it necessary for us to discuss some details of how we work with it at the further stages of Process Meditation.

The principle underlying all the log sections in the *Intensive Journal* system is that they are fact gatherers. On that basis all entries made in log sections are to be as concise as possible. They should also be as objective as is feasible, considering that many of the facts being recorded in the log sections are in actuality subjective experiences that are taking place even as they are being described. Because they often are expressing inner events that are in process of happening, *Meditation Log* entries have a tendency to be more expansive than other log entries. The movement of the writing is part of the progression within the experience. As we read back to ourselves, however, we notice that in certain entries there is a point where the nature of the content subtly changes. Without realizing what is taking place, we shift from the direct description of our inner experience to a more intellectual type of discussion regarding the significance of what has taken place. That should be a sign to us that we have gone far enough in the *Meditation Log*. Its function is to catch the raw material of experience. Whatever is to be done beyond that is for *Peaks, Depths and Explorations*.

The essential reason for which *Meditation Log* entries are to be brief is to record the facts of our inner life as effectively as possible. If we find that, despite our desire to be concise, a *Meditation Log* entry insists on extending itself, that may be an indication that it has more to tell us. We should then treat it as a transpersonal lead and take it to the *Peaks, Depths and Explorations* section.

If we find that over a period of time the entries in our *Meditation Log* continue to return to particular themes, perhaps addressing the questions from different angles but returning to the same general subjects again and again, that may also be a message. It indicates that the theme of those entries has a persistent inner importance to us and that we should therefore work with that theme in *Peaks, Depths and Explorations*.

We should be aware that the transpersonal leads that we are following are not merely passive pointers. They are not merely like road signs that indicate the direction in which a particular town is to be found while leaving it to the driver to decide whether to go there. These are active leads that contain an energy of desire and need within themselves which carries the work forward. They do more than road signs that merely point the way. The transpersonal leads might better be compared to self-directed engines that take you where they themselves want to go. The differences among them lie mainly in the fact that some transpersonal leads move with large heads of steam giving them energy while others barely chug along.

The work we do with some transpersonal themes proceeds with

great strength when we take them into the *Peaks, Depths and Explorations* section. They carry considerable momentum and move directly into active experiences. Other themes may have the same potential, but their inner timing has not yet generated as great an energy. That may come later, depending on the rhythms within the life-cycle of the themes that are being carried to us by the transpersonal leads. Some may be ready for active extension immediately after a workshop experience while others may go into an extended time of gestation before they are ready to take another step. In the *Peaks, Depths and Explorations* section, it is essential that we be sensitive to the tempo of the themes with which we are working so that we can adjust our procedures to their needs and rhythms.

We have a guideline format to help us in carrying out our work in *Peaks, Depths and Explorations*. It provides a framework for the variations that are required as we proceed in our open-ended exploration of transpersonal themes. The format consists of a few basic steps that we should keep in the background of our minds as we carry out the various combinations of exercises.

Our first step is to identify the transpersonal themes that we feel to be important for our inner development. We rely for this on the transpersonal leads which we draw from the entries we have made in our *Meditation Log* over a period of time.

When we have determined the transpersonal themes with which we shall work, we set up a sub-section for them in *Peaks, Depths and Explorations*. Each theme is given its own sub-section so that the continuity of the varied exercises we carry out in relation to this theme can be coordinated.

Our next step is to choose the exercise with which we shall begin our work in *Peaks, Depths and Explorations*. Our primary clues for this will undoubtedly come from the transpersonal lead that originally called our attention to this theme. Its tone will give us our starting point. Perhaps its first effect is to recall us to earlier times in our lives. If it is personal memories that are awakened here, we go to the *Life History Log* for our next entry. If it is transpersonal memories, we go to Gatherings. Possibly what we describe in Gatherings will evoke additional memories in us, and these will lead us to further exercises in other segments of the *Connections* section, in Spiritual Steppingstones and in Re-Openings.

After we have carried out an exercise, there is an additional reportorial entry that we would ordinarily make in the *Meditation Log*. But now, having established the sub-section for this theme in *Peaks, Depths and Explorations,* we make that entry here. From this point on, everything that relates to this theme is brought together in this sub-section, at least from the point of view of reporting what has taken place and recording the development of its continuity. As we decide on the individual exercises that we shall use, we move out into the various sections of the workbook.

Following the indications of our transpersonal leads, we may use any or all of the techniques available to us through the *Intensive Journal/* Process Meditation system, applying them in ways that seem appropriate to the particular materials. These practices may include:

1. Twilight imagery in any of its aspects, including twilight thinking and twilight dreaming experiences.
2. Life history work in its various phases.
3. Personal and transpersonal dialogues.
4. Mantra/crystal meditation.
5. Journal interplay and cross-referencing.

Moving from exercise to exercise in this way with a theme in *Peaks, Depths and Explorations,* we find that we are taken back and forth through many of the sections of our *Intensive Journal* workbook. In the course of this movement, a number of other aspects of our lives may be stimulated into activity and awareness. But a report, a response, and a further reflection is always brought back to the sub-section in *Peaks, Depths and Explorations.* This is how we maintain and coordinate the continuity of our exploration. All the experiences that take place in us with respect to that theme are fed back into that sub-section where we extend our consideration of it with imagery and thought and the full range of twilight experiences.

Proceeding in this way, we find that one experience and awareness leads to another. Each is drawn forth by what took place before it. We realize that the sequence of exercises for each transpersonal theme is unfolding out of the life and the needs of the theme itself. By the continuity and the interior reference of our exercises, we have set a self-contained process into motion. This process began with the intimation that came to us by means of the transpersonal leads indicating that we could have a deeper understanding and relation to a particular area of reality. We began to explore that, and now the process is moving from one exercise to another as though by its own power and direction. It is enlarging its scope, incorporating data and images of which we did not know at the start.

As we proceed, the process of transpersonal exploration expands out of its own nature, drawing us from one exercise and perception to the next. There is an open-ended creativity in the process as its continuity carries it at each step another length beyond itself. Time and again we are brought to a surprise. As these unpredictable insights are given to us, we recognize that the essence of our spiritual method lies in its freedom within a structure. Had we tried to set our agenda of exercises in advance, we would have eliminated the breakthroughs that cannot be anticipated.

Working in *Peaks, Depths and Explorations,* we find that there is a uniqueness and creativity in the way that each transpersonal theme unfolds its life for us. Depending on the degree of open receptivity with which we follow its leads from exercise to exercise and commit ourselves to helping it bring forth its message, it becomes an artwork. It proceeds out of the seed of its potentiality and, once we have enabled it to establish its life and its integrity, it moves with its own tempo and style. We have then become the servant of the quest that we ourselves began, as every artist must eventually become the servant of his or her artwork. We find that the spiritual work we do in *Peaks, Depths and Explorations* parallels the principles and process that are involved in the artist's life of creativity.

THE JESUS PRAYER AND THE BLESSING MANTRA: A PERSONAL EXPERIENCE

Since the major part of the work in *Peaks, Depths and Explorations* is carried out in an atmosphere of depth, the recrystallizing factor that we have spoken of as MTI, the molecules of thought and imagery, often seems to be at work here. New formations of awareness come into existence in the course of the deepening, the intensity, and especially the personal commitment of the work. It is not uncommon for persons to recognize that they have followed particular pathways simply because they had a vague intimation that a valuable truth would be found along that road. At the outset they did not know what it would be, nor what form it would take, nor even what the name of the road was. Continuing to pursue their intuition, however, and working at it, they have sometimes found truths of unexpected size and quality, the good fruit of the spirit.

The *Peaks, Depths and Explorations* section can serve as the workplace of integration, to give continuity and support for that inner work especially as we move through the difficult phases of our quest.

There are times in human experience when we cannot say, "This alone is true," or "This alone is how it is to be done." At those times we can only say, "This is how it has been with me."

The following are excerpts from my personal work in *Peaks, Depths and Explorations*, extending certain themes that have been dealt with in other contexts in the course of this book. One point that should be observed is the interweaving of material and experiences from varied sections of the *Intensive Journal* workbook, as personal history, spiritual history and new awarenesses come together to set their own course.

AN ENTRY IN THE MEDITATION LOG

I have been studying the text of the Russian Pilgrim and considering the implications of his experience. I find his life and his commitment to be deeply moving. In some way he is a symbol to me of something more than himself. I know that his way of practice is significant for modern use, but I think that his appeal to me is more personal than that.

I find myself coming back to a passage that he quotes from St. Simon containing some instructions: "Sit down alone and in silence. Lower your head, shut your eyes, breathe out gently, and imagine yourself looking into your own heart. Carry your mind, i.e., your thoughts, from your head to your heart."

I keep returning to consider that again and again. It seems to touch a chord in me that connects with many other things.

It leads me to think of Dostoevsky and to wonder at his linkage to the doctrine of the heart.

It reminds me especially of Pascal and his "reasons of the heart."

When I was beginning to study Jung in the nineteen-forties, I went back and forth to Pascal as a philosophic source. And I recall my old professor, Albert Salomon, as he lectured on Pascal. He didn't care for Jung, but he saw the connections I was exploring then. That was why he backed my studies.

The "heart" doctrine reminds me also of the Talmudic doctrine of "conquering the heart." I studied that in the "Ethics of the Fathers" when I was in the Army. Those old rabbis and the Russian *starets:* what an ironical linkage!

Apparently that passage keeps coming back to my mind because it evokes something in me. It seems to be a common source for my earlier philosophical studies, for my seeking to reach the depths of persons by means of psychology, and for seeking an experience of unity on a spiritual level.

It seems strange that I feel such a strong emotional connection to an old Russian *starets* from the Greek Orthodox Church.

(Note: At this point in my *Meditation Log* entry I realized that something of larger significance to my inner life was being opened here. That feeling is the main indication that something more than a *Meditation Log* entry is involved, and that we should consider to which other section, or sections, of the workbook the material should be taken.

In this case there was also a second sign that the entry was moving beyond the *Meditation Log*. It was becoming longer than just a few paragraphs, Length is not the only criterion in this regard. Quite often an Inner Process Entry in the *Meditation Log* is dealing with a current experience that requires a considerable description and discussion, and such an entry does not necessarily lead beyond the *Meditation Log*.

In this case, however, my entry was becoming long not because there was a great deal to describe in the current experience but because it was opening areas of my thought and my inner life. That was the primary reason for my feeling that the entry needed to be taken to a section other than the *Meditation Log* so that it could be explored further and so that I could follow the various leads that it was opening to me.

The question of the section to which I would take this entry in order to continue it was settled easily for me in terms of the distinction between personal and transpersonal leads. If it had indicated that material of a personal nature was primary in what was discussed here, I would have had several possible sections to which I could take it. But the issues here involved the aspects of my life that were reaching toward meaning in ways that other persons in history have also done over many centuries. My experiences and concerns were indeed personal in the sense that they were private to me, even intimate in the intensity of their feelings. But they were not limited to my personal life. They concerned my personal existence as a human being rather than merely as an individual. In that sense the content of my *Meditation Log* entry was transpersonal. That was clear to me and therefore there was no decision needed as to where to carry that entry. It could only go to *Peaks, Depths and Explorations.*

In that section, therefore, I set up a sub-heading which I entitled, "Entering the Heart." To begin the sub-section, I made a brief note to indicate that the subject of discussion was first noted in the *Meditation Log* and that I was now continuing it here. I continued then to make further entries in *Peaks, Depths and Explorations* and also derivative entries in other sections as the continuity of the work would suggest them from time to time. Whenever I would make a derivative entry in another section, I would also record it briefly in *Peaks, Depths and Explorations* and perhaps summarize it there. In that way the line of perception could build itself and new awarenesses emerge.)

A PEAKS, DEPTHS AND EXPLORATIONS ENTRY

I find myself thinking about the conception of "the heart" as it is spoken of by the Russian Pilgrim and his *starets*. It is more than a doctrine or a concept to them. It is an image with which they work very actively and directly. I started to describe my thoughts in the *Meditation Log*, but it seems to involve a great deal more. I'll follow it up here.

The phrase from Pascal returns to me. "The heart has reasons that the reason does not know." I recall the days in graduate school when I was trying to determine what the dimension of depth should or can be in a philosophy or a psychology.

A GATHERINGS ENTRY

I see myself listening to old Professor Albert Salomon as he is lecturing on Montaigne and Pascal. He is analyzing the intellectual development of their thought and he is painstakingly describing their recognition of an intuitive factor, something more than the rational, working in the human mind.

I am listening to him on one level as he describes the history of the ideas, and I am conscious of other levels of thought moving around inside of me. The thought occurs to me: Aren't the reasons of the heart just the things that a depth psychology should help us understand? And not to psychoanalyze their origins but to go deeper to draw out what the heart's reasons may be?

That was a first insight for me into what a depth psychology can become, placing it in the history of Western thought. Later Salomon supported this viewpoint, and that was how my dissertation on Jung became possible.

A GATHERINGS ENTRY

I see myself in the Army. I am twenty-one years old and I have not been in it very long. Somehow I have been given a job getting the fires started in the barracks in the morning. I like that because it enables me to follow the practice of the spiritual disciplines I have marked off for myself. I have to get up around five o'clock while it is still dark and rather cold. My job is to get a few coal fires started and wait for them to become strong enough so that I can build them further.

The in-between time when I am waiting for the kindling wood to take fire is the time that is important to me. The particular discipline I am practicing is to choose a passage from a spiritual text, whatever it may be, and to read it until I find some particular lines that strike me as being profound or especially meaningful. Then to read and reread those lines and consider them in silence, letting their implications work inside of me.

I remember sitting in front of a stove waiting for the kindling wood to catch while I was reading a passage in the Talmudic segment called "The Ethics of the Fathers." I came to the lines:

> Greater than he who conquers a city is
> he who conquers his own heart.

What does it mean, I thought, to "conquer one's heart"? It cannot be sufficient merely to follow some pattern of rituals. Nor just to give up or forswear certain pleasures. It must involve more than that.

I remember pondering the meaning of "conquering one's heart" while I was sitting in front of a stove waiting for the fire to be thoroughly kindled

A PEAKS, DEPTHS AND EXPLORATIONS ENTRY

I have written about Salomon and Pascal in Gatherings, going over the concept of the heart in relation to depth psychology.

Some time I should do an Inner Wisdom Dialogue with Pascal.

And old Professor Salomon would be good to talk with in Dialogue with Persons.

In Gatherings also I wrote about meditating on "conquering one's own heart," while the fires were being kindled when I was in the Army. It occurs to me now that a primary aspiration of Hasidic mysticism is "enkindlement of the heart."

"The kindling wood of the heart." Is that a mantra/crystal that will open for me?

Or perhaps a mantra/crystal that carries the active sense of timing in life, "Waiting for things to kindle."

My thoughts return to the *starets* as he was explaining his method of breathing while saying the Jesus Prayer. His instructions are to breathe in fully, and then on the exhalation to say the prayer. That exhalation is like a sigh, a great sigh. I am reminded of the colloquial phrase that the Puerto Ricans use to express what might be called their tragic sense of life, "Ay, benito!" It also is a great sigh in the way they say it, a sigh of resignation at the pains of life. And I think of the various Yiddish phrases that I know that are also a great sigh of surrender to the limits of life, and to the pains of history. The exhalation is the sigh of life. How appropriate that the *starets* connected it with the Jesus Prayer.

I take note of the fact that the balance of the inhalation-and-exhalation in conjunction with the Jesus Prayer also builds the continuous pendulum effect of our mantra/crystal work. The difference is only that the *starets* seems to have said the prayer phrase only in the exhalation phase of the breathing cycle, whereas in our mantra/crystal cycle we balance the mantra phrase through both phases of breathing in and breathing out. Possibly there are advantages to both procedures, depending on the circumstances and the conditions in which the meditations are being carried out. Individuals can test them in their own practice and see for themselves which way is better for them. It occurs to me that connecting the phrase with the exhalation may work well if you are saying the mantra or prayer while you are in the midst of the activities of your life, or doing something like walking across Russia, as the Pilgrim was doing. But if you are working with a mantra/crystal in a quiet position, the balancing of the whole mantra phrase with the two phases of breathing has the advantage of carrying the continuity of the meditation for us with a self-sustaining movement like a perpetual motion machine on the spiritual level.

I begin to work with a mantra/crystal that comes to me:

> Here in the depth of my heart

It has a quieting effect. In a little while it seems as though all my being and all my consciousness is focused at the level of my heart. I feel it physically but it is an imagery experience. At the twilight level I feel something moving out from my heart—or through my heart—like a large pipe or a passageway, a connecting road that goes through my heart to the hearts of others and through them and on and on.

> The open road of the heart

That is the mantra/crystal that comes to me. And it remains with me. I breathe with it. I sit in quietness with it. In stillness, it seems to have an emanation, an outward movement on the interior level. It stays in one place, and yet it endlessly moves outward from within itself. I sit in stillness traveling the open road of the heart.

I feel myself to be moving through the time and space of history. I am within the heart of the *starets* as he is saying his Jesus Prayer. I feel the person in his heart, there in that time of history, in that isolated byway of civilization, feeling his fears, and his love.

> Lord Jesus Christ have mercy,
> Lord Jesus Christ have mercy.

I am within the heart of the *starets,* feeling his life and being one with his mantra/crystal, being one with his Jesus Prayer. It is a deepening connection, an extended silence. I realize how all of his life and the continuity of the generations is carried in his Jesus Prayer. I feel the limitedness of his physical life, his non-existent power in outer things.

He has only his inward power, the power of his Jesus Prayer. From being within the heart of the *starets*, I find myself moving through the generations of Russian history that came after him. I see images of the massacres and the murders, and I hear the Jesus Prayer, "Lord Jesus Christ have mercy," sounding in the background. I hear the cries of pain and I hear the chanting of the Jesus Prayer. Lord, what would have happened in Russia if the *starets* and his fellow saints had not maintained at least that small leaven of love in the world?

Within myself on the twilight level I find that a small scale has become present. Something is carefully being weighed and I see that the two scale-pans are going up and down. They are in movement because the substances being weighed are apparently nearly equal so that very small amounts can make a decisive difference. Now a voice in the background tells me what is being weighed and balanced. It is the relative power and impotence of love in the world. It seems that the power and impotence of love in the world are approximately equal to one another. That is why the scale moves up and down so much, almost like a seesaw. Apparently a small amount of love can make a very great difference. One additional atom of love may carry just enough weight to influence the scales of history. I wonder at the atoms of love that have been added to history by the *starets* and his Jesus Prayer. And I wonder how much violence and pain those atoms of love have outweighed on the scales of history, considering how much conflict and suffering there remains. I wonder whether the atoms of love of the Jesus Prayer have a lingering effect, and whether they are still working toward an atmosphere of peace within Russia—and in the world.

Now I feel myself to be within the heart of the *starets*, and within the heart of the Russian Pilgrim making his goal-less journey on the road.

In the heart of the *starets*.
In the heart of the Pilgrim.

I cannot say that I know where they were in their life. But I feel that I am there with them. I feel myself to be in the heart of the *starets*, in the heart of the Pilgrim.

This condition of being continues for some time. (Many things were shown to me, and I have been able to record some of them.)

Being in the heart of the *starets*, I find that the events in the life of the person, Jesus, are being recapitulated within my mind. I see the infant child, and then the small boy listening and later speaking in the synagogue. I see in rapid sequence the events of his ministry, and I find myself feeling his wonderment at what was taking place. I feel his confusion, and his pain, and I hear his outcry, "My God, my God, wherefore hast thou forsaken me? Eli, Eli, lomo asavtauni?"

> Feeling the heart of Jesus,
> Feeling the heart of Jesus.

I realize that tears have welled up in me, and that as I feel the suffering with the heart of Jesus I also feel a welling up of love. It is a harmonizing love, healing and restoring, waning and returning, as the sun coming into the world in the midst of pain.

I am sitting in silence, altogether within the atmosphere of that life, when another sequence of events moves rapidly, one scene after another, on the screen of my mind. It is the life of Moses. I see the infant child in the rushes, the child in Pharaoh's court, the young man violent in righteousness, and then a series of inner experiences by which the spiritual Moses evolves. I realize that I am retreading a path I had marked off some years before in my studies and writings on the life of Moses. But now something additional is present. I am

> Feeling the heart of Moses,
> Feeling the heart of Moses.

I sit in silence, feeling his struggle and his love, his power and his impotence. (Many things also were shown to me at this time, and I was able to record some of them.)

When the movement of these events within me had subsided, I found that I was sitting in silence reciting two mantra/crystals alternately:

> Feeling the heart of Jesus,
> Feeling the heart of Moses,
> Feeling the heart of Jesus,
> Feeling the heart of Moses.

They alternated in a regular balance carrying each other; I felt a movement back and forth between them. They seem to be part of a single unity, a cyclical process that begins anew when it seems to have come to a close.

I find that I am saying another mantra/crystal now. I did not know I was saying it, but now I hear it moving through my lips.

Baruch Atau Adonai

I had never thought of this as a mantra/crystal before, although I know these Hebrew words well. They are the three words that introduce most of the prayers and benedictions in the practice of Jewish religion. They may be translated as: "Blessed art Thou, O Lord God." I have never heard nor conceived those words in this way before, but now I recognize that "Baruch Atau Adonai" is a seven-syllable mantra/crystal based on blessing the unnameable and infinite Lord of the Universe. It is a Blessing Mantra.

I sit in silence letting the mantra-breathing pendulum carry the phrase back and forth.

Baruch Atau Adonai,
Baruch Atau Adonai.

At first I said it in Hebrew. Then I said it in English.

Blessed art Thou, O Lord God,
Blessed art Thou, O Lord God.

Then I returned to the Hebrew. That is how it feels best. That is how it feels right unto itself.

I feel the Blessing Mantra as a benediction from within my heart on all that has taken place. It is a blessing upon Jesus, and a blessing upon Moses. It is a blessing upon the *starets,* and it is a blessing on the Pilgrim. It is a blessing on the atoms of love they have generated and that they have sent out into the world to move endlessly through time.

As I say it, I find the Blessing Mantra becoming a prayer within me. May the saying of the Blessing Mantra atone for all the prayers and all the blessings that have been neglected and have not been said. And may it add the missing elements to prayers that have been said in the past quickly and by rote and not from the depths of the heart.

I am continuing to say the Blessing Mantra. Baruch Atau Adonai. Baruch Atau Adonai. It seems to be saying itself. It seems to have the power to continue of itself within me. I welcome it. It is like waves rising and falling within me. I feel them as waves that belong to the vast ocean. These waves carry water and energy that will not dissipate.

> Baruch Atau Adonai,
> Blessed art Thou, O Lord God.

The waves of the Blessing Mantra roll on.

* * *

Some days have passed and I realize that I have been able to continue the Blessing Mantra a fair percentage of the time. And when I have not continued it, it seems to have continued itself. I say that because, when I think of it, I realize that it is there. And it seems to have been there, even though my mind was on other things. It seems that the Blessing Mantra is present and has been present even when I have not been conscious of it. At the moments when I recognize its presence, there seems also to be an atmosphere of sustaining strength, an energy, and a feeling of non-judgmental love carried by the Blessing Mantra. It is quieting and supporting. A number of feelings and awarenesses come in this atmosphere. More than I can record. But some I have recorded, and will try to explore them later.

A further realization about the Blessing Mantra. Like the Jesus Prayer, it is a mantra/crystal, but both of them belong to a special class of mantra/crystals. These are mantra/crystals that may be present with us all the time, like our blood and our breathing. We may have a number of other mantra/crystals, but these have a special place in our inner lives.

It occurs to me that these should be called "Staff Mantras" to set them apart from all the other mantra/crystals with which we may work. They are *staff mantras* because they are like the staff that Moses carried with him wherever ne went. It provided something for him to lean upon. It gave him support and balance, steadiness and strength. The staff of Moses was an ever-present instrument that he carried with him into all the activities of his life. It was part of him, as the Jesus Prayer was part of the being of the Russian Pilgrim. And sometimes the staff served Moses with a special power of its own, as when it brought forth water out of a stone. In a comparable way, the Russian Pilgrim felt that from time to time the Jesus Prayer performed large and small miracles for him as needed. I wonder whether he knew that the fundamental miracle lay in the Jesus Prayer itself and in the fact that he could experience it. We do not require special miracles from the Blessing Mantra, but it may also serve as a *staff mantra*, a mantra/crystal that is present for us through the continuity of our life.

These entries drawn from the various sections of my *Intensive Journal* workbook are excerpts from the inner process, a few buckets of water drawn from the river.

We each have access to that underground river. It has a tributary that flows in the depths of our life, and through that we each connect with all. That is the place of transpersonal connection. We may reach it as we explore the themes that present themselves to us in the course of our Process Meditation. Therefore let each of us place ourselves in our individual interior process, following the transpersonal leads that call our attention to the ultimate issues of our lives. Many of these carry messages we would never have suspected to be there. And they may have wisdom for us of which we could not dream.

Chapter  **19**

Testament

We turn now to the *Testament* section in our *Intensive Journal* work-book. This is where the varieties of our Process Meditation explorations come together, to crystallize, to find their essence and give us the message of the whole. It is here that we restate our beliefs and awarenesses as they are shaping and reshaping themselves within us. Our philosophy of life takes form here and adds its increments to the building of our spiritual history, thus taking the first step into our spiritual future.

When we are at a Process Meditation workshop, our *Testament* practices draw together the unit of inner experience through which we have just passed. They serve that role for us also if we have been carrying out the practices by ourselves.

The conception of a workshop in the *Intensive Journal* system does not require that a number of persons be present. A workshop is taking place whenever our attention is concentrated for a period of time in following a focused agenda for working in the depths of our life, whether in the company of others or in our active privacy. By that definition, it can surely be said that those of us who have been practicing the procedures described in this book have been engaged in a work-shop. And it is now time for us to draw together the fruits of that unit of our experience.

We take a moment of quiet to pause in our inner process. Many thoughts and memories, emotions, images and new realizations have been brought to our consciousness in the course of our Process Meditation work. Much is intermingled here, but the metaphor of "muddy water" does not seem appropriate now. Our water is not muddy; it is, however, "full of things." It is full of the contents of the inner experiences that have been stirred to life in us. We do not wish these to settle to the bottom like formless mud. We have activated these varied contents from the depths and heights of our consciousness so that they can come together in new forms and combinations, as new MTI's, as molecules of thought and imagery that carry new patterns of awareness for our consciousness. This is their time to come together and show us the new shapes they are taking.

As we become quiet, we let ourselves feel the presence of the varied contents that have been stirred to life in the course of our workshop. We do not think of any of them specifically. We do not try to identify any of them individually. We merely feel their presence and we let them move around within us in the twilight range of our consciousness. There is a moving flux in the depth of us beneath our surface self. In the metaphor that we used earlier, it is like the molecules moving within the apparent solidity of a piece of wood. These molecules contain the contents of our beliefs, our visions of what can be painted or sculptured as art, our understandings of what can be stated as truth, our hopes of what may be possible in the activities of our lives. These are the "things" we feel so full of, especially now that we have stimulated them to experience with our Process Meditation exercises. We feel their presence and their movement as we sit in the stillness.

Gradually we let outselves drift into a twilight state. The various symbols and images, memories, ideas and intuitive knowings are there within us, moving about, looking for new combinations that will feel right to them. The molecules of thought and imagery are seeking to fit together with others to make new forms, new joinings at the twilight level, to bring new perceptions and new understandings to us. Presently we become aware that new combinations of thought and imagery are being set before us. They may take the form of symbols that appear visually, phrases that are spoken to us, concepts that we find ourselves thinking, a statement of an idea or a doctrine or a belief. Mantra/crystal phrases may present themselves to us, or lines of poetry or a prayer or a metaphor that states our inner perception of reality, our sense of what is becoming true for us.

We record whatever comes to us in this silence. Our perceptions may be of many kinds, but we give each its place and describe as much as is given to us. As they move through us, coming together in new combinations that may seem strange at first since we are not accustomed to them, we recognize that new units of thought and imagery are being formed within us. As we describe them, we find that more of their meaning declares itself to us and we begin to sense what they can eventually become in our lives. We find that, as we are describing what is being manifested to us, the possibilities of the future increasingly become present. They are taking *shape*. Images that were vague at the outset come into sharper focus, taking a definite form so that they can become the base point for an artwork. Ideas and beliefs that were little more than hunches before now articulate themselves as we describe them. Their outlines are being filled in with content. This is because, as we proceed in the silence at the twilight level, the various molecules of thought and imagery are moving about and coming together within us. New structures are being formed, combining symbol and idea with the actualities and needs of existence. As these elements are integrated into a single unit, they become the interior molecules that will provide the new content for our beliefs and our actions.

Like molecules forming and re-forming themselves, new integrations of awareness both symbolic and conceptual are taking shape in us. This is a silence that should be allowed to continue long enough to establish itself and to hold in its atmosphere all the contents of our Process Meditation experiences. We are feeling the fullness of our Process Meditation work in the silence, letting the many aspects come to expression in a symbol or a phrase and articulate themselves further if they wish. We are open now to all that has taken place within us, letting it re-present itself in order that we can take a further step with it. We are sitting in stillness, writing in *Testament*, in the silence.

*   *   *

We have allowed as much to be presented to us as wished to come, and we recorded all that we could. In that silence we have held ourselves open in the twilight range in order to gather as much non-conscious material as possible. Now, however, we re-approach what we have written from another point of view. Rather than encourage the movement to enlarge itself further, we seek to winnow it down to its essence.

We are adapting for our *Intensive Journal* use the doctrine from the history of philosophy known as Occam's Razor. "Principles should not be unnecessarily multiplied," said William of Occam at the turn of the fourteenth century. We now take his razor in hand as we read back to ourselves the extended entry we have just recorded. As much as possible we re-approach it as an impartial third party. What is the heart of the matter? What has been unnecessarily multiplied in it? We cull out the images and thoughts that are essential, and we draw them together into a single, concise statement, a sentence or two or three, not much more. It need not be prose. It may be poetry, some phrases of a prayer, a mathematical formula that is deep in your consciousness, some bars of music that express the core of your inner vision. Whatever language takes you closer to life/reality as you are now perceiving and experiencing it is the language you should use in making your crystallizing statement.

You will very likely find that a number of different experiences are coming together in what you write now. You are drawing together and consolidating into one unit the various elements that are adding to and re-forming your view of what life is and what truly matters to you now in the atmosphere of your Process Meditation work. What is consolidated may at a later time need to be refined and integrated more sharply. Or you may recast it into an altogether new form. What is important is that you express now, in however compressed a form, the essence of your present view of life/reality. To that degree it may bear resemblances to a mantra/crystal, but your statement should be much more fully articulated. A mantra/crystal may, however, be contained within it.

You may bear in mind, as you read back what you have recorded, that the two steps we are now taking in *Testament* are modeled after the sequence of movements that we perceive in the molecules of thought and imagery as they form their integrations within us. First they reach out to a broad range of elements, as many as may fit into the formation of the new units they are seeking; then they proceed to integrate these into a consolidated form. In our twilight experience we made contact with as many interior contents as we could. And now we are applying our discerning intellect to assist the integrative process. The statement at which we now arrive should be a concise articulation of our present envisioning of life/reality as we perceive it in its personal and transpersonal aspects.

Now we sit in stillness, turning our attention to the many contents we have recorded as they were presented to us from the twilight range. As our conscious mind moves through this material, discerning and separating, emphasizing and discarding, it is acting as the instrument of the process of integration. It is acting on behalf of the organizing factor within us that is drawing the molecules of thought and imagery together into meaningful forms. The resources have been drawn from the twilight depths. Now it is our conscious mind that does the organizational work.

We review and consider the various symbols and ideas, memories and emotions that have spoken to us most strongly in the course of our practice of Process Meditation. We have sensed a factor of meaning moving through our experiences and establishing itself as the reality of our lives. Now we seek to identify that factor in order to describe it and articulate it in the concise crystallizing statement that we are preparing to write. We write our statement now in the silence.

*　　*　　*

The best thing to do with this statement, once we have completed it to our present satisfaction, is to set it to one side. Keep it in the *Testament* section of course, but try to resist the temptation to read it back to yourself. At least for a few days. It is good to let some time pass after the intensity and inner concentration of our Process Meditation experience. Even spiritual work has to be followed by a Sabbath!

After we have rested from our Process Meditation workshop and sufficient time has passed to place some distance and objectivity between us and our subjective work, we may return to it. The post-workshop use of Process Meditation is of great importance, especially because it sets into motion the continuity of our lifelong meditation. Very often we find that the best point at which to resume our Process Meditation work is by reading back to ourselves the crystallizing statement we made in *Testament,* and moving from there into the ongoing process of our inner work.

Let us speak, before we part, about the first steps you take following a Process Meditation workshop. Those first steps will set you into motion, and after that the practice of Process Meditation is freedom, disciplined freedom.

When you read back to yourself your crystallizing statement in *Testament,* there will undoubtedly be additional responses that will arise in you. Take note of these, but do not record them in the *Testament* section. You now work in the *Meditation Log* again, and your response to reading your *Testament* statement should be recorded here in the Inner Process Entries segment. As you describe the stirrings within you it may occur to you that you would now like to alter your original statement or at least add to it. Record these thoughts here in the *Meditation Log* and let your *Testament* statement remain as it is, unchanged. You may, however, add a cross-reference in the *Testament* section indicating the date of the additional entry you are making in the *Meditation Log.*

As you are responding to your statement and considering it, the question of Journal Feedback is bound to arise in you: Where else in the *Intensive Journal* workbook can I go to explore the life issues and concerns that are raised in my *Testament* statement? What personal leads are given to me there? And what transpersonal leads? To which Journal sections do they take me?

As the answers to these questions come to you, record them in the Inner Process Entries segment together with your other considerations. You may wish to follow those leads now, at least some of them, and carry out their full additional exercises while their energy is still strong. Or you may prefer to make a brief indicative entry in the appropriate section and return to it later. Generally these decisions are determined by the momentum of the Journal work as you are continuing in its process.

You may now be ready to take a further step in your post-workshop process. You may now read back to yourself, proceeding either systematically or by browsing through the Journal sections, choosing any or all the of the experiences that you recorded in the course of your Process Meditation workshop. Take note of the responses that stir in you as you read them back to yourself. In many cases you will find that thoughts and feelings and awarenesses will come to you now that were not present in the original experience. Be sure to record all that comes to you now. As you return to each section it is especially important that you remember to ask yourself the Journal Feedback questions: Where else can I go with this material? What personal leads, and what transpersonal leads does it give me?

With the perspective we have now after having worked in *Testament*, we observe another possibility as we read back the experiences we have recorded. Some of them, most of them probably, seem to be incomplete, still developing, still in quest of and in need of further work and exploration. These are the experiences that give us the personal and transpersonal leads to other Journal sections where they can be carried further. There will be other experiences, however—perhaps only a very few at first—where the experience seems to have had a wholeness, a completeness in itself. These will be experiences in which our statement of our view of life/reality took place spontaneously, emerging out of our Process Meditation practice as an awareness of an essential truth. We may come upon such statements interspersed as random jewels of poetry among our Process Meditation entries. These should be copied and added to our *Testament* section following our original crystallizing statement. As we copy them over, we find that we wish to add to them, perhaps inserting comments and explanations as well as elaborations. It is good to do this, but keep the identity of the original experience and entry distinct, adding your new material separately. When you copy these over into the *Testament* section, make sure to enter both dates, the date of the original experience and the date of the transcription. And insert a cross-reference indicating the Journal section from which it was taken.

As we proceed in our Process Meditation work we find that such integrative statements expressing our perceptions of essential truth increasingly enter our experience. They are part of the new events that take place as we continue our practice of Process Meditation. We find more and more of them especially as we extend our explorations in the *Connections* section, since it is there that we uncover and remind ourselves of the connective experiences in our spiritual history. Sometimes we come upon integrative statements of this kind that are fully written and complete unto themselves as of the moment they took place. Such entries seem just to be waiting for us to copy them over into the *Testament* section. At other times, the experience that we described was integrative, but our statement of the essential truth that it carried was not adequate to convey the fullness of what was involved in it. Now we write that statement, whether in prose or poetry, and we place it in *Testament*.

As we proceed in our Process Meditation work, then, we gather together in the *Testament* section two types of statements. The first are the integrative statements that crystallize our experience at a Process Meditation workshop. They come to us one workshop at a time. Those of the second type, which become more numerous as we proceed in our Process Meditation work, are statements that express our experience or perception of an essential truth as these realizations are given to us at any point in the course of our life. Going back over our Process Meditation entries, we may find at first just a few statements of this second kind. We add them to the *Testament* section as we discover them in pages that we have already written, or as they come to us afresh in the continuity of our Process Meditation work.

As we proceed in collecting into our *Testament* section the record of our experiences and our statements of essential truth, we find over a period of time that a significant spiritual resource is being brought together. Its contents are very personal to us as individuals, but they are also much more than personal. They are the events in which we transcend ourselves because we are experiencing our lives and our consciousness in relation to realities larger than ourselves.

Each of these interior events that is a connective moment in our life is an increment to our spiritual history. Taken by themselves, like individual bricks, they have little strength or significance. But taken together, like many bricks that have been properly arranged, they become a substantial edifice. Working in the continuity of our Process Meditation, unitary experiences of essential truth will inevitably accumulate. They are the fruit and the flowers of our interior practice. They give us both truth and beauty. They are the personal scriptures being created from within us, out of the substance of our lives with the help of our commitment and our inner desire.

As our experiences continue and are gathered together, we extend our spiritual history into the openness of our spiritual future. In this we can recognize the meaning of the term, *Process-plus-one*. All that we have experienced in the past and all that we are working at in the present are part of process in the universe. But as individual human beings living with an intention toward essential truth, we add to the totality of process, experience by experience. Abstractly we add to process in the universe. Specifically we add to process in our civilization. And concretely we add to process in our individual lives, particularly with respect to the dimension of meaning, the spiritual essence of human existence.

Process-plus-one means all of our past, plus the next experience for

which we are now preparing. Since that next experience is still unknown, indeterminate, unpredictable, infinite in its possibilities, the
plus-one factor is our doorway to freedom and creativity. We do not
know when, beyond all the determinism contained in process, the
bonus of an *extra* will be given us, an *emergent*. Both the evolution of life
and our individual human condition wait for such emergents. And
better than waiting, we each do our interior work.

When we began our practice of Process Meditation, we possessed
the past experiences that our life had given us up to that point. Since
then we have had the additional experience of actively recalling some of
those events, drawing them together into accessible formats, re-entering some, re-opening others, and especially we have had the additional
experience of reaching into our twilight depths where new constellations of awareness have taken shape for us beyond our conscious
knowledge. All of these are part of the vital process that adds to itself in
freedom one present moment at a time as it creates our personal spiritual history. Now, with our Process Meditation experience added to it,
we have given ourselves tools and a methodology by which we can
continuously add to our spiritual history, one *next experience* after
another.

APPENDIX

The Registered
Intensive Journal
Workbook

(white)

INTENSIVE JOURNAL® WORKBOOK

Your Registered Journal is _____

(green)

PERIOD LOG

PERIOD LOG

(yellow)

DAILY LOG

DAILY LOG

(orange)

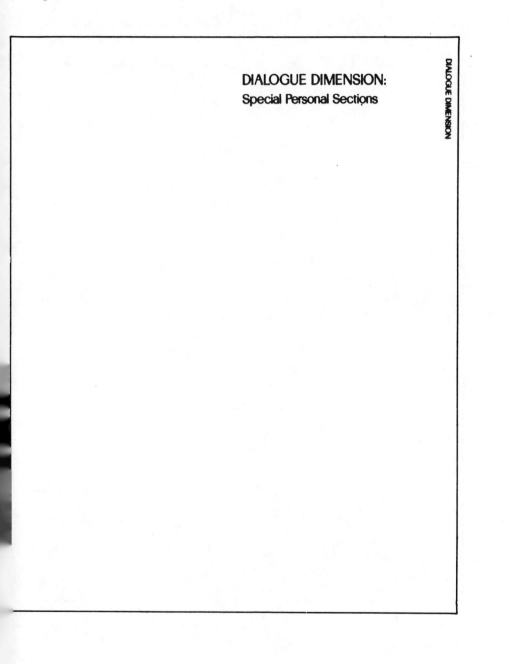

DIALOGUE DIMENSION:
Special Personal Sections

DIALOGUE DIMENSION

(orange)

DIALOGUE WITH PERSONS

DIALOGUE WITH PERSONS

(orange)

DIALOGUE WITH WORKS

DIALOGUE WITH WORKS

(orange)

DIALOGUE WITH SOCIETY
Group Experiences

DIALOGUE WITH SOCIETY

(orange)

DIALOGUE WITH EVENTS
Situations and Circumstances

DIALOGUE WITH EVENTS

(orange)

DIALOGUE WITH THE BODY

DIALOGUE WITH THE BODY

(blue)

DEPTH DIMENSION:
Ways of Symbolic Contact

DEPTH DIMENSION

(blue)

DREAM LOG
Description, Context, Associations

DREAM LOG

(blue)

DREAM ENLARGEMENTS

DREAM ENLARGEMENTS

(blue)

TWILIGHT IMAGERY LOG

(blue)

IMAGERY EXTENSIONS

IMAGERY EXTENSIONS

APPENDIX

(blue)

INNER WISDOM DIALOGUE

INNER WISDOM DIALOGUE

(red)

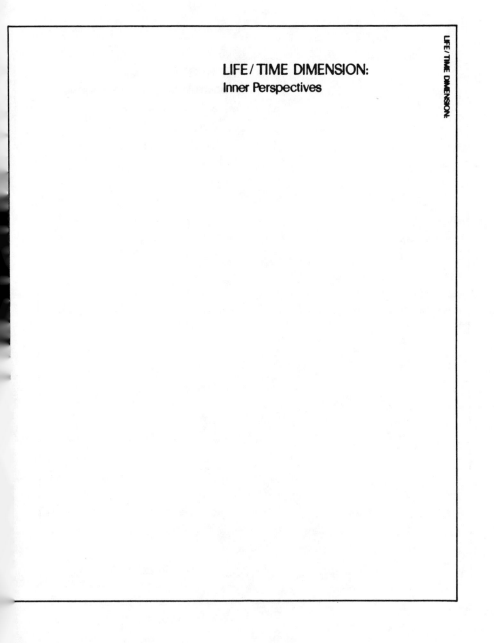

LIFE/ TIME DIMENSION:
Inner Perspectives

LIFE/TIME DIMENSION

(red)

LIFE HISTORY LOG
Recapitulations and Rememberings

LIFE HISTORY LOG

(red)

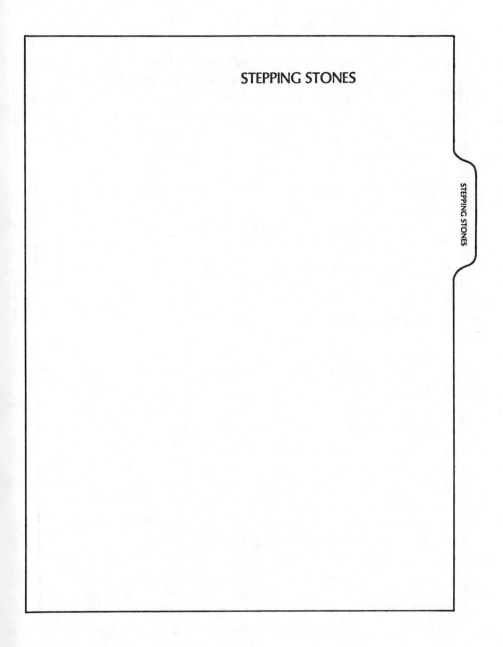

STEPPING STONES

STEPPING STONES

APPENDIX

(red)

INTERSECTIONS
Roads Taken and Not Taken

INTERSECTIONS

(red)

NOW: The Open Moment

NOW:
The Open Moment

(purple)

PROCESS MEDITATION

(purple)

MEDITATION LOG
Entrance Meditations
Spiritual Positioning
Inner Process Entries

MEDITATION LOG

APPENDIX

(purple)

CONNECTIONS
Gatherings
Spiritual Steppingstones
Re-Openings: Spiritual Roads Not Taken

CONNECTIONS

(purple)

MANTRA/CRYSTALS
Mantra/Crystal Index
Workings

MANTRA/CRYSTALS

APPENDIX

(purple)

PEAKS, DEPTHS and
EXPLORATIONS

(purple)

TESTAMENT

TESTAMENT

About the Author

Dr. Ira Progoff has long been in the vanguard of those who have worked toward a dynamic psychology of creative and spiritual experience. In his practice as therapist, in his books, as lecturer and workshop leader, as Bollingen Fellow, and as Director of the Institute for Research in Depth Psychology at the Graduate School of Drew University, he has conducted pioneer research and developed new techniques that are widely used.

The core of Ira Progoff's theoretical work is contained in a trilogy of basic books. *The Death and Rebirth of Psychology* (1956) crystallizes the cumulative results of the work of the great historical figures in depth psychology and sets the foundation for a new psychology of personal growth. *Depth Psychology and Modern Man* (1959) presents the evolutionary perspective and formulates the basic concepts of Holistic Depth Psychology. *The Symbolic and the Real* (1963) pursues the philosophical implications of these ideas and applies them in developing new techniques for personal growth.

Proceeding from the Holistic Depth Psychology which he had developed, Dr. Progoff then created the *Intensive Journal* concept and process in 1966, publishing *At a Journal Workshop* as the basic text for its use in 1975. He first evolved the concept and method of Process Meditation in 1971 as a means of fulfilling the *Intensive Journal* process. After years of testing and development, it is now described in *The Practice of Process Meditation: The* Intensive Journal *Way to Spiritual Experience* (1980)

Dr. Progoff is Director of Dialogue House which, from its New York headquarters, administers the national and international out-reach of the *Intensive Journal* program including Process Meditation.